Themes in Social Anthropology
edited by David Turton

Initiation

Themes in Social Anthropology

Buddhism in life
The anthropological study of religion and the
Sinhalese practice of Buddhism
Martin Southwold

Sacrifice in Africa
A structuralist approach
Luc de Heusch

J. S. La Fontaine

Initiation

Manchester University Press

1985

Published by arrangement with Penguin Books Ltd

Published by
Manchester University Press
Oxford Road, Manchester M13 9PL, UK
and 51 Washington Street, Dover, N.H. 03820, USA

British Library Cataloguing in Publication Data
La Fontaine, J. S.
    Initiation.—(Themes in social anthropology; 3)
    1. Initiation rites
    I. Title ° II. Series
    392'.14   GN483.3

Library of Congress Cataloging in Publication Data
applied for

ISBN 0 7190 1966 4

Printed and bound in Great Britain
by Biddles Ltd, Guildford and King's Lynn

CONTENTS

This book is for
Amanda and Ginny
with my love

PREFACE

So much help has been given me, in different ways, over the years this book has been in preparation that it is a difficult, though pleasant, task to acknowledge it all. The initial idea was Professor I. Schapera's; he has encouraged and urged me on throughout the process of writing. So too did Dr Audrey Richards, whose influence on my work will be obvious. It is sad that she did not live to see the final product.

The preparatory reading was largely done while I was Visiting Professor at Ohio State University. I am grateful to the University for their invitation and for the facilities they gave me which enabled me to read so widely. Linda Kimball, my research assistant there, was an indefatigable collector of material; to her, and to colleagues and graduate students in the Department of Anthropology, particularly Ed Hale and Jim McLeod, I offer warm thanks. A series of seminars on the subject of initiation, which I held during the academic year 1972–3, was a further stimulus and I am happy to be able to thank the participants, particularly Jean and John Comaroff. A number of colleagues have given me the benefit of their expert knowledge and comments on different chapters: I owe particular thanks to John Beattie, Elizabeth Meyerhoff, Paul Spencer and Woody Watson for this help and offer them my apologies for any errors that may remain. Dr Anne Akeroyd has drawn my attention to much relevant material and has always been ready to discuss it with me. To her and to Professor Ioan Lewis, who read an early draft of the first chapters, I offer grateful recognition of the work entailed.

Without the ungrudging hospitality and friendship of Jack and Esther Goody I would never have completed the final draft; it is difficult to express my appreciation of their support without appearing fulsome. Professor Lucy Mair spent much time on the final draft in an heroic effort to improve my prose and correct my punctuation; I am most grateful to her, while recognizing that the book probably still fails to come up to her high standards in these matters. Amanda Sackur took the time to go through the final draft and I was much helped by comments which were both amusing and to the point. She and Ginny Sackur have given me unstinting support and encouragement, which has been a great source of strength. Finally the manuscript was typed, and often retyped, by several members of the secretarial staff of the Anthropology Department of the London

School of Economics. I particularly want to thank Hilda Jarrett and Joan Wells, Pat Blair and Caroline Simpson.

None of the persons mentioned is responsible for the opinions and conclusions expressed here. It is often difficult to pinpoint the source of ideas but I have tried to indicate particular intellectual debts. The book shows the influence on my thinking of the Cambridge Department of Anthropology under Professor M. Fortes, of the work of Professor Sir Edmund Leach, and of nearly fifteen years spent at the London School of Economics among colleagues whose different theoretical approaches and varied intellectual concerns have ensured the constant stimulus of lively academic debate. The final responsibility for the work is, however, my own.

JEAN LA FONTAINE
Camberwell, 1984

INTRODUCTION

This book is concerned with religious behaviour, with the details of the persons involved, the objects used and the acts performed in an ordered sequence which has purpose and meaning for the people concerned. The term 'ritual' is commonly used by anthropologists to refer to this, but the word, and its synonym 'rites', have been used in a variety of ways by scholars of different disciplines so that it is important to make clear the sense in which it is being used here. Even within anthropology there remain serious problems in determining the nature of ritual[1] in such a way that we can always say what is, or more importantly, what is not, ritual. This discussion is not directed to that technical debate but aims to define, in a rough and ready fashion, the term that will be used.

Ritual is social action; its performance requires the organized co-operation of individuals, directed by a leader or leaders. There are rules indicating what persons should participate and on what occasions; often the rules excluding certain categories of people are of as much significance as those which permit or require others to take part. Ritual is also social in that there is a general recognition of a correct, morally right pattern that should be followed in any particular performance. While changes in ritual procedure do occur, whether to accommodate particular contingencies or, on a more long-term basis, to adapt to changes in the organization of society, there is generally a sense that ritual has a fixed structure. The prescriptive nature of ritual, that it must be done, is recognized in most anthropological definitions of ritual. All of them agree on its social nature, which distinguishes this view from that of ethologists or psychiatrists, who use 'ritual' to denote repetitive and formalized behaviour. Conventional behaviour, however regularly repeated, is not ritual.

Social relationships are represented in the organization of ritual; the constitution of the congregation, the allocation of roles in the performance, and the identity of those directing it, are modelled on the structure of the society concerned. Ritual occasions, like secular events, mobilize this structure in action; in some cases rituals are the only times when this happens. The annual service, in St Paul's Cathedral, of the Order of St Michael and St George is a dramatic realization of a hierarchy of honour, linked to Church and State; it assembles in one place for common action, ordered by rank, a category of people normally dispersed among the

British population. In this, as in other cases, a common ritual tradition is an important element in a community's sense of its own identity.

Such effects are, however, rarely recognized by the participants for whom ritual has its own purpose. Rites are acts directed to some aim, whether that be rather vague and general, such as peace and goodwill among men, or specific, such as inducing rain to end a drought. The relation between ends and means which is characteristic of ritual is usually described by contrasting it with what has been called rational or technical action. Goody (1961: 156) has pointed out that we are inclined to use the category of ritual as a repository for those items of behaviour we do not understand or, one might add, in whose efficacy we do not believe. Ritual action is not irrational, it is purposive, but its success or failure cannot be measured in western scientific terms. Some confusion has been added to the discussion by attempting to substitute the social effects of rituals (as perceived by the observer) for the purposes, as expressed by those who perform them, and writing as though the symbolic means used in ritual constituted its sole purpose.

Some anthropologists have argued that ritual is a form of communication, a symbolic code which can be read, and that it resembles language more than action. In this connection G. Lewis (1980) has rightly pointed out that ritual differs from language in a number of significant ways and that it is important to distinguish between the expression of meaning and communication, which implies an intent to transmit a message.

While the words, objects and gestures of ritual cannot be dismissed as meaningless and irrational, the repetition of traditional behaviour whose origins lie beyond recovery,[2] determining the meaning of ritual is a difficult task. Even where the participants offer interpretations, they will vary according to age, social position, knowledge of ritual or sensitivity to such matters. In some societies there is no tradition of exegesis or discussion; knowledge may be reserved for specialists or a few senior men or women, or questions may even be frowned on. It is all too easy for the analyst to impute meaning for which there is little or no evidence, imposing interpretations borrowed from another culture, usually his or her own. This is not to say that all attributions of meaning should be avoided, but that care must be taken to distinguish between perceptions which are the anthropologist's and those which are made explicit by the people concerned. The materials, form and use of objects, the everyday relations of persons and their use of language, constitute a context in which ritual is performed, and understanding of that context is implicit for those who perform it, taken so much for granted that they are not aware of it. An examination of the social and material setting of ritual is essential therefore; associations with it are a legitimate source of understanding for an analyst.

A particular difficulty lies with the idea that there are 'universal symbols'; that is, that all ritual uses a similar repertoire of concepts, referring to the natural environment, or to the human body and its capacities. There is a good deal of evidence which seems to support this view, but the meaning carried by these 'natural symbols' (Douglas, 1970) cannot be assumed, wherever we find them. There is, for example, a considerable history to the interpretation of sexual symbolism, which is no longer taken as referring simply to fertility. It will be part of my argument that the human beings who perform the rituals described here, and those who are ostensibly a ritual's objects, are themselves representations of concepts and ideas, and therefore symbolic. Like the performers of a morality play, the actors stand for something other than themselves.

In analysing ritual there are a number of different dimensions to consider; a successful analysis consists of keeping them distinct but also showing the relationship between them. First there is the ritual action, whose essential quality is that it constitutes a sequence which accomplishes a purpose – the latter phrase refers to one dimension of the participant's account of ritual: what it aims to do. As an explanation this account is essentially circular: the Gisu of Uganda[3] initiate boys to make them into men, i.e. so that they shall not remain uninitiated boys. It is a fairly simple matter to show that the structure of the rite is such that its explicit purpose is achieved.

It is more difficult to relate the second dimension, that of meaning, both to the action in ritual and the nature of society. Here we are concerned with meaning, whether this is made explicit or, as is common, consists of sets of overlapping metaphors. This is best demonstrated using an example. During the initiation of boys among the Gisu, the initiands are smeared with mud, with chyme and with the millet yeast used to make beer, not necessarily in that order. The substances belong to a set, in that they can be observed to substitute for one another. Their meaning is, in one sense, what they have in common: they are substances containing elements of creative transformation (mud is the mixture of water with earth that results in the land being fertile, chyme is the stomach contents of an animal and embodies the digestive process, and yeast is the agent of fermentation, a generative process which is, in Gisu thought, analogous with sexual intercourse). Each substance has also its own referent: the mud is taken from a place sacred to the ancestors and refers therefore to the relationship between the descendants of those ancestors and the land; chyme is produced by the killing of animals with its referent both of

ancestral sacrifice, and hospitality and commensality between members
of a descent group and between kinsmen in different groups; beer is brewed
for work-parties and all celebrations, whether involving a sacrifice or not,
and invokes, by its reference to sexuality and wives who brew it, the idea
of marriage. All these occasions properly involve a range of people whose
relationships are defined in social, not individual, personal terms. The
application of the substances is purposive: to bless the initiand and prepare
him for the ordeal of circumcision. They are thought to have an effect on
the boy which has been interpreted both mystically and pragmatically
(Heald, 1982); that is, they 'work'. They are applied by a senior man with
authority over the initiand (a kinsman from his own descent group),
whose knowledge of ritual has been gained largely through experience of
many performances since his own initiation. The act demonstrates the
relationship, not between two individuals but between the roles they
occupy, senior and junior agnate. The social order is a tissue of ideas of
this sort, by which behaviour is described and evaluated. They form an
integral part of the universe of meanings to which ritual and myth refer.
The whole corpus of ideas evoked in ritual is the traditional knowledge of
a society, not organized in the manner we are accustomed to associate
with science but expressed and put to use.

The subject of the book is rituals of initiation in the common sense of
the term; that is, rituals of admission into secret societies are included as
well as those which mark the passage between childhood and maturity.
Where the latter are concerned, the sociological distinction between
rituals which concern a set of initiates (even though in particular
instances there may be only one or two members of the set), and those
which are specific to individuals, is important. Individual transitions to
maturity usually concern girls[4] and are closely linked to events in the life
cycle, such as the development of the breasts or the onset of menstruation,
which are believed to need ritual treatment. Such rites are best described
as puberty rites and will be excluded. Some societies perform both puberty
and initiation rituals. In Zambia Bemba girls undergo puberty rites
individually at first menstruation; they are a necessary preliminary to
initiation, which is performed later when several girls are ready to go
through it together. While the timing of the menstrual rites is determined
by physiological events, initiation can be arranged when it is convenient
(Richards, 1956).

Although initiation may take place when the candidates for initiation
(the initiands) are about the age of puberty, the focus of the rites is a social
rather than a natural change. Both boys and girls may be initiated before
or after they have reached physical maturity. Among the Gisu of Uganda
youths may reach the age of twenty-five and be the fathers of legitimate

children while still uninitiated, while in contrast in Madagascar Merina boys are now initiated as toddlers (Bloch, n.d.). Bemba initiands are physiologically mature, while in traditional Nayar communities in India little girls might have their *tali* tied (the phrase which stood for initiation) at the age of three or four (Gough, 1955). The significance of the distinction between puberty ritual and initiation is discussed more fully in Chapter V, but throughout the book the term 'initiation' is restricted to cases where boys or girls are initiated in sets, or new members are admitted to groups.

Initiation cannot simply be defined as admission to groups, whether secret or not. The conferment of adult status may involve membership of no social unit and these are precisely the rites which have been referred to as initiation by anthropologists and others for years. To exclude them would go against common usage and limit comparison to particular societies, such as those of New Guinea (Allen, 1967), the Mende of Sierra Leone (Little, 1951), or the Hopi (Parsons, 1939), where adult status entails membership of secret cults.

In addition there is such a striking similarity in the rituals of admission to secret societies and those marking the passage to maturity, that it is necessary to consider them together. The resemblances, however, do not mark off initiation rites as a category distinct from all others. On the contrary, certain symbolic themes, such as an enactment of death and rebirth, are found in rituals which are not normally referred to as initiation (see Bloch & Parry, 1982). The reasons for this will become clear later; but the features common to initiation rites require further consideration in order to justify the definition of subject matter.

Secrecy is not an invariable accompaniment of initiation rites in the sense that the ritual is always performed in secret, although it often is. Many initiations into adulthood are public affairs, and in others, where a parade may be made of secrecy, the knowledge that is so jealously guarded may be trivial, or the secrecy a generally maintained fiction. Yet all initiations purport to transmit knowledge and powers that are exclusive to the initiated. It is helpful to distinguish between information, such as the names of members and the nature of ritual objects, songs or words, and understanding of truths revealed or mysteries explained, and the experience itself, which may not be communicable and is in some sense mysterious. Knowledge may include any one of these elements or all three. Secret societies are classified as such because of their concern with secret knowledge, as much as because they entail covert or subversive activities, although they may be involved in both.

Oaths and affirmations are also commonly found in initiation rituals. A variety of acts, from a solemn oath to an act of commitment which is not a verbal formula but merely a sign of assent to words uttered by the initiator, can be included here. In some cases they are so important that they overshadow all other elements. In Kenya during the guerrilla warfare which preceded Independence, initiations into the secret organization known as Mau Mau were usually referred to as oath-taking ceremonies, although there was more to them than the taking of an oath (see Chapter III). The essence of an oath is that it commits the individual, binding him or her to other members, and its breaking usually involves powerful sanctions; these may be misfortune or even death, whether at the hands of the group itself, or through some supernatural agency. The oath is likely to be an important element in the rituals of admission to secret societies, and where secret information is revealed, since the individual must be committed to preserve that secrecy. However, oaths are not always a part of initiation rites, even if using a wide definition of the term; where they are absent, other mechanisms compel the initiate to recognize his or her changed state and new obligations, which is essentially what an oath does. The adoption of new styles of dress or of wearing the hair, distinctive behaviour or restrictions, are all ways of committing the individual to his or her new role, but in this case publicly, rather than privately among fellow-initiates.

Tests and ordeals of varying severity occur in all these rites, although they may be very attenuated. In initiations into maturity it is common to find that the ordeal involves suffering some operation on the body which marks it permanently. Scars may be cut, or teeth knocked out, or there may be more radical mutilations such as circumcision or clitoridectomy. Such physical changes are not an invariable accompaniment of initiation. The Karimojong and Turkana of northern Kenya and Uganda perform rituals in which the central act is the sacrifice of an animal by the initiand. He is expected to kill it with one thrust of the spear so that the act is not only a sacrifice but a test of his skill. Bemba girls are set tests, like jumping over hoops made of branches, which must be performed correctly. These tests leave no marks to show who is an initiate but, like the more severe ordeals, they simultaneously test the qualities of the candidates and provide an essential element of the whole experience which effects the change in them.

Initiation defines boundaries: between members of a group and outsiders, between different statuses and between contrasted ideas. The rites also involve ideas of hierarchical order, for the initiates are not only transformed but gain status. At its simplest there is a single distinction between initiates and the uninitiated, but many rites serve to reveal further gradations of status to which individuals may aspire. The equality of the initiates may be emphasized and contrasted with the higher rank of those who are the officiants. The latter's superiority is based on their greater ritual knowledge, and initiands are made to feel ignorant and confused to underline their inferiority in this respect.

Knowledge often appears to be equated with power, power based on the control of mystical rather than material resources (see Mauss, 1950). However, the concept of spiritual power conflates two ideas which are best kept distinct in analysis, however intertwined they are in social life. The first of them is power which can be defined as coercive force, whether as the result of physical or economic pressure. The other is authority which is the recognized right to command, legitimized by appeal to principles which are part of the moral order. Power need not be legitimate, as for example in the case of a gang of thieves, and authority may confer little in the way of power. These are extreme cases; usually power and authority are associated, for power is legitimized by an appeal to moral principles, and authority gives access to economic and political power. Ritual is concerned with legitimacy, reaffirming the divisions and hierarchies that are indispensable to a system of authority. The rituals may also regulate access to assets more tangible than knowledge: the support of a large organization, control of property, the establishment of a household, fees for specialist services. These rewards of initiation must be derived from the social setting of the rites, rather than the details of what is done or said, which are overtly concerned with what may be termed 'ultimate values': birth, death, mystical powers and human development. It is this emphasis, perhaps, which has misled many interpreters, who focus on the symbolic meaning to the exclusion of the social concomitants of initiation.

The legitimacy conferred on ritual officiants is that of traditional knowledge: the information, understanding and experience needed to ensure the correct performance. Objectively, their power may derive from their roles as owners of land or herds, as heads of households, as experts in many fields, or as the leaders of powerful groups. The ritual, however, contrives to demonstrate the effectiveness of their knowledge and confirm their authority as legitimate.

In order to discuss the context of ritual, one must, inevitably, present a considerable amount of detailed information. To allow for this, the ethnography is limited to one or two cases per chapter. Each is used to make certain points, so that the ethnographic detail is not identical in each case. Although the material presented is restricted in this way, the conclusions are based on a study of a much wider range of evidence and some reference is made to this from time to time. However, the book is not, and does not pretend to be, an encyclopaedic survey of initiations. Moreover, while it is concerned with one kind of ritual, this should not be taken as an indication that this one kind is somehow different from others, however defined. The argument is intended to suggest a way of understanding ritual in general.

NOTES TO THE INTRODUCTION

1. For a recent discussion see the sensitive account in G. Lewis (1980: Chapter 2). An earlier work, which considers the central issue of the connection between belief and ritual, is that of the philosopher, Skorupski (1976). See also Firth (1973).
2. This assumption has not always been made. Lewis Morgan, the American whose book *Ancient Society* (1877) has had a great influence on Marxist thought, wrote: 'Religion deals so largely with the imaginative and emotional nature, and consequently with such uncertain elements of knowledge, that all primitive religions are grotesque and to some extent unintelligible' (pp. 5–6).
3. I did field-work among the Gisu from November 1953 to September 1955.
4. Among the Iatmul (Bateson, 1936) the first performance of significant activities is marked ritually for both boys and girls.

CHAPTER I

THEORIES
OF RELIGION
AND THEIR
CONTRIBUTION
TO THE STUDY
OF INITIATION

Theories of religion are usually one-sided; that is, they stress either the social significance of religious action, the ritual, or the intentions of the performers, their ideas and beliefs. This double strand in the interpretation of religion can be traced as far back as the beginnings of anthropology in the nineteenth century. The most recent approaches belong, generally, to the latter, intellectualist stream, although the modern focus is usually the meaning of ritual symbolism, rather than statements of dogma or the nature of beliefs in spiritual beings. Yet the two approaches have also drawn closer together and there is a great difference between modern anthropological thinking and the earlier tradition which it resembles. A consideration of the history of these ideas may serve to indicate the variety of ways in which initiation has been interpreted and related to other religious practices; it may also serve to demonstrate the differences of the two kinds of approach.

A second reason for setting out a brief review is that the ideas of the first generation of anthropological thinkers still influence the general public's views of the religions of other societies. It is common to find terms like 'magic' and 'superstition' used to refer to these practices and beliefs, and there is often an idea that they are survivals from the past, from which western nations have advanced further. A general interest in the exotic is given greater strength by the belief that progress in western scientific learning will destroy traditional religion. Such views are supported by the films shown on television which almost invariably concentrate on rituals, some very theatrical and dramatic in effect, others less so. The general impression conveyed is that such rituals play a more important part in the life of these peoples than in our own. This is largely a product of the film's need to hold the audience's attention, by cutting out the humdrum and the boring routine of daily life. The result is that people are more aware of exotic rituals without necessarily understanding them. The great changes that have taken place in anthropological thinking in the last fifty years are largely unknown outside a relatively small circle; much of what is held to be 'common knowledge' about other societies consists of outworn, often nineteenth-century, theories, which have percolated into general thinking without those who hold them being the least aware that they have long been superseded. A second aim of this chapter is thus to set these ideas in context and provide a general background for this book.

Sir James Frazer, author of that massive treatise on religion *The Golden Bough* (1907–15) described initiation as 'the central mystery of primitive society'. Like many nineteenth-century scholars, he sought the origins of European civilization in other societies. His researches in comparative religion were undertaken in order to demonstrate an evolutionary sequence from the earliest, most 'primitive', to the latest, most 'civilized', society. Like earlier evolutionists he assumed that the simpler societies, described by the missionaries and explorers whose accounts he drew on for data, were surviving examples of earlier stages of development through which the more 'civilized' peoples had already passed. He used his own extensive knowledge of the classics to furnish further stages in a sequence which charted a progress from lower to higher orders, with all the implications of moral superiority that these terms entail.

Religious ideas were the key to this sequence for Frazer, as they were for his distinguished contemporary E. B. Tylor. Both scholars belonged to a tradition which saw the evolution of human society as essentially a matter of progressive enlightenment, a freeing of the mind from the errors of the past. Frazer saw this development of the intellectual powers of men as passing through three stages: magic, religion and science. He pointed to the increasing secularization of society, linking the decline of religion to the development of science as a distinct mode of thought and, like Tylor, he regarded religious practices as survivals which would disappear with the triumph of scientific thinking. Religious practices, like initiation, contained within them magical elements which were survivals from a still earlier stage. Such survivals were the clues to development from one stage to another. Elements of the rituals of classical antiquity could be seen as linking them to the religious practices of peoples classified as still more primitive, which showed similar features. He included within his purview initiation into adult status of both boys and girls, which, he argued, was the most archaic form, since it was the most widely distributed, initiation into secret societies or cults, which he claimed as a later development, and finally, induction into office in such Ancient Greek cults as the Eleusinian mysteries, from which, he argued, developed first the idea of priesthood, and then divine kingship. The central feature which underlay all these apparently different phenomena was the idea that they all concerned a passionate interest in, and desire to control, life, death and the forces of nature. The development of rites followed from the progressively greater understanding of the natural world and showed changing techniques designed to produce the desired result: the enhanced fertility of people, animals and crops.

Frazer's interest in initiation rituals lay in the evidence they provided of the development of religious institutions and hence of intellectual progress. Rituals were, for him, actions consequent on certain cosmological beliefs, manifestations of ideas about the nature of the world and the possibility of controlling it. His assumption that religious beliefs were the key to an understanding of religion as an institution had its direct opponents in some of his contemporaries, like the Scot, Robertson-Smith, and Durkheim, the great French sociologist who argued the priority of religious action over dogma. The latter developed a sociological approach which was to supersede evolutionary theory of which Frazer was only one of a number of exponents; hindsight allows us to see that when *The Golden Bough* was published it was already out of date. Although there has recently been a revival of interest in some aspects of Frazer's work, the reasons for rejecting the framework of his evolutionary theory are still valid: the underlying assumptions are unfounded and the data he used were incomplete and unreliable.

There is still not a great deal of evidence about the early history of parts of the world where there is no tradition of written records, but more is known than was known in Frazer's day. The evidence indicates that it is wrong to assume that a single line of development is followed by all societies or that modern non-literate people have not had at least as long a period of evolution behind their distinctive life-styles as we have behind ours. Other societies are not fossils in the human record, frozen at particular stages of development. The distribution of human differences in space cannot be reinterpreted as the result of differences in stages of development over time.

Frazer, like most early writers on the subject of human evolution, but unlike modern anthropologists, did not collect his data himself. His sources were travellers who often understood little about the people they described and did not speak their language, or missionaries who regarded them either as benighted heathens, children of the devil, or else, though this was more common in the eighteenth than in the nineteenth century, as innocent reminders of a Golden Age. Whatever the particular prejudices of the observer, they made it unlikely that the anthropologist sitting in his study would obtain full and detailed descriptions of the rituals, and even less likely that he would have an understanding of what these rituals meant to participants in them. Thus when Frazer referred to the thought underlying magical or religious acts, he was speculating from the conviction that such actions must derive from the ideas held by ignorant savages. He usually had no information on what they thought at all. The superficiality of early accounts also partly explains why Frazer could ignore the fact that the peoples he characterized as 'magical' in their thinking could not have survived without a detailed and practical knowledge of plants and animals, seasons and soils. Moreover, in modern society science has not superseded religion in the manner Frazer predicted it would, although religious beliefs are now more varied and more a matter of personal conviction than in his day; science and religion have come to be recognized as distinct, not competing, modes of thought. All societies have a body of practical ideas and also beliefs which are dogmas of faith.

The ideas of both Frazer and Tylor are still influential today, although modern anthropology has discarded the broader theory of which their work was the exposition. Modern anthropological studies of religion may not acknowledge their debt to Frazer, although Horton saw the modern interest in systems of thought as 'Neo-Tylorianism' (1968); however, they contain many insights into the meaning and logic of symbolism and the intellectual preoccupation with the natural world, which resemble those of these Victorian predecessors. Anthropologists today work through the language of the people they study; observation of rituals and discussion with the people who perform them, as well as a greater understanding of the social context of the rites, have resulted in much richer data than were available at the turn of the century. Audrey Richards, writing about the initiation of girls among the Bemba of Zambia, pointed out how much fuller her data on the rituals were than the accounts of similar rites in neighbouring areas, published by sympathetic missionaries and colonial administrators, and even than those of the Bemba themselves. Lack of detail and reticence about certain episodes in the ritual made her informants' accounts mere sketches of what actually happened, as her observation of one lengthy performance made plain (Richards, 1956: 135–8).

The evolutionary approach itself survives in the work of writers outside what has become, since Frazer's day, the specialized discipline of anthropology. Mircea Eliade, the distinguished religious philosopher, published in 1958 a book called *Rites and Symbols of Initiation* which reads curiously like the work of nineteenth-century anthropologists. He retains all the assumptions of that time; in particular he assumes that western Europe represents the greatest development of civilization, and Christianity the highest form of religion. He places other societies on a historical ladder according to their modes of making a living. Thus for him, as for Durkheim who is discussed below, the Australian Aborigines represent the earliest form of human society because they traditionally neither cultivated the soil nor kept domesticated animals. He assumes that their initiation rituals, which he sees as coterminous with their religion, must reveal the crude forms of ideas which receive their highest development in Christianity. Thus, what he is doing is to take the idea of life after death, of spiritual rebirth, which he sees as central to Christianity, and seek counterparts to it in the other rituals he studies. What purports to be a study of development from most primitive to most civilized is, in fact, an interpretation of other religions in the light of the assumption that Christianity is the end-product towards which those religions will ultimately develop. Hence, while his discussion provides us with interesting insights into religious symbolism it is prejudiced from the beginning. One can accept with interest from an authority on the subject the statement that religion is essentially concerned with the problem of death, but cannot but reject such speculations as are contained in many other passages. For example, after stating, rightly, that in many African societies circumcisers are associated with wild animals, he goes on: 'The masters of initiation are divinities in animal form, which supports the hypothesis that structurally the ritual belongs to an archaic hunter culture' (Eliade, 1958: 23). He thus ignores the contemporary significance of wild animals in favour of guesses about the past which support his evolutionary hypothesis.

Like his predecessor Frazer, Eliade is concerned with initiation in its widest sense, for secret societies and cults are necessary to his argument about the essential steps in the spiritual development of humanity. His work leaves quite unexplained a question at least as important as that which he claims to have answered: if the various societies of the modern world represent stages in a single process of development, what has determined their different rates of progress, so that some remain at earlier stages than others? No evolutionary theory of society has produced a satisfactory answer to this question.

Durkheim, Frazer's contemporary, whose work forms part of the foundation of modern social anthropology and sociology, argued that religion could not be understood by speculations about the origins of beliefs but only by considering its relation to society.[1] He built on Robertson-Smith's argument that religious acts were prior to the formulation of a coherent body of beliefs, in order to explain the social nature of rituals. Society, to Durkheim, was a structure of social divisions and groupings, consciousness of which was both collective and part of the individual make-up of each member. Religious action, he asserted, was the means of reviving and strengthening the basic moral precepts on which social life is founded and endowing them with a compelling authority which appeared to derive from outside each participant. Beliefs in the sense of ideas about spirits, ghosts and gods, which intellectualist scholars took as fundamental, were, to Robertson-Smith and Durkheim, later elaborations. They could not therefore be used to explain rites. By placing the emphasis not on intellectual speculation about the world but on the representation of groups and social relationships in ritual action, Durkheim's work gave a new direction to studies of religion. His ideas, popularized in British anthropology by his admirer Radcliffe-Brown, still form the basis of much modern work; this book is no exception to the rule.

The most influential early work on initiation, rather than on religion in general, was written not by Durkheim or Frazer, but by a man who is known largely for one book. The Belgian Arnold Van Gennep published *Les Rites de Passage* in 1909, three years before Durkheim's famous work *Les Formes Elémentaires de la Vie Religieuse*. He was clearly in sympathy with the sociological approach of the school founded by Durkheim[2] and had also read Frazer's work. His own book combined an interest in symbolism with a perception that ritual must be analysed as an activity, not merely as a manifestation of primitive thought. He set out to demonstrate that rituals can only be understood in their entirety. Many of the acts which had been interpreted as survivals of magic should be understood as marking stages in the rites, whose characteristic form was determined by their purpose, 'to ensure a change of condition or a passage from one magico-religious or secular group to another' (Van Gennep, English-language ed., 1960: 11). The similarities between initiation into adult status and into secret societies thus derive from the fact that both are rites of passage, transition rituals. The term includes in a single class a variety of rites accompanying crossings of boundaries, changes in time and in social status.

Van Gennep starts by noting that the boundaries of territories and villages are often marked by shrines, and that borders are considered dangerous so that people will make offerings at the shrines to protect themselves before crossing them. Similarly, society is made up of a series of social boundaries, between categories and statuses, so that social life can be seen as a series of transitions as individuals change their state. Events such as births, marriages and deaths, or changes from one season to the next, involve the potential of danger to those in transition. The rituals of transition both mark the changes and protect the individuals concerned. The danger of such changes Van Gennep sees as deriving from the sacredness of all social acts in simple societies; what is sacred is also dangerous and must be dealt with ritually. Like many anthropologists of the time, and since, Van Gennep believed in the greater religiosity of simple societies.

The characteristic structure of *rites de passage*, as analysed by Van Gennep, is tripartite. The three stages are marked by rituals but need not be of uniform length or emphasis, either at similar transitions in all societies or in different rituals in the same society. The first phase is characterized by the stripping away of the initial state: of childhood in rites of maturity, of the responsibilities of life in many funerals, and so on. These are rites of separation since the individual who is undergoing the ritual is separated from his initial state and left in transition, a state which Van Gennep called 'liminal' from the Latin *limen*, meaning a threshold, where one is neither in nor out. He also described it as 'marginal'. The liminal or marginal stage is characterized by danger and ambiguity, symbolized, for example, by being blindfolded or removed into the bush or forest away from normal life, or by having to undergo various unpleasant trials. A further ritual, which he called a rite of 'aggregation' or 'integration', ends this phase and emphasizes the individual's integration into his new state. Thus the tripartite form of rituals of transition – separation, liminal phase and integration – dramatizes the transition by creating a margin, a boundary between the two states concerned, and transferring the individual across from one to the other. The next chapter demonstrates in detail these stages in the rituals of initiation into membership of the Masons and of the Chinese Triad society; ethnographic evidence has demonstrated over and over again in different parts of the world the validity of Van Gennep's assertion that this tripartite structure was to be found in all rituals of transition.

Unlike Durkheim and his followers, however, Van Gennep was interested in discovering the meaning of the symbolic acts which make up a ritual. He saw their meaning as establishing the three phases of the ritual, although he pointed out that, to the participants, there were special purposes associated with each occasion. Thus the marriage rite, while concerned with the transfer of the bride from her natal family to that of her husband, is also aimed at ensuring the fertility of the couple, and funerals are purifying as well as markers of the change from life to death. In addition, he argued that ritual acts show remarkable conformity across cultures according to the phases of the ritual they designate: washing, head-shaving, circumcision and other bodily mutilations, the crossing of streams and other obstacles, all indicate separation, while anointing, eating, dressing in new clothes, are common integrative actions. These acts are symbols which can most effectively be interpreted by their position within the total ritual. However, symbols also have some independent meaning, for the same symbol may occur in different rituals and have a similar meaning in each. Thus the head-shaving of a baby at a naming ceremony resembles the head-shaving of a corpse before burial, not merely because of beliefs in reincarnation, but by reference to the beginning and end of social life which is being ritually marked. Later anthropologists such as Douglas and Leach have elaborated a suggestion implicit in Van Gennep's association of the social with physical transitions, the idea that the body is made to represent social changes, as the circumcised penis may represent adult status and movements in space may represent changes in social position. This is a theme taken up in more detail later in the book; here it is sufficient to notice that ritual acts are symbolic; they express significant social ideas by associating the physical with the social.

Van Gennep's contributions to the understanding of initiation in particular, rather than rites of passage in general, are now so taken for granted that their origin is often forgotten. He pointed out that what is central to them is a change of social status rather than concern with physical changes. Since initiations usually concern sets of individuals, it is clear that the initiands will be at various stages of physical maturity; moreover, in many societies the rites are held well before, or after, the age of physical maturation. In any case it is difficult to identify any single physiological sign of maturity which is unequivocal. He attacks Frazer for explaining initiation as a form of fertility ritual, although he agrees that it is not surprising that ritual to enhance fertility should be associated with a change to social maturity, as an additional but secondary purpose. The operations on the body which accompany such rites are to be interpreted as symbols, not as acts which reveal a faulty understanding of biology.

Van Gennep's class of rituals of transition is very widely drawn; it includes rituals of greeting guests, celebrations of the harvest and new year, and a variety of others. Indeed most rituals can be included under the rubric if the tripartite structure is used as a means of identifying them. The tremendous scope of the term came to be seen as a weakness in Van Gennep's work, even by those who accepted its general findings. Gluckman, introducing a collection of articles in his honour, noted the complaint that 'all Van Gennep established was that all rituals had a beginning, a middle and an end' (1962: 9). While he goes on to defend Van Gennep against this charge, Gluckman's own criticisms show that he too had not recognized the potential of the book. Its success lies in having related symbolic meaning to wider social significance, a feat which few before or since have emulated.

Van Gennep did not, however, offer a satisfactory explanation of the rituals he classified together as rites of passage. His expressed aim was a more limited one, that of showing the value of considering the whole sequence of rituals in order to determine their structure. Classification should be based on the 'patterns' revealed in this way. His references to the reasons for their performance at all are perfunctory and disappointing.

His argument is essentially circular. The purpose of *rites de passage*, shown in their characteristic structure, is to effect the transition from one state to another. The states concern the relation of individuals and groups to the sacred world, and to one another in relation to the sacred. Events and the developments of the life cycle constantly involve changes in conditions which 'do not occur without disturbing the life of society and the individual, and it is the function of rites of passage to reduce their harmful effects' (1977: 13). Van Gennep does not elaborate on what he means by these harmful effects but they seem to be the consequences of not performing the rituals, of leaving changes unregulated. If this is so, then they must be seen as the obverse of the performers' intentions, to regulate changes in status, and should not be confused with the effects of the rites. Audrey Richards reported that the answers of Bemba men to her questions about the reason for initiating girls 'amounted often to little more than saying that the girl is initiated to prevent her remaining uninitiated' (1956: 121). The suggestions Van Gennep makes in his conclusions are no clearer, although he alludes to the way in which rituals link the social and natural worlds so that the former becomes as ineluctable as the latter, a fact of life. What Van Gennep seems close to saying is that what is permanent in social life is the set of ideas concerning the divisions and categories of society; ritual, by regulating the relation of individual events to these basic divisions, maintains social order, locating individuals in relation to positions within it. It is a short step from this to perceiving that the effect of the ritual is to maintain the boundaries. The ritual transfer of individuals across them is the means by which they are made manifest and reaffirmed as significant. It is this view that will be argued in the following chapter.

Van Gennep's book has had lasting influence. The missionary Junod, who had worked among the Ba-Ronga of southern Africa for fifteen years and published a book on them, rewrote it after a period of study in Europe, during which he read *Les Rites de Passage*. In the second edition (1927) he paid generous tribute to Van Gennep, whose influence is particularly clear in the section on initiation, which has gained in clarity. Gluckman's study 'The Role of the Sexes in Wiko Circumcision Ceremonies' uses the tripartite schema to order his analysis (1949). In 1956 Richards remarked that anthropologists were still using Van Gennep's terms and concepts; they had, however, elaborated his classification to suit their different approach.

Until the later 1950s, most British social anthropologists, like Gluckman in the paper referred to above, were interested in developing Durkheim's ideas about the relation of religious action to social organization and structure. This meant a concern with the social roles and group identities of the performers rather than with details of the performance.

Van Gennep's unitary class of transition rites was subdivided on the basis of the different social functions and institutions involved, until finally even the term *rite de passage* came to have a meaning which was much narrower than it had originally been given. This elaboration of the classification directed attention away from similarities in the rituals concerned, towards a range of other problems, while still paying lip-service to Van Gennep's pioneering work.

The first distinction within the general category of transition rites resulted from the separation of those concerned with the natural world, such as harvest rites or new moon ceremonies, from rituals celebrating human or social changes. The division between natural and social is important in western culture, though not always in others, and the distinction between 'calendrical rites', as they came to be called (Gluckman, 1962: 3–4), and *rites de passage* is not based on differences in the rites themselves, but on perceptions of their different social functions. Calendrical rites usually aim to ensure success and prosperity in the future, or to protect against danger and failure which could harm crops or animals. Their effect is to break up the flow of time into regular periods; hence the term used for them. However, this effect is not uniquely characteristic of calendrical rites. Any regular event, social as well as natural, may have significance as a means of marking the passage of time. Initiation rituals, for example, mark accession to new status of successive sets of individuals at regular intervals; like the reigns of kings, the order of the sets can serve as a human calendar against which events are located in time. The attribution of this function to only one type of ritual, the seasonal, seems to justify the distinction made on other grounds, but is not sufficiently well-grounded to do so when examined more closely.

The shift from classifying *rites de passage* as a single category on the basis of the common purpose of all the rites, to subdividing them in terms of a social function attributed to their effects, is seen in a further elaboration of the classification which has occurred since Van Gennep wrote. Rituals concerned with groups, such as initiation into secret societies and into cults, are normally considered separately from those concerned with the status of individuals, the term 'rites of passage' being reserved for the latter. The distinction made here concerns the function of ritual in maintaining the constitution of groups, following the work of Durkheim. A similar functional distinction can be seen to be implicit in the practice of considering rites concerned with the conferment of office, such as the installation of kings, priests or chiefs, and those which involve most, if not all, members of a society at different stages of the life cycle. The use of the term 'life-crisis rites' for the ritualization of stages in the life of an individual, as though it were synonymous with *rites de passage*, is an indication of this further dismemberment of the original classification for which the older term was coined.

Together with the restriction of the term 'rites of passage' to refer to rituals marking stages in the life cycle, the term 'initiation' came to mean 'rituals at adolescence' (Gluckman, 1962: 3). Narrowing the focus to life-crisis rites also raised a problem for analysis which seems largely the product of this modification in the original classification, which drew attention to the global distribution of such rites. Almost all societies ritualize the beginning and end of life, celebrating birth and mourning death; most also celebrate marriage with ritual, even if not all couples in a particular society have formal weddings. Rituals marking stages between birth and marriage, initiations, are much more unevenly distributed, occurring at various different stages or even, in some societies, not at all. The search for an explanation of the presence or absence of initiation rites has generated its own literature, which will be discussed in Chapter V. It has also focused attention on the definition of initiation on which there is little agreement, as will become clear. In the present context it serves to mark the nadir of interest in the details of the rituals themselves, since all that is considered significant is whether or not there *are* rituals and what other social features can be shown to determine their presence.

In general, the concern with social functions has encouraged social anthropologists to consider narrowly defined subclasses of *rites de passage*, such as initiation or funerals. They are analysed in terms of their significance for a range of social institutions. The book of essays published in 1962 in honour of Van Gennep and edited by Gluckman illustrates this general trend well; only one[3] of the four articles it contains deals with more than a single category of life-crisis rituals.[4] In addition, the article by Turner shows the well-established practice of discussing initiation rituals for boys and for girls separately, even if the society in question performs rites for both sexes. Recent work (Hays & Hays, 1982; Comaroff, forthcoming) has shown how essential it is to consider the male and female rites of one society as part of a single complex. But, with certain exceptions, the general resemblances in *rites de passage* which caused Van Gennep to treat them as a single class of phenomena seem to have been forgotten.

The emphasis which came to be put on the social function of ritual, and its consequent effect on the classification of rites within the broader category of rites of passage, also influenced interpretation of them. A particular ritual might be susceptible of classification in a number of ways. The Swazi *ncwala* was first described as a ritual of kingship (Kuper, 1944, 1947, 1973), and then as a periodic ritual rebellion, providing a harmless outlet for popular opposition to authority (Gluckman, 1954); still later it was analysed as a calendrical rite, showing its cosmological meaning (Beidelman, 1966). The different social effects perceived are not necessarily mutually exclusive but indicate that particular instances of ritual may not fit easily within the rather elaborate schema of classification that has developed. Many initiations are both life-crisis rites and admissions to secret societies and cults (Allen, 1967; Barth, 1975). Yet once the attempt to reconstruct the evolution of all social life from contemporary examples had been abandoned, the problem of definition and classification necessarily came to the fore. If the aim is not historical reconstruction but cross-cultural comparison, then like must be compared with like. The problem of defining, in a satisfactory manner, the object of analysis has been particularly acute in the case of initiation.

Some of the factors involved can be illustrated by a closer examination of one attempt to make a rigorous cross-cultural comparison of initiation, based on sociological function rather than the interpretation of symbolism. Allen's work (1967) aims to explain why initiation rites are performed in some societies and not others; he limits his analysis to the peoples of New Guinea, where a wide variety of such rituals is found. Allen implies that such diversity in the details of ritual performance prevents him from using the rites themselves as the means to answer the question why some of the peoples in New Guinea perform initiation rites and others do not. He argues, too, that a failure to distinguish between puberty rites and initiation proper has confused earlier analyses. He uses sociological criteria to do this: puberty rites 'are usually performed separately for each individual at an appropriate stage in the life cycle' (1967: 5) while initiations are performed simultaneously for a number of individuals who are admitted to membership of an exclusive group, a secret cult. Allen thus defines as initiation only those rituals which are both life-crisis rites and admissions to a secret society. He would thus exclude from consideration many rites of passage in other parts of the world which are concerned with changing the status of sets of individuals but do not admit them to secret groups. These rites are usually referred to as 'initiation'. But having established his unusually narrow definition, Allen cannot keep rigorously to it. Two of the societies[5] included in his study perform rituals which fall outside his formal definition of initiation; they are nevertheless included as initiation because they fulfil another criterion, that of being concerned with the transmission of secret knowledge. The sociologist Simmel, whom Allen cites, demonstrated that secrecy creates a boundary between those who share secrets and those who are excluded; the boundary need not be that of an organized group. It thus seems that such a narrow definition was unnecessary.

A further difficulty in this type of analysis can be seen in the correlations

Allen establishes. He demonstrates a close correlation between initiation and the existence of unilineal descent groups.[6] The association clearly depends on the fact that the secret cults which are included in the definition of initiation are an aspect of descent-group organization in much of New Guinea. Detailed studies of single societies in New Guinea (Barth, 1975; Herdt, 1982) have shown clearly that participation in the ritual is an important group activity, assembling large numbers of the clan or lineage's members. The association between organization based on descent groups and initiation rites has been shown to exist outside New Guinea; Cohen has shown a world-wide correlation between initiation rites and organization on the basis of descent, and this has also been confirmed by detailed ethnography (e.g., Hugh-Jones, 1979). The empirical association is strong but the two elements are not mutually determinant; organized groups based on descent exist without the institution of initiation ritual,[7] however defined.

Allen also associates this form of social organization with a pronounced division between the sexes, which is probably more strongly marked in New Guinea than most other areas of the world. By virtue of the correlation of both these features with initiation, he argues that 'all initiations maintain the sex division in one form or another' (1967: 121). Expressed in this way the statement is banal, a tautology that derives from the very definition of adult status conferred by initiation. However, in the particular form it takes in New Guinea, which, Allen argues, receives institutionalized expression in secret initiation rituals, the proposition is false, for initiation rites with many of the features found in New Guinea occur elsewhere without the very marked sexual opposition characteristic of these societies.

Allen's study has done little to advance the general understanding of initiation rites. This form of cross-cultural comparison fails to take into account the long-established fact that societies are not bundles of features which can be considered independent variables and then tested for their strength of association. Even if they were, a correlation has to be explained; it does not of itself constitute an explanation. Allen is the first to admit that he can offer no conclusive evidence for the explanation he produces for the association between his 'variables'.

Allen's study is discussed here to demonstrate the ultimate failure of methods of explaining ritual which do not take into account either the ritual itself or the social context from which it takes its meaning. Most British social anthropologists have not used this quantitative approach but have made detailed studies of the rituals of particular societies. In considering them, one can also draw on a similar tradition of work on the nature of descent in order to provide a more satisfactory suggestion as to the way in which it is linked to initiation. What is critical is the structure of authority. Ranking by order of accession to adult status and a notion of the collective wisdom of experienced seniors, whether formalized or not, is produced by regular initiation rituals. The legitimate authority of seniors may not coincide with the distribution of effective power[8] which may be exercised chiefly by holders of office or by self-made leaders. In some descent systems, authority flows along genealogical channels, linking men with their ancestors through their fathers; effective power rests in the hands of the 'fathers' until their deaths. Such systems provide the negative case; in the classic instance, that of the Tallensi (Fortes, 1945, 1949), there are no initiation rituals.

Nevertheless, there is a limit to the amount of understanding of initiation, or any *rite de passage*, that can be obtained through the study of its purely social correlates. The symbolic nature of ritual requires a means of analysing its meaning. Whether this meaning is merely expressed in ritual, or communicated as a message or a tradition of knowledge, is still a matter of debate.[9] The discussion was made possible by the accumulation of many careful accounts of such rituals by trained observers, but it was stimulated by a revival of the interest in the ideas behind ritual that characterized the early scholars. More than half a century later, however, what was of central concern, was not speculation about beliefs but the interpretation of symbolism.

The publication in 1956 of the study by Audrey Richards of Bemba girls' initiation, which has already been referred to, marked a change of direction in the study of ritual and the beginning of a development of an anthropological interest in symbolism.[10] It uses insights which no longer rely entirely on the expression of a people's 'beliefs' or on speculations about the meaning of objects and acts, but on deductions which rest on a combination of the participants' explanations, the observation of other contexts in which the same symbols appear, and the observer's understanding of the people's environment, their social life and its common preoccupations, tensions and conflicts. It is in fact dependent on modern field-work and its method of participant observation.

Richards points out that it is characteristic of symbols to evoke multiple meanings. Frazer had argued that rituals at adolescence denoted a concern with fertility; Van Gennep denied this, claiming that the symbolic enactment of birth and death which Frazer had used as evidence of this should rather be interpreted as denoting the stages of a ritual of transition. While he accepted that such rites might have other purposes, such as the promotion of health and fertility, he resembled Frazer in seeking *the* meaning of ritual. Richards' contribution, like that of Turner and Wilson who took similar views, was to emphasize that ritual's power depends on its ability to convey a range of meanings. Some of these can be expressed by everyone but others will be known only to a few, depending on their age, social position and special expertise or interest. After all, as she remarks, 'the Archbishop of Canterbury does not give the same account of the meaning of the Holy Eucharist as the verger who watches at the church door, the worshipper in the church or the young boy or girl who has just been confirmed' (1956: 113–14). Some other meanings will only be accessible by a study of the social and ritual contexts, by observation of the actors' demeanour, by noting casual remarks in conversation, and by acquired experience of the whole natural and social environment.

Richards also argued that initiation rituals among the Bemba aimed to transform girls into mature women but had the effect of making public and legitimate a natural change that had already happened. She pointed out the connections with a system of chiefly authority and a social structure which combined the tracing of descent through women with placing the control of domestic and political groups, from the village upwards, largely in the hands of men. While she drew tentative conclusions about underlying tensions between men and women, the major part of her analysis concerned the way in which social values are expressed and maintained in the symbols of the drama. It is clear from her account that these rituals have a far wider significance than impressing the candidates with their change of status. Indeed, she notes that the girls themselves, for whose benefit the ritual is ostensibly performed, fade into insignificance and become virtually invisible. They are the occasion for the rites but not the only audience for its message.

The symbolic association between nature and social life which is made apparent in the *chisungu* ritual had earlier been remarked by other social anthropologists.[11] One of the effects of the interweaving of religious and other institutions in society is to identify social institutions with the natural world – to make them facts of life, in the same sense as the seasons, or the biological differences among human beings. Turner's work among the Ndembu of Zambia, a people similar to the Bemba, developed this insight into a theory of symbolism. He argued that all symbols combine referents to bodily products, such as blood, milk, semen and faeces, which also have emotional significance, and referents to more abstract social and cultural values. The latter are thus imbued with the natural inevitability and psychological force of the former. For example, the *mudyi* tree's chief characteristic is that it exudes a white latex; it is a central symbol in girls' initiation rites where it represents milk, breasts, motherhood, matrilineal descent and, finally, the Ndembu people as a distinct entity (Turner, 1962: 131). The *mudyi* tree thus combines, as a symbol, a range of meanings from the most narrow sensory pole (milk) to the most abstract and widest (tribal identity).[12]

Turner developed his theory of symbolism in the course of studying the initiation of boys and girls, for the Ndembu initiate both sexes. He presents his theory in the course of an interpretation of 'symbols of passage' in boys' initiation, which includes circumcision. The article is published in the book of essays honouring Van Gennep, so he takes up, appropriately, Van Gennep's argument that the symbolism of death and rebirth so common in such rituals represents in dramatic form the change of status that is being enacted. Turner shows that these ideas can have rich and deep significance in a particular social context. His conclusion, however, is not an advance on Van Gennep's, but a rephrasing of it in more mystical terms: 'This is death to the indistinct and amorphous state of childhood (implicit in the meaning of *mudyi*) in order to be reborn into masculinity and personality' (Turner, 1962: 173).

Turner's work shows a progressive tendency to isolate symbols from their context of mobilization in ritual and to concentrate on their mystical and philosophical implications. He designates as the symbol one attribute (colour) of the objects used, and postulates a universal colour symbolism of red, white and black. A later article (Turner, 1969; and see La Fontaine, 1972, and Heald, 1982) which attempts to demonstrate how this applies to the Gisu is a failure; he is forced to admit that triple colour symbolism is not part of the Gisu ritual repertoire and substitutes a trinity of substances instead. The mistake, it seems to me, lies in the separation of symbols not only from the ritual sequence but also from the social context, which results in an assumption that through symbolism one can, as it were, look into a universal human mind. In the process the social purposes and effects of ritual acts are lost; all rituals, among them initiation rituals, become merely vehicles for the display of symbols.

The detachment of symbols from their ritual context is most clearly seen in the work of structuralists who have used Lévi-Strauss's method of analysis to discover the meaning of symbols. Lévi-Strauss himself only rarely discusses ritual,[13] reserving his formidable analytic powers for an exhaustive study of myth. However, his influence on students of ritual can be seen in the work of such writers as Leach and Tambiah. Essentially the method rests on the fact that meaning can be seen to consist not merely in the properties of objects used as symbols but in the way such qualities are identified and contrasted. The arrangement of units in a sequence, whether in the narrative of a myth or the dramatic sequence of a ritual, is thus immaterial; what matters is the series of oppositions and identifications which constitute what Leach has called 'the logic by which symbols are connected' (Leach, 1976). In order to reveal this pattern the analyst must rearrange the units, thus disconnecting them from ritual. In the extreme version of such a method one loses not only any connection with action, values affecting behaviour or the constraints of the natural environment, but also the differences in culture which characterize many varieties of human society. The residue consists of universal symbols expressing human thought.[14]

Concentration on meaning ignores much that is fundamental to religion: specifically that it is social action. On the other hand, purely sociological analyses fail to deal with the characteristic symbolic form of that action, by which ritual is most often defined. This book attempts to present an approach which is more integrated. It derives an initial impetus from the stimulus of articles by Fortes on rituals of installation in West Africa, in which he points out that they endow individuals with office by drawing and emphasizing a clear distinction between the office and the particular incumbent of it. The ritual confers on the incumbent the right to exercise the powers defined by that office but draws attention to his responsibilities. Fortes concludes: 'Ritual presents office to the individual as the creation and possession of society or a part of society into which he is to be incorporated through the office. Ritual mobilizes incontrovertible authority behind the granting of office and status and thus guarantees his legitimacy and imposes accountability for its proper exercise' (1962: 86). The conferment of office is not the concern of this book but the same distinction between living individuals and their roles is made in initiation; the same 'incontrovertible authority' lies behind them, and the aim is to show how it is mobilized.

Ritual is purposive; the participants believe that they are accomplishing their aim in what they do. Bloch has argued that this is an illusion. 'Circumcision ceremonies do not, as Van Gennep was at pains to point out, make adults out of little boys, curing ceremonies do not cure, etc., and any attempt to pretend that they do (as is done in the work of so many anthropologists) is wrong from the first. By contrast the interesting question is the disconnection between the religious statement and the real world, a disconnection which is produced by the mode of communication of ritual' (Bloch, 1974: 4).[15] However, the terms 'boy' and 'man' are given meaning by the culture in question; where to be a man is to be circumcised, then circumcision does indeed 'make adults out of little boys'. The disconnection to which Bloch refers is part of the process of mystification which Marxist theory perceives to be the function of religion. The 'real world' in this statement I take to be the distribution of power at any particular point in time which depends on a whole range of contingencies from climatic factors and crop yields to numbers of individuals concerned and their personalities, to name but a few. Day-to-day social life is perpetually changing; what is relatively constant in it is the part played by ideas through which particular individuals both perceive events and evaluate their own and others' behaviour – what has been referred to as the moral order. To refer to it as false, and the untidy process of living as real, is to make a judgement of value by comparing non-comparable entities, which cannot be helpful.

The insistence with which participants state that ritual effects change cannot be ignored. Richards records: 'I believe that the women in charge of this ceremony were convinced that they were causing supernatural change to take place in the girls under their care, as well as marking those changes' (1965: 125). The means by which this was done was the correct use of the 'things handed down'. Knowledge of this is the basis of the authority of the mistress of ceremonies and also the activating power which effects the transformation. It is thus an indissoluble part of the 'incontrovertible authority' which guarantees not only the legitimacy of office but also the moral order.

NOTES TO CHAPTER I

1. Like Frazer, Durkheim relied on the information collected by others. His monograph on religion, however, is based on detailed descriptions of Australian Aboriginal religion; in any case, his theory made much less use of interpretations of symbolic material which requires a thorough understanding of language and the social context of meaning.
2. Much of the work of this school, on religion, had appeared before Durkheim's book on the subject, both in the *Année sociologique* and elsewhere.
3. The exception is Gluckman's Introduction which is both an exposition of Van Gennep and an attempt to explain, more convincingly than he did, the apparent dearth of ritual in industrial society. He argues that the significant characteristic of small-scale, non-industrial societies is that social roles overlap: people are neighbours, kin, workmates and political allies to the same group of other men and women. Thus any change in the status of one individual has wide repercussions which must be emphasized and clarified in ritual. By contrast, in societies which are more complex, different roles are played by distinct sets of people; a neighbour is unlikely to be kinsman and workmate as well. Hence, in such situations, changes of status are less disruptive and do not require ritual definition. The hypothesis sounds plausible but is controverted by the evidence of elaborate initiation rites, such as those of the Freemasons, discussed in the next chapter. Amanda Sackur has pointed out to me that members of a secret society have relationships which are non-specific and wide-ranging, like the multiplex relations of small-scale societies; hence ritual definition is appropriate, as it still is for what Monica Wilson called 'rituals of kinship' (life-crisis rites)

(Wilson, 1957). It would seem that it is the character of the relations being defined in ritual rather than those of the society at large which is the more important.

4. Fortes' article in the collection referred to is a partial exception to this generalization. He suggests that the conclusions he has reached with regard to installation rites might well hold for initiation, an idea taken up below (see Chapter III).

5. These are the Orokaiva and the Koko (Allen, 1967: 73–5).

6. These are groups recruited either through men only (patrilineal) or through women only (matrilineal). In the former, children belong to their father's group, although a daughter is, to some extent, transferred to her husband's group at marriage; in the latter, children are members of their mother's group and a man's children belong to his wife's group, not his own.

7. For example, the Ganda and others of the Interlacustrine Bantu (Taylor, 1962).

8. See Almagor, 1978; Baxter & Almagor, 1978.

9. See Barth, 1975; G. Lewis, 1980.

10. Her pioneering work is cited by the authors of monographs on initiation in all areas of the world (Gell, 1975; Hugh-Jones, 1979; Barth, 1975).

11. Turner, 1962; Wilson, 1957, 1959.

12. Semen is also represented among the Ndembu by white fluids, most often by what they call 'white beer'. The association of whiteness with female physiology is only unequivocal in the girls' initiation rites. Elsewhere semen is considered a nurturant fluid, as is breast milk (Herdt *et al*, 1982). Turner's failure to relate the initiation rituals of boys and girls in a single analysis is a weakness in an influential corpus of work.

13. But see Lévi-Strauss (1958, 1971).

14. Indeed, Lévi-Strauss has argued that the binary logic exemplified in both symbolism and language is probably an attribute of the structure of the brain. Recent work has cast doubt on the primacy of binary logic and it must be remembered that the work in linguistics which influenced Lévi-Strauss was developed in order to analyse phonemic, not semantic, structures, so that his hypothesis is unlikely to be confirmed.

15. I take a rather different view of Van Gennep's remarks on this point (see p. 109). Van Gennep seems to me to be pointing out that the change being effected by initiation is a social, not a physical, change: i.e., a change of status which requires a change in the term used to designate it. See also La Fontaine, 1977.

CHAPTER II **THE SECRETS OF INITIATION**

The term 'secret society' allows us to class together a wide range of organizations which are comparable only in that they emphasize secrecy. Yet many organizations protect themselves in some ways by secrecy and we do not call them secret societies. British Cabinet ministers are expected to keep the proceedings of Cabinet meetings secret, businesses often go to considerable lengths to protect their own secrets and obtain those of their rivals; yet we would hardly call these organizations secret societies. This is because the activities of the organizations are known, even if the details are not. By contrast the Ku Klux Klan has no publicly accepted function but may undertake a wide variety of actions; Masons meet in private and no one who is not a Mason should know what the subject of their discussions may be. In short, secret societies are *defined* by their secrecy, whether they are legitimate or illegal, and whatever their origins and aims, which may be political or religious, in support of the established authorities or in opposition to them.

Although secret societies take many forms and the only quality they have to distinguish them from other organized groups is secrecy, they do show common characteristics. These characteristics can also be found in other, non-secret, groups, so that they are not peculiar to secret societies but are commonly found together with the element of secrecy. Firstly, almost all secret societies are single-sex organizations, generally of men. If women are admitted, it is usually to a separate chapter or even a parallel organization.[1] Among the West African peoples where the Poro secret society exists, only men may join it; women are initiated into a parallel organization, the Sande. However, a woman must officiate in the Poro initiation rituals; it is likely that she is given the role because she is an official in the Sande society but she may be chosen because she is the wife of one of the Poro officials. In their segregation of the sexes, the secret societies show a characteristic that is very widespread in social life. Even where boys and girls are initiated together, as in the confirmation ritual of the Christian Church, they are commonly separated into two groups. Most initiations into adulthood make a much sharper distinction than that between boys and girls. Another feature of secret societies is that their organization is hierarchical. Initiation into the organization merely places the new member at the foot of a ladder of positions, each rung of which is characterized by its own secrets and initiation rituals. The elaboration of this internal structure reaches amazing complexity in some secret societies. Among the Freemasons one set of rites, the Ancient and Accepted Rite, which is only attained after passing through the basic three stages of Masonic initiation, contains thirty-three higher degrees. In the Poro society, discussed in Chapter IV, there are said to be even more. Not every such organization is as elaborate as this, although all of them seem to distinguish newcomers from more senior members in terms of the greater degree of knowledge which they have attained. The secrets of the society are thus not immediately available to someone who has passed through its initiation rituals; they are acquired gradually.

There is a close parallel between the structure of secret societies and those of some tribal peoples where an elaborate hierarchy of rituals initiates men[2] into higher degrees of knowledge. Among the Baktaman of New Guinea studied by Fredrik Barth in 1968, soon after contact was made with them, there are seven stages of initiation into ritual knowledge. Each stage adds to the initiates' knowledge of the meaning and power of the objects used in the ancestral fertility rituals. Only after the seventh may a man make sacrifices to the ancestors. Progressively fewer men attain the higher degrees, just as the hierarchy of secret societies like the Masons or the Poro tapers to the small number of high officials. Barth's remarks about the Baktaman can be applied also to the better-known secret societies and are worth quoting in full, for they succinctly explain the effects of a system of secret knowledge. 'The value of information seemed to be regarded as inversely proportional to how many share it. From this, it would follow that if you seek to *create* highly valued information, i.e. basic sacred truths, you must seek to arrange worship [or rituals of initiation] so that a few persons gain access to these truths.'[3]

One secret which secret societies guard most carefully is their initiation ritual; the proceedings invariably include an oath not to tell any outsider of the ritual and other secrets on pain of the most severe sanctions. The newly initiated Mason swears not to 'reveal, write, indite, carve, mark, engrave or otherwise delineate any part of the secrets in Masonry' and accepts that the penalty for breach of faith will be 'having my throat cut across, my tongue torn out by the root and buried in the sand of the sea at low water mark, or a cable's length from the shore where the tide regularly ebbs and flows twice in 24 hours'; the alternative, which is referred to as being more effective, seems tame after this – being 'branded as a wilfully perjured individual void of all moral worth and totally unfit to be received into this worshipful Lodge'. In the other secret society with whose rituals we shall be concerned in this chapter, the Triad society of China, the new initiate is shown, not told, what the punishment for failure will be: a cock's throat is cut in front of him as an explicit reminder of the need to keep the secrets with which he is now entrusted.

So important is the oath of secrecy as part of the initiation ritual that in at least one case it is seen as the whole of the ritual; the association of guerrillas known as Mau Mau, which fought a terrorist war against the British in Kenya for seven years, was founded on what was always referred to as the administration of oaths (see Chapter III). I refer to it here to highlight the significance of this aspect of initiation into secret societies, and to point out that the emphasis on secrecy has encouraged fantastic speculation about what the rituals really consist of. Much of the writing on Mau Mau during the time of the Emergency in Kenya was concerned with descriptions of bestial orgies which were said to accompany oath-taking ceremonies. In earlier times, in Europe, the Masons and the Carbonari in Italy were also believed by outsiders to indulge in sinful and blasphemous rites. In 1783 Pope Clement XII forbade Catholics to join or support Freemasonry, describing Freemasons as 'depraved and perverted', since, he argued, it was clear that if they had secrets there must have been something sinful to hide. When the Templars were accused of heresy by Philip IV of France they were also forced to confess under torture to homosexual acts as well as to blasphemy and devil-worship. Many of them died; others confessed. One of the latter, Jacques de Molay, recanted publicly before being burnt at the stake, proclaiming that his infamy had been only a false confession made in order to avoid torture. Initiation oaths and secrets have thus been shown to have powerful effects on men's minds; initiates have died rather than reveal what they have promised to keep secret, and outsiders have believed that what was being hidden was full of evil. Secrecy has allowed free rein to contemporary fantasies and obscured much of what actually happened.

As well as keeping silence about the rituals of the society, members were pledged not to reveal other secrets and mysteries. Some of these referred to signs and words which acted as recognition signals for members. The handclasp of the Masons is one of these; it demonstrates a man's member-ship and rank to a fellow-Mason but is meaningless to an outsider. The Triad society invested certain words with a special significance to members. They could be used quite innocently in ordinary conversation but would reveal the user as a member if another member were listening. These codes of recognition and other esoteric items of knowledge are considered vital secrets; indeed they *are* vital, for it is only they which mark off members from non-members. The line which an initiate must cross to join a secret society is an invisible boundary, that between ignorance and knowledge; it does not change a man's appearance and with some rare exceptions, such as that of the Templars, it does not change his way of life. Membership *is* the common knowledge of secrets and the exclusion from them of outsiders. Were non-members to have access to these secrets, then the dividing line would be blurred. The very existence of secrets is thus crucial for the society to define its own existence.[4]

Initiation rituals and secret signs most often refer to the traditions of origin of the society, its history and early heroes. The two societies I shall now discuss both trace their origin back to the earliest times of their nation's history and beyond. Neither the organizations nor their rituals can be understood except in the light of these traditions, mythical though they are. Each society's history, as perpetuated inside it, serves to justify a claim to power through ancient knowledge. There is much similarity between them, as indeed Freemasons who have made a special study of the Triad society have emphasized, even going as far as to claim for them a remote common origin. It is not uncommon to find similarities in social forms 'explained' by historical connection but, unless such connections can be validated by evidence, this is speculation, not explanation. In this case the similarities undoubtedly stem from the similarities in organization and function; there are also important differences which the Freemason, J. S. Ward, who puts forward the theory of common origin, does not consider.

Secret societies have been a part of Chinese society for two thousand years at least. Their nature and activities have changed at different periods of Chinese history. Sometimes they have presented a threat to the ruling dynasty, which they have eventually overthrown. At other times they have been used by the rulers as a source of support or, more usually, they have provided a refuge for the persecuted and acted as a covert opposition, offering support for the weak against the powers of officialdom. Societies were prepared to take strong action in support of their members; assassination was one of the weapons with which they were traditionally credited. Their protection was generally effective and this goes a long way towards explaining their large and widespread membership. Through the long course of Chinese history different societies rose to prominence and declined again. In the fourteenth century AD the Yuan dynasty succumbed to the revolt led by the White Lotus society; the Manchu dynasty was overthrown in 1912 by forces including those of the Triad. Yet other societies had political importance in different parts of China and at different historical periods. In taking the Triad society as the focus of my discussion I am taking only one example among many but it seems to be fairly typical of most Chinese societies.

The origin of the Triad society, which is also known as the Hung Family, the Heaven and Earth Society, or the Three United Association, is placed in the seventeenth century by the writer William Stanton who, in 1900, published one of the first full accounts of the society by a westerner. However, its own view of its foundations incorporates traditions which go back much earlier in China's history. In the second century A D, some five centuries after the establishment of the Chinese Empire as a single state, there was a rebellion against the Han dynasty, associated with a society called the Yellow Turbans, from the yellow bands the members wore round their heads in battle. In the chaotic times that followed, there arose three popular heroes who became national leaders associated with the defence of popular justice and morality in government. These three, Kwan Yu, Liu Pei and Chang Fei, whose doings were later to form the theme of the great Chinese medieval novel, the *Romance of the Three Kingdoms*,[5] became the mythical ancestors of many secret societies dedicated to brotherhood. The oath they swore in a peach garden is the prototype of the oath in the rituals of initiation in the Triad society, as in many others. The symbolism quite clearly involves the heroes and legends associated with them; Kwan Yu became the god of war Kwan Ti, patron of all brotherhoods, who presides over the altar at initiation rituals. The name of the Triad society is itself an allusion to the three heroes. There are various other symbolic echoes of the cycle of legends about them which formed the stock-in-trade of Chinese story-tellers long before they were written down. Hence the Triad society claims a much longer history by implying that it is the heir of the remote heroes. As we shall see later in the chapter, this is also true of the Freemasons.

The historical, as opposed to mythological, origin, of the Triad, according to the detailed account given by Stanton, lies in the opposition to a (Manchu) Ching emperor soon after the overthrow of the Ming dynasty, which fell in A D 1644. He found himself in desperate straits because a former tributary ruler had not only rebelled but had made several successful incursions into the Emperor's territory. The Emperor offered great rewards to those who would expel the invader and free China from this threat to peace. The monks of the famous old monastery, Shao-lin-tze, who had studied the arts of war, succeeded in doing so, but instead of rewarding them, the Emperor turned against them, razed and burned their monastery and sent soldiers to pursue and kill those who survived. The main body of the society's history concerns the adventures of five[6] monks, who were several times saved from death by miraculous happenings. The man who founded the society as a military group which aimed to avenge the monks was Chen Chin-nan, who had been banished for protesting against the Emperor's treacherous act and who took the despairing monks to his home, White Stork Grotto, to rest. The name of this place becomes part of the Triad greeting. The correct response to the question 'Whence do you come?' is 'From the White Stork Grotto'. The second lodging given the monks by Chen Chin-nan, the Red Flower Pavilion, together with a strange red light which appeared in the sky as a sign of mystical protection, is alluded to in the ritual surname taken by the members of the Triad society. This surname, Hung, has the same sound as the Chinese word for 'red', a colour with favourable mystical implications. In the Red Flower Pavilion the monks and their rebel supporters performed the first ritual of the society; they mingled their blood and tasted the mixture, thus making a bond of blood-brotherhood which became the basis for membership and the central act of the initiation ritual.

After two abortive attempts to overthrow the Emperor and restore the Ming dynasty which had been ousted by the Manchus, the legendary founders of the society dispersed to await a more propitious time for action. Before they parted, some of the monks composed a verse, which is written on the certificate of membership given to each new member. The Triad society remained a secret opposition to the Manchu Ching rulers but its members were never successful in their attempts to restore the Ming emperors, who had been helped to power by the secret societies in the fourteenth century but had been unable to resist the powerful Manchu invaders. Manchu emperors ruled China until the end of the Chinese Empire in 1911 when the last dynasty collapsed, overthrown by a Republican revolution. The Triad society was among other societies whose role in events[7] is still debated by historians (see Chesneaux, 1965; Chesneaux and others, 1970).

In modern times the Triad society has been divided into local chapters, each with its own name. It is sometimes difficult to decide whether these are separate societies or parts of a single organization with a central direction. Probably the degree of central control varied at different times. However, like the traditional government of China, which was established two centuries before Christ and lasted two thousand years, the Triad society was built up from small local groups into a large organization. Each division had its own officials so the hierarchy of officials was very similar to the Chinese bureaucracy. Both systems ultimately rested on a belief in the spiritual powers of the leadership derived ultimately from Heaven but promoted by sacrifices to gods and, in the case of the wider Chinese society, to ancestors. At the pinnacle of the Chinese Empire was the Emperor, a vessel of divine will, whose rule was believed to be divinely ordained and whose orders were the commands of Heaven. Emperors might forfeit divine support by their actions; if they failed in moral righteousness they might lose the mandate of Heaven. Conversely, a successful usurper might claim that the mandate had demonstrably passed to him. Hence in the government of China temporal and spiritual power were associated.

In the Triad society the favour of the patron god and other tutelary deities was also thought to be the cause of a man's promotion to high office. The rituals of initiation into each successive grade of membership both confirmed and enhanced his spiritual strength. However, the religious philosophy which provided the framework of spiritual protectors for the secret societies was drawn from Taoism and Buddhism rather than the official doctrine of Confucianism which supported the Imperial government. The White Lotus society, the most powerful of them all, is said to have been founded as a religious brotherhood, to meditate upon and invoke the name of Buddha. It was this society which was largely behind the successful installation of the Ming dynasty in the fourteenth century, although it appears to have withdrawn its support towards the end of the period and to have been involved in the rebellions which led to the Manchu conquest. The secret societies thus represented an alternative source of spiritual and political power but they did not challenge the main principle of government, that rulers were divine instruments. Like the Poro of West Africa and other secret societies that will be discussed later, the Triad society shows clearly the influence of the wider society in its organization and in its symbolism.

In some important ways, however, the Triad society was the antithesis of the official bureaucracy and it is important to make this clear before we go on to describe and analyse its initiation rituals. In the official system, only the Emperor approached Heaven directly; Triad members all stood before the altar of their tutelary deity as they made an individual approach to the guardians of the society. Traditional China was characterized by infinite awareness of rank; even brothers were ranked by order of birth. Birth was generally important in conferring rank but wealth and success might raise a man's status. The path to advancement lay also through the annual examinations in classical Chinese studies. The various levels of examination provided those who passed with the necessary qualifications for a range of different posts, although it did not ensure that a post was available. The examinations required a scholarly knowledge of the classics and skill in calligraphy so that a career in the bureaucracy was only open to those with the wealth, and hence leisure, to study.

Some of the disappointed scholars who had passed the examinations and failed to obtain an appointment no doubt provided the leadership for the secret societies. But the Triad otherwise emphasized quite other qualifications for membership. Many members were illiterate, the history and legends of the society were committed to memory as well as to writing, and lowly birth was not a bar to advancement in the society. In addition the society's ritual stressed brotherhood and equality and explicitly excluded any member's outside social position from consideration. Loyalty was the prime requirement. In many respects, then, these organizations seem to have offered an alternative chance of power and prestige to those who were debarred from such rewards in the wider society of China.

The setting for initiation into membership of the society as reported by modern authors[8] is a symbolic representation of the history and legends of the society. The place in which initiations are held is variously described as representing a walled city, a palace or a temple, thus referring either to the Emperor or the religious origin of the founders. The inner courtyard is called the Red Flower Pavilion, which recalls the home of the founders, the refugee monks. The robes of the officials are of the Ming dynasty and the shrines are Buddhist but recall various deities including the god of war, the transformed hero of the peach-garden oath. There are shrines to two sets of Five Patriarchs, the Before Patriarchs being the monks and the After Patriarchs five generals who saved them from the Emperor's soldiers. (The number 5 is significant in Chinese numerology: it refers to the five planets and five elements which govern astrology, and to the five branches of government; here it also implies the five branches of the society itself.) At the altar is placed a peck of rice and into it are set the flags representing the five sections of the society, each associated with a Before and an After Patriarch. The peck may itself serve as an altar. Before it on a table are placed a variety of symbolic objects, each referring to the legend as well as to auspicious objects in Chinese religious thought. The objects may themselves be only symbolically represented by the characters which stand for them, written on pieces of paper.

The three chief officials of a local group have titles but are also referred to as Great Elder Brother, Second Elder Brother and Third Elder Brother. (This is a reference to the first initiation ritual in which the monks and their earliest supporters took the role of elder brothers to the new recruits.) At initiations, the Great Elder Brother assumes the name and status of the society's founder. Each candidate must be sponsored by an officer of the society. Several people are initiated at once and each receives instruction from his sponsor.

The account which follows is a shortened version of a long and complicated ritual with a very rich symbolic texture and great variation from place to place. The Red Flower Pavilion is ideally reached through an ante-room and two other rooms, each of which is guarded by members with drawn swords. However, Stanton says that it is common for these other rooms to be represented by hoops of bamboo, held by the two guards at each 'doorway'. The candidates enter the first room after making the appropriate answers to questions asked by the guards. They must bend low to pass through the door, in a gesture of humility and supplication. In the first courtyard their shoes are removed and their hair is released from its pigtail, which, since the pigtail was a Manchu introduction[9] is a sign of their opposition to the Manchu-dominated wider society. The rite is clearly a rite of separation in Van Gennep's terms.

The sponsor then leads the candidates towards the second room where they are challenged for the name of their sponsor. At the entrance to the ante-room they are asked a question, the response to which has the implication of a vow to suffer death rather than divulge the secrets of the society. The Vanguard, who ranks below the three principal officers, then conducts the candidates to the threshold of the inner room. They must shuffle along on their knees. They pass the guards and a long dialogue takes place between the Vanguard and the Second Elder Brother, consisting of questions and answers, often in verse, which refer to the aims of the society and to its past. Finally the Vanguard leads the candidates, still on their knees, right into the room and under a bridge made of swords.

The marginal stage, during which they do not walk and do not speak but have questions answered for them by a sponsor, is now over, with the passing through the doorway of swords into the Red Flower Pavilion, symbol of the society itself. The next stage completes their integration into the group; as new members they undertake the ritual acts themselves.

The Second Elder Brother recites a prayer which invokes the favour of the gods and the Patriarchs on the new members whose induction they are asked to witness. The prayer stresses that they will become part of the new family, whose Father is Heaven and Mother the Earth. They must replace their old loyalties to their families with new fidelity to the Hung Family. Following the prayer, the Second Elder Brother reads from a scroll the thirty-six oaths to which the candidates must show their assent. This they do by rising and thrusting three burning incense sticks, which they have been given to carry at the beginning of this stage, one at a time into an incense vessel in front of the Patriarchs' shrines. Then each candidate takes them back and dips them in a bowl of water, extinguishing them and saying as he does so: 'May my life go out like the fire of these incense sticks if I prove a traitor or false to my oath.' The Second Elder Brother puts a paper on which the oaths are written into the incense vessel and breaks a basin on the floor, saying as it smashes: 'May such be the fate of all traitors.' He sets fire to the papers. A cock's head is then cut off with a sword, a further reminder of the fate of traitors. It must be done in a place open to the sky – under a smokehole or skylight – and some of the blood is dripped into the bowl of water in which the incense sticks were extinguished. The second finger of the right hand of each candidate is pierced and blood allowed to run into the bowl; ashes from the burned oath papers are added. The initiates must either dip their fingers in the mixture and lick it or else sip a little. This action makes them blood-brothers – to each other and all other members of the society. They are now full members and are greeted as such, although they may have to undergo further teaching later. They now pay their fees (some authorities say the fees are paid at the beginning of the ceremony) and the Twenty-One Rules, Ten Prohibitions and Ten Punishable Offences are read out. They reiterate the rule of strict loyalty to other members and the punishments which follow any breaches of it.

Even this shortened version gives some idea of the multiple meanings of this ritual. There are many grades or ranks within the society, known by numbers and entered by their own initiation rites, each with distinct features. In all these, a complex, many-layered system of symbols contains references to the history of the society, to cosmology, astrology and puns on words and numbers, together with play on the intricate calligraphy of key terms. A brief consideration of some of the symbolic meanings of numbers may give some idea of the complexity of the system. The secrets of the society consist largely in knowing the right puns and associations with key words and numbers. One name of the society is the Hung Family, and as I have already said, Hung sounds like the word for red, which recalls the auspicious red symbols of the society's founding; it also was the surname of the ruling Ming dynasty that the Triad society swore to restore. The character Hung is formed from the characters for the numbers 3, 8, 20, and 1. A verse on the character refers to the relevance of these numbers to the first battle of the society with the Manchus. Another name for the Triad Society is the Heaven and Earth Society; in Chinese numerology Heaven is the number 36, Earth 72, and the sum of these 108, is the title of one level of Triad officials. The symbolism of the society makes much use of the numbers 36 (the oaths of membership), 72 and 108; as well as the religious symbolism of the numbers, there were 108 bandits (36 major and 72 minor) in the band led by the three legendary heroes of the peach garden, whose aims of brotherhood and protection of the weak are associated with the Triad society in many ways, as we have seen. The multiple referents of the number 5 have already been noted. The number 3, the symbol of the society itself, also appears frequently: three chief officials, three incense sticks, three legendary heroes; many of the other significant numbers we have mentioned are multiples of 3. A full analysis of the symbolism would be beyond the scope of this book and require the expertise of a sinologist but I have given some examples to show that what the new member of the Triad society is committed to is an elaborate cosmology expressed in complex symbolism. An ordinary member is probably hardly aware of the full implications of the symbols, but the higher he rises in the ranks of the society, the more its meanings will be revealed to him. To begin with, the society appears to the initiate as steeped in the most powerful mystical knowledge, its members as heirs to a long heroic tradition.

Glick and Hong (1947) offer an interpretation of the ritual itself that echoes Van Gennep. According to them the parts of the initiation represent three stages in the evolution of man: death to the world, purification and rebirth – although they do not make it clear whether this interpretation is offered by members of the society. Stanton also records that the Triad slang for initiation is 'to be born'; one member may ask another where he was born, a question with an innocent meaning to listeners who are not members but which asks a member where he was initiated. In the ritual the symbolism of birth is clear. The candidate must have a sponsor, known as his 'mother's brother'; this recalls the significance of this kinsman in the Chinese family system. Chinese marriage, like marriage in most societies, is an alliance between two groups, represented at the wedding by the bridegroom and his brothers, and the bride's brother, who will be mother's brother to future children of the union.[10] Moreover, in the Triad ritual the senior official is referred to as 'Father', so that the initiate is provided with the two male kinsmen who are vital to a child. The Cantonese version of the ritual makes the theme of birth even more explicit: the second official is referred to as 'Mother' and the initiands must crawl between his legs to reach the inner sanctum. This mime of birth reinforces the idea of the Triad society as a family; the officials normally carry the titles of Great (First), Second and Third Elder Brother, thus emphasizing both the equality of members and the ranking by birth (initiation) order which distinguishes brothers in the Chinese kinship system. The bonds of kinship for Chinese are strong moral ties; so are the ties between members of the Hung Family.

Although all initiation rituals show the tripartite pattern of *rites de passage*, varying emphases may be placed by different cultures on the stages in them. Some rites, like those of the Poro (see Chapter IV), elaborate some episodes into subsidiary transitions, with subordinate rituals of separation, marginality and integration linking major phases. Not all stages show equal elaboration; the separation rites in the Triad initiation are brief and simple by comparison with those of the transitional stage and the elaboration of the integrative rites. The effect is to underline the incorporation of the initiated into a new moral community.

It is difficult to interpret the initial rites in Triad initiation as symbolizing death, even though they clearly indicate separation. One is led to suspect that the interpretation offered by Glick and Hong is influenced by a Christian viewpoint which sees ritual birth as implying death and resurrection, rather in the manner of Mircea Eliade whose interpretation of initiation it resembles. The Freemasons, by contrast, elaborate the stages of separation from the outside world and marginality and do seem to see them as a symbolic death. Indeed, the initiation of the third degree of Masonry enacts the symbolic murder and burial of the candidate who is made to lie either in a real coffin or the representation of one, until he is resurrected as a Master Mason by the initiator. The theme of death and resurrection in Masonic ritual may be much clearer because Freemasonry developed within a Christian society, while the wider referents of Triad ritual symbolism are elements of a different religious (and social) tradition. The account of Masonic initiation which follows is a condensation of that published in America in 1875 by Charles William Heckethorn in his book entitled *The Secret Societies of All Ages and Countries*. (I quote from the modern edition of 1965.) Some of the details do not appear in the accounts of other writers on the subject but all authorities agree that there is variation between Lodges and it also seems that the ritual performed in the twentieth century is curtailed, by comparison with earlier forms.

The novice is led into the building by 'a stranger' (a Mason he does not know) and left alone in a small chamber. Then he is stripped of all metal objects he has on him – money, watch, cuff links; his left breast and right knee are uncovered, and his left shoe has the heel trodden down (other accounts say a slipper is put on the left foot). This symbolizes that he is deprived of worldly possessions and is accepted into the Lodge poor and humble. We can also see it as a symbolic stripping of the attributes of the outside world, with its distinctions of wealth and clothing, to leave him naked, without significance except as a potential Mason. His eyes are bandaged and he is led into 'the closet of reflection' where he is told to stay blindfolded until he hears three knocks. After a little while he hears the signal, uncovers his eyes and sees, on the walls hung with black, various injunctions. One that Heckethorn cites is 'If thou value human distinctions, go hence; here they are not known'. His eyes are then bandaged again and a cord in the form of a noose[11] is passed round his neck. He is then led out of the Lodge and back so as to disorientate him. At this point the novice is entering the marginal stage, associated with ordeals; he cannot see, his sense of direction has been confused, and he has been dressed like a victim for execution.

A large square frame covered with paper is brought forward and after an exchange between the sponsoring member and the Master, the latter orders: 'Shut him up in the cave.' Two Masons throw the novice through the paper (as a circus performer jumps through a paper hoop) into the arms of others who catch him. The doors of the Lodge are then slammed and the noise of closing locks indicates that the novice is locked in a dungeon. Silence ensues. Then the Master raps with his mallet and orders the candidate to be brought to kneel before him. He is asked several questions in the form of riddles, to which he must repeat the correct answers he has learned beforehand. The significance of the answers is then explained. One such question is 'How was he clothed?' ('he' being the Master whom the candidate has said he has seen). The answer, 'In a yellow jacket and blue pair of breeches', refers to one of the sacred objects of Masonry, the compasses: an object with brass body and steel (blue) points. As in other secret societies, it is considered vital that the candidate answer without a mistake. The possibility of failure is part of the 'testing' of the candidate, which appears in other initiation rituals. I continue in Heckethorn's own words:

> The candidate is then offered a beverage with the intimation that if any treason lurks in his heart, the drink will turn to poison. The cup containing it has two compartments, the one holding sweet, the other bitter, water; the candidate is then taught to say: 'I bind myself to the strict and rigorous observance of the duties prescribed to Freemasons: and if ever I violate my oath' – (here the guide puts the sweet water to his lips and having drunk some, the candidate continues) – 'I consent that the sweetness of this drink be turned into bitterness and that its salutary effect become for me that of a subtle poison.' The candidate is then made to drink of the bitter water, whereupon the master exclaims: 'What means the sudden alteration of your features? Perhaps your conscience belies your words? Has the sweet drink already turned bitter? Away with the profane (the defiler). This oath is only a test; the true one comes after.'

Heckethorn then describes how the candidate is led round the Lodge, dragged over blocks of wood, told to mount what are described as 'endless stairs' and throw himself off the top, only to fall just a few feet. He is passed through fire, has his arm pricked and appears to lose a lot of blood. All the trials are accompanied by much noise, shouting and beating together of the squares, compasses and other symbols of Masonry which are carried by members of the order. Through all this the novice is blindfolded and must be pushed or led; he is helpless like a corpse or a baby and made to feel so. Finally he takes the oath of secrecy.

The final stage begins with the candidate being led again to face the Master, standing between two pillars, with sword points placed against his breast. The blindfold is loosened (but not removed) and a lamp is held up in front of him. The Master asks whether the novice has shown himself worthy of membership and when the sponsoring Mason replies 'Yes,' the Master asks: 'What do you ask for him?' He is answered 'Light,' and says:

'Then let there be light.' The Master gives three blows with his mallet, at the third of which the blindfold is removed, and light shines into the novice's face. The swords are lowered and the Master leads him to the altar where he kneels and the Master proclaims: 'In the name of the Grand Architect of the Universe and by virtue of the powers vested in me, I create and constitute thee Masonic apprentice and member of this Lodge.' Then he strikes three blows with his mallet, raises the new member and puts on him the apron of white lambskin, giving him a pair of white gloves to wear in the Lodge and a pair to be given to the lady he esteems most (the gloves for the lady do not appear in most other accounts). He is then led again between the two pillars to be introduced to the other members.

This account makes clear that, as the Master declares, the initiation ritual creates a new member. The novice is first stripped of the attributes which identify him with the world outside the society. He is then separated from his former existence but he is not yet given a new identity; he is in a marginal stage. Like the Triad rites, Masonic initiation stresses the distance a candidate must travel to reach his goal, the inner sanctum where he will become a member; the Masonic novices make the journey blindfolded, and various devices are used to make it seem longer and more difficult. The Triad novice travels through three arches on his knees, not walking like the sponsor; the Masonic initiand is blind. In both cases the initiands become diminished, abnormal beings. Both must travel what are made to appear long distances.

The final stage in all these rituals is one in which the novice is endowed with new powers. The newly made Mason is given light, which symbolizes his new life as a Mason. The phrase used by the Master, 'Let there be light', is the same as that attributed to God at the creation of the world, in the account given in the Book of Genesis. 'The Grand Architect of the Universe' is the Masonic title for God, in whose name the Master creates a new apprentice Mason out of the blindfolded, confused human being, whose determination has been tested in a series of ordeals on his journey towards light, which is Masonic knowledge. This symbolism has been treated by writers hostile to Masonry as a blasphemous use of Christian religion. Here I consider it only as showing that the ritual symbolizes an act of creation which transforms the novice from an outsider into one of the group. The corresponding transformation in the Triad ritual uses the symbolism of blood-brotherhood; the new member incorporates into himself the mixture whose making, in the presence of the tutelary gods, changes him into a member of the society. Both rituals represent the initiate as a new-born child.

Although the rituals of these two secret societies resemble each other, it is also obvious that their symbolism draws on very different intellectual or philosophical traditions. The symbolism of Masonry is derived from the technical tools and skills of a craft. Although the Freemasons as such originated only in the seventeenth century, they claim links through the medieval guilds of stone masons back to the mathematical knowledge, the 'mysteries', of Ancient Egypt; like the Triad, they assert an ancient origin. The guilds of masons were associations of itinerant craftsmen, more similar to modern trade unions than to the Freemasons of today. They were concerned to ensure that building, stone-carving and other such work remained in the hands of their members, and admission to the guilds was also a guarantee of skilled training, so that employers could be sure of good workmanship. To maintain the organization they developed secret recognition signs and symbols of their status.

The guilds included not only masons but builders and their employers, whom we might now call architects. The development which led to the formation of Freemasonry was the establishment of honorary membership of local groups of masons, or 'lodges' as they were called from their meeting-places, where members could find lodging when travelling outside their home districts. Mervyn Jones writing on the Freemasons records the admission of an honorary member of an Edinburgh lodge as early as 1600. In 1619 the London masons formed a parallel body for 'gentleman masons', who did not practise the trade but paid double the usual fee for initiation. The movement for what is now referred to as 'speculative masonry', as opposed to the craft of 'working masonry', grew rapidly, fed by the spirit of enquiry of the Enlightenment. A new interest both in the principles of architecture and the hidden knowledge of past ages fanned the flame. It spread swifly through English society, where it soon became first respectable and then fashionable; then to Europe and to the United States. In some of these countries it aroused the suspicion of the authorities and at various times it was banned in France, Italy and Spain. The Vatican fought a long battle against Freemasonry although at one time there seems to have been an alliance between the Catholic Society of Jesus and Scottish Freemasons. In both France and America, leaders of the radical thought of the times, who voiced and encouraged the movements which led to the French and American revolutions, were Freemasons. Men such as Diderot and Voltaire in France, and Benjamin Franklin and George Washington in America, joined the Masons to further the spread of knowledge and encourage the pursuit of freedom, the twin aims to which they were dedicated. However, Freemasonry as an institution seems to have been politically neutral, and in both England and Germany Masons included members of the artistocracy and even the royal families.

Nevertheless, Freemasonry's emphasis on equality and on thought which was freed from the authoritative pronouncements of the Church made it an instrument for intellectual innovation. It must not be forgotten that Freemasonry as a movement began in England at a time when the effects of the Agricultural Revolution and of recent political developments had instituted far-reaching changes in the structure of society, although not perhaps such violent ones as the military struggles which accompanied the creation of the Triad society. Early Freemasons seem to have been trying to combine a search for a solution to the new moral problems of a changing society with a revival of the lost wisdom of the past, a combination which anthropologists also find in other situations of social change.

The symbolic system of Freemasony is taken from the craft of masonry, but also includes references to the Old Testament and to Ancient Egypt. In Mozart's opera *The Magic Flute*, which is in part about Freemasonry, the temples of Isis and Osiris represent salvation. The square symbolizes the honest, 'square-dealing' methods of Masons in their relations with each other; the compasses, chisels and mallets represent other moral qualities which Masonry upholds. Each grade within Freemasonry has its own tracing-board, a design which incorporates the signs of Masonry particular to its own rank, the explanation of which is part of the instruction given by the Master of a Lodge to initiates at the end of the ritual. The square and compasses are general symbols of Masonry which appear in many contexts. They are included in the illustration on the title-page of Diderot's Encyclopaedia where they represent the search for the hidden mysteries of Nature and Science. The founder of Masonry is said to be Hiram, architect of Solomon's Temple, who was murdered for the secrets of his craft.[12] The pillars through which an initiate passes at the last stage of his initiation represent those of the Temple of Solomon and hence the skills of Hiram the Master Builder. The Masonic tradition is believed to descend from that time; to quote the Master's speech, from 'three thousand years after the creation of the world'. During its history, different schools of Masonry have incorporated a number of different 'mysteries' so that there is considerable variation, in both rite and legend.

The three stages of both these initiations constitute powerful dramas, which fulfil the expressed purpose of transforming outsiders into members of the group by enacting the transition symbolically. The change in the novices also serves to define the group as distinct from the wider society to which it appears to be opposed. The marginal stage, represented symbolically as a journey, is also the boundary enclosing members; the transfer of individuals across it emphasizes its existence and underlines the solidarity of members whose loyalty to one another is declared in the formal oaths of allegiance.

The ritual itself is a display of esoteric lore, which is only partly explained to the initiated. Much of it remains mysterious, indicating deeper levels of understanding, associated with higher rank in the organization. The roles of officiants in the rites make this clear, for although the initiates are given some instruction so that they are no longer ignorant outsiders, the officiants show themselves to be even more learned. Ostensibly the body of knowledge, the hidden meaning of symbols, the legends of the society's origin and history, and the experience of rituals like the one they have just undergone, are the secrets to which members are admitted. Yet this seems hardly sufficient to explain large and powerful organizations which have such a long, documented existence.

The Masons and the Triad both have more important secrets which are entirely secular. While the names of prominent Masons may be published in the British press, it is difficult to find out who are the members of particular Lodges. Formerly there were parades of Masons on ceremonial occasions, particularly at the funerals of their members, when full regalia were worn. This practice has been largely discontinued and Masons do not reveal their identity to outsiders; some authorities say that Masons are not allowed to recruit others for the organization, not even their own sons. Clearly some recruitment must take place if Lodges are to continue but the membership and the activities of Masons remain largely unknown. The identities of Triad members have always been closely guarded secrets, which allowed the society to organize in opposition to past governments. It was this very secrecy which protected Triad members from harassment and presented such a problem to the authorities of Communist China when they attempted to disband the secret societies (Lieberthal, 1973). What initiates learn at their induction is precisely what is kept from the general public: they meet their fellow-members and learn the substance of their meetings.

Professor A. Cohen has studied Freemasonry in Freetown, Sierra Leone, where large numbers of Creoles are joining the many Lodges that have been established there. The Creoles are a mixed people with no common cultural traditions on which to base a separate identity; yet they have an interest in maintaining, as far as possible in an independent African state, their earlier status as an influential upper class. Cohen argues that joining the Masons is a significant, if not deliberate, means of achieving this. The personal contacts that membership affords and the confidentiality of Lodge meetings facilitate transactions and discussions of all kinds, enabling Creoles to maintain their exclusiveness and cohesion. In the United States, similar considerations seem to be attractive to the businessmen who make up a large proportion of Masons. The mutual loyalty of Freemasonry can be used to infuse trust and 'square-dealing' into business dealings in a world in which the general ethos is one of cut-throat competition. In Freetown recruitment was more open than in the United States or Europe but the confidentiality of the meetings, which took place several times a week, was closely guarded.

The lack of particular aims and precise policies has meant that secret societies can provide strong but flexible organizations which can be mobilized for a variety of aims. Working masons were originally protecting craft skills but the gentlemen Freemasons who joined them were eccentrics who did not accept the orthodoxies of their day and may have found it a sympathetic milieu in which to develop their ideas in private. In recent times Masons have given financial support to the widows and scholarships to the children of their members. In Chinese settlements overseas the Triad has acted as a welfare agency, helping to find jobs and housing, or arranging loans. At certain periods, as in Singapore in the early days of British rule, the great secret societies have virtually provided the government of the Chinese community (Freedman, 1960).

Some of the activities of organizations like these have earned public disapproval and suspicion. Some governments of China, including the Communist regimes, have seen the secret societies as dangerous traitors. In the latter half of the nineteenth century the Triad was involved in the criminal world of California and has often been suspected of drug-dealing, although Dr Watson, who has studied the Chinese in Britain, regards reports in British newspapers that the Triad were behind such activities in London as mistaken.[13] Recently the Masons have come to public attention with moves to investigate their activities within the police and local government in Britain. Reports that Masons form a covert organization within these institutions have resulted in demands for Masons to declare their membership.[14] As a result of mounting pressure, the United Grand Lodge published, in October 1984, a leaflet for the general public, entitled 'What Is Freemasonry?'. It denies that a Mason's primary allegiance is to his Lodge and to fellow-Masons, stating clearly: 'The use by a Freemason of his membership to promote his own or anyone else's business, professional or personal interests is condemned.' An article in a Sunday newspaper, discussing the new policy of the Masons, commented that 'Freemasons vigorously deny that they belong to a secret society' and pointed out that the names of senior members, such as the Duke of Kent, who is Grand Master, 'are not particularly secret. The more persistent can find out the names of senior craft officers, including at least 40 judges.' Despite the new openness, however, the Masons will not release the membership lists 'of their 8,000 Lodges, with over half a million members', nor are they prepared to reveal how one can join or what goes on during their meetings (P. Lashmar, *The Observer*, 18 November 1984). Whether there is any foundation for the allegations made against the Masons or not, it is argued that the mutual loyalty of members to one another may conflict with their official duties and that such interests should be made public. The anonymity which is the strength of their organization seems likely to be maintained; no doubt it will continue to lay Masons, like members of other secret societies, open to accusations of conspiracy and corruption.

Both the Triad society and Freemasonry began in large-scale societies, dominated from the centre by hereditary rulers and a self-perpetuating upper class. The egalitarianism of both is in direct opposition to the ideas which support such systems, yet neither organization is simply a rebellion of the poor and oppressed. They did provide opportunities for those who suffered disabilities but they also offered a means of mobilizing support for those who were contenders for political and economic power in the wider society. Today Freemasonry in Great Britain is led by aristocrats and members of the royal family while secret societies elsewhere have declined in significance or, like the Triad in China, been forcibly suppressed. In many cases the rituals of initiation continue to be performed, creating a barrier which prevents the intrusion of outsiders and encloses members in privacy and mutual support. Their full significance can only be understood if we consider their effects as well as their purposes, the sociological relevance of the symbolic actions.

NOTES TO CHAPTER II

1. Some of the examples discussed below, such as Mau Mau and the spirit cult of the Nyoro, are unusual in this respect.
2. Rituals for women do not usually support such an elaborate hierarchy.
3. Barth, 1975: 217: my comments in square brackets. Barth is not implying that the Baktaman elders consciously sought to create such a system. To do that would be to confuse effects with aims, which is a common source of theoretical weakness.
4. Often it is not very difficult for the curious, or the researcher, to find out what these secrets are. William J. Whalen in a (largely hostile) account of Freemasonry in his book, *A Handbook of Secret Organizations*, writes, 'Any scholar can soon discover all he wants to know about the secret passwords, rituals, grips, etc., of the Lodge' (1966: 63). He goes on to argue: 'No one should agree to self-destruction to keep secrets which are not secrets at all and call upon God as a witness.' I would argue that it is the ideal of secrecy to which members swear, and the oath itself which sets them off from outsiders and draws them into a clearly defined group. Later we shall see that the Masons do still have secrets, even if their rituals are not part of them.

5. The Three Kingdoms were established in China early in the third century AD, persisting longer in the South by about fifteen years. By the end of the century the Ching dynasty had come to power. A translation by Pearl Buck (1948) is entitled *All Men Are Brothers*

6. Stanton, significantly, says three monks in one passage.

7. The Republic was declared in 1912. Sun Yat-sen is alleged, in some accounts, to have been a Triad officer, but his role and that of the society are now thought to have been exaggerated (J. Watson, personal communication). Detractors of Mao Tse-tung have made similar allegations about his connection with the Triads; in such cases proof is obviously difficult.

8. Stanton, Glick & Hong, Ward, Ward & Stirling, Davis.

9. Initiates wear their hair in Ming style for meetings.

10. Dr J. Watson comments that a mother's brother, who is outside the patrilineal group, acts as intermediary and sponsor for his sister's sons all their lives (personal communication).

11. Heckethorn merely calls it a cord but all other accounts call it a running noose.

12. This legend dates, not from the foundation of Freemasonry, but from the early eighteenth century.

13. J. Watson, personal communication; and see Watson, 1977.

14. See various articles in the *Guardian*, 1984.

CHAPTER III OATHS
AND
INDIVIDUALS

The Triad society and the Freemasons form subgroups within large and complex societies. In discussing them, I concentrated on showing the relationship between the initiation rituals and the constitution of the group. The ritual creates the boundaries which separate outsiders from members, for it emphasizes in dramatic form the distance that separates the two statuses between which initiands must pass. Experience of the ritual and knowledge of its meaning both constitute secrets, possession of which is the right of every member, and is denied to non-members. A more practical advantage which the society offers its members lies in the moral commitment of members to one another, which has no specific aims and therefore can be used in many ways.

Symbols do not simply mark the stages of initiation but reverberate with meanings derived from other social contexts, both secular and sacred. Both the Triad society and the Freemasons legitimize their existence in terms of traditions which are explicitly opposed to the religious system of the wider society: the Triad society uses Buddhist symbols in a wider society whose authorized religion is Confucianism, and the Freemasons emphasize the eclectic nature of their beliefs against the orthodoxy of Christianity; but in both cases their ritual can only be explained in terms of the wider society to which they are opposed. Although secret organizations define themselves by stressing their differences and their secret knowledge, the ritual which represents the division drawn is at least partly based on common ideas. Thus, although the specific meaning of emblems such as the square and compasses is not known outside the Lodges, much of the symbolism of Masonic ritual is intelligible to western European readers, for it is part of their general culture.

An important characteristic of such associations is that they must be formally joined; no characteristic such as age, sex or occupation of a particular office or status qualifies individuals as members. Both the Triad and the Freemasons accept new members as individuals, stripped of their outside qualities, and in principle any member may achieve high office. They thus stress individual commitment, ability and achievement in contrast to a wider society in which hereditary rank and wealth were major determinants of political position. Their system of authority thus conflicts with that of the wider society and may be seen as a challenge to it. This opposition does not necessarily entail political conflict, although it may do so. The central political authorities may see its existence as a threat, as the Masons were perceived to be at certain times and in different places; or the leaders of secret organizations may actually mobilize their members in organized rebellion, as Triad leaders have done at some periods of Chinese history. Their ideas, however, usually present a challenge to the established order, as some knowledge of their beliefs, however inaccurate, filters out to non-members. In the first case discussed in this chapter the individual achievement of power challenges the principle of hereditary succession on which the established political organization rests; indeed, the spirit possession cults of the Nyoro and similar peoples to the west of Lake Victoria do seem to have been involved in political rebellion from time to time. The second case is that of Mau Mau, the guerrilla movement that waged war against the British colonial authorities in neighbouring Kenya for several years. For members of Mau Mau, secrecy was a vital political necessity. In both cases, individual commitment to the leaders of the movement was inculcated in the initiation rites, much as we have seen secrecy enjoined on initiates into the Triad society and the Masons. However, the first is a religious cult, whose purpose is healing and the alleviation of misfortune, the second a (mainly) political organization. Consequently, the first ritual stresses the mystical power of the initiator, the second the commitment of the individual.

The spirit possession cult[1] of the Nyoro was, like Mau Mau, rigorously repressed by the colonial government; like Mau Mau, it survived sufficiently well for the anthropologist John Beattie to be able to obtain information about its ritual. He also records that most people could tell him who were the senior cult members in the locality, which indicates that it had persisted underground. The material thus raises a further question to be dealt with in this chapter: how are the initiation rituals effective in securing loyalty and secrecy from members? In the case of Mau Mau the strength of these sentiments presented such political problems to the government of Kenya that the authorities devised counter-rituals to release members of Mau Mau from their oaths of allegiance. The relative lack of success of these cleansing ceremonies, as they were called, gives some indication of the effectiveness of the initiation rituals of Mau Mau.

The Nyoro of western Uganda resemble many other peoples of the world in that their culture includes institutionalized techniques which are believed to enable experts in them to establish direct and public communication with spiritual beings.[2] These techniques may be incorporated in public worship which upholds the main moral code of a society, or they may be exercised on the periphery, involving individuals (and spirits) who are marginal, or opposed, to the central political and religious institutions.

The Nyoro traditionally believed in two categories of spirits: 'white' or pure spirits who upheld the ideals of kingship and collectively controlled the well-being of the whole kingdom, and 'black' or dangerous spirits. As is common with such beliefs, many of the black or dangerous spirits were seen as foreign; they were never approached in rituals involving important social groups and were associated with misfortunes of various kinds. Thus the categorization of spirits had social referents as well as representing contrasted mystical powers.

The Nyoro are one of a number of peoples known as the Interlacustrine Bantu, from their location around and between the great lakes of Uganda and Tanzania and from their languages which belong to a single sub-group of the Bantu family of languages. They were organized traditionally as a kingdom state, with a hereditary royal clan, the Bito, and an aristo-cratic class who provided the chiefs and other political subordinates of the Mukama, the king. Their authority derived directly from him in a ritual of installation. The bulk of the population, known as Iru, were peasant cultivators, living in scattered settlements ruled over by village headmen, the lowest officials in the political hierarchy. Iru were often village head-men and could in theory rise further but rarely reached the top of the political ladder.

Nyoro believed in several categories of spirits, of which the most important were those of dead ancestors, the *mizimu*, and those powers referred to as *mbandwa*. Mbandwa spirits had names and individual identi-ties but they were described as being 'like the wind'; that is, not located in any form or place. They were capable of manifesting themselves in a number of different ways. The white *mbandwa* are also referred to as 'Cwezi spirits', a term which links the cult to the Cwezi, a supposed race of marvellous people with miraculous skills who, Nyoro believe, came to their country many generations ago. After ruling the Kingdom of Bunyoro for a period they vanished, leaving behind them the techniques of spirit possession so that the Nyoro might appeal to them for help and blessings. The nineteen white *mbandwa* bear the names of Cwezi, either those who were rulers or their wives and slave girls, although they are not thought of as the ghosts of Cwezi but as non-human powers. These white Cwezi are divided into 'great' and 'little' according to their powers, and are also associated with natural phenomena. Their worship was believed to promote health, happiness and fertility. Traditionally each Nyoro clan was associated with one or more Cwezi spirits and every household had its spirit medium, usually installed as a child, whose duties were to communi-cate with the clan Cwezi spirit in order to promote the well-being of the household. As well as this general concern for particular clans, the Cwezi spirits are associated with particular spheres of influence. For instance, Nyabuzana, the most powerful female Cwezi spirit, is associated with childbirth, and Wamara is associated with rain. The household cult of the Cwezi has virtually disappeared under the opposition of the Christian missionaries and the British Administration.[3] The Cwezi spirits and the black *mbandwa*, however, have always possessed individuals as well as household mediums and still did so when Beattie studied the Nyoro in the early 1950s. The legal proscription[4] of spirit possession cults has thus affected different aspects of the cults differently.

The 'black' or dangerous *mbandwa* are of two main types, traditional and recent. Many of the traditional ones were associated with foreign origins, particularly with neighbouring peoples. The new black *mbandwa* show by their names that they represent the essence of the new experiences. Thus there are two *mbandwa* of white people: one is generic, and one the *mbandwa* of white women in particular. There are *mbandwa* of European medicine, of tanks and aeroplanes, and of Christian missions and Islam. The word 'power' that Beattie uses in preference to 'spirit' is a precise description, for the *mbandwa* represent the forces with which the Nyoro had, and still have, to deal.

The possession of an individual by an *mbandwa* spirit is said by Nyoro to be revealed in misfortunes, illness, dreams or visions, which are the means the spirit uses to make its 'demands' known. Both 'white' and 'black' spirits afflicted individuals in this manner and so were said to 'select' those people they wished to have as mediums. Misfortune afflicting a household would traditionally have been attributed to the desire of a Cwezi spirit to establish a domestic medium, if one had not been installed. Only established mediums could communicate with the spirits, and this entailed initiation into the group of the mediums, known, like the spirits, as *babandwa*. Nowadays initiation is usually the cure prescribed for a period of illness or misfortune afflicting individuals rather than households. A diviner is employed to find out what is causing the trouble and may indicate a spirit.[5] Initiation into the cult allows the spirit to express itself and promotes alleviation of the misfortune, but it is not necessary for the sufferer himself or herself to be initiated. Another member of the household may be initiated, particularly if it is a question of the illness of a child. Children were thought particularly suitable as mediums for white Cwezi spirits because of their purity.

An initiation requires the participation of all the mediums in the area, one or more of whom would be senior mediums (*basegu*). It is an expensive affair, for there is a substantial fee to be paid to the initiator and large quantities of food and beer must be prepared to entertain the mediums as well as the kin and neighbours of the initiand. There are in effect two distinct sets of rites, each of which can be seen as an initiation: the first induces the spirit to enter the new medium for the first time, and is an induction into the role of medium, carried out with a public audience; the second, which is wholly secret, is an initiation into the local group of *babandwa* to confer entry into a society, whose membership is known but whose knowledge is secret.

Formerly it seems that the professional mediums of a locality were organized into a group with a loose hierarchy of senior members, usually men, although women seem to have predominated among ordinary members. No initiation into mediumship could take place without them and they were much respected and feared. They were described by Grant, who visited Bunyoro in 1862, in these terms:

> A class of mendicants or gentle beggars called Bandwa ... They adorn themselves with more beads, bells, brass and curiosities than any other race and generally carry an ornamented tree-creeper in their hands. Many of their women look handsome and captivating when dressed up in variously coloured skins and wearing a small turban of barkcloth ... They wander from house to house singing and are occasionally rather importunate beggars, refusing to leave without some present. A set of them lived near us at Unyoro and seemed to have cattle of their own, so that they do not entirely depend upon begging for subsistence. The natives all respect them very much, never refusing them food when they call and treating them as religious devotees. Anyone may join their number by attending to certain forms; and the family of a Bandwa does not necessarily follow the same occupation. I knew of one of them, the captain of a band of soldiers.[6]

In 1888, Emin Pasha described them in similar terms as members of the court of certain Bito princes.

It seems clear that the mediums might have exercised considerable power in traditional Nyoro society. Their profession gave them access to wealth, through the fees paid for initiations and for treating patients. The cult itself provided an organizational structure and, as we shall see, the ritual of initiation inculcated great personal loyalty to *basegu*. Grant's reference to military leadership is also suggestive, for it implies that mediums might mobilize support for political purposes, and in fact the Bito princes at whose court Emin Pasha met *babandwa* were rebels against the Mukama, the Nyoro king. The nature of the mediums' authority was quite different from that of the king and the great nobles whom he chose as his subordinates. In the central institutions of the Nyoro state, rank at birth conferred privilege, wealth and authority; the *mbandwa* cult was open to anyone regardless of birth with the interesting exception of the royal clan. Leadership in the cult was a mixture of seniority and proven expertise and, as with the Triad society, it seems that it has always attracted those who would otherwise have had little chance to exercise any influence: women, and men of lower rank.

That spirit possession cults have represented an alternative source of power for the weak is one of the main conclusions of I. M. Lewis' book on *Ecstatic Religion*, He points out, however, (1971: 112–13) that while for the most part these cults were kept subordinate to the central authorities, it is dangerous to think of them as merely compensatory mechanisms, consolation prizes so to speak. Indeed to the south of the Nyoro state, at the end of the nineteenth century and in the early years of the twentieth, a very similar cult caused a long period of political upheaval. Elizabeth Hopkins (1970) describes it as having first appeared in the area marginal to the great pastoral kingdom states like Ruanda and Ankole. The spirit Nyabingi possessed a number of mediums who rapidly became powerful in these areas where the royal writ did not run. The mediums claimed unique access to spiritual powers but seem also to have used an organization very similar to that of the *mbandwa* cult to mobilize forces against their opponents. One medium, Ndungutsi, was accompanied by a force of sixty men armed with bows and arrows like Grant's 'captain of a band of soldiers'. When the European powers, German, Belgian and British, entered the area they threw their support behind the traditional authorities and urged them to re-establish control; full-scale revolt was provoked and in many areas the cult was only finally suppressed by military force. Hopkins writes that 'the cult represented throughout the region the major vehicle for opposition to the established authority structure of each tribe' (1970: 68). The rebellions seem also to have involved the leadership of dissident princes and princesses so that to label this spirit possession cult a popular uprising against royal oppression is too simple. Moreover, in the case of the Nyoro it was the traditional authorities themselves who opposed British colonial authority, in a number of military encounters. However, the historical background makes clear two important features of the cult: that it was a potential political force and that it might either be used by the royals in their internecine struggles or form the vehicle for protest against the authorities. This might well explain the measures designed by the British rulers of the Nyoro to suppress it.

As well as the usual elements of a transition rite, the initiation rituals of the *mbandwa* cult show similarities with those of both the Triad and the Freemasons. In the first part there are clear and frequent parallels drawn with marriage and the birth of children. The senior officiant is a medium of the spirit diagnosed by the diviner as afflicting the patient, but he and those whom he chooses to assist him are addressed by the initiand in kinship terms.

The senior medium may be called *nyinenkuru*, 'great mother' or 'grand-mother', while the others will be addressed as 'mother'; some Nyoro told Beattie that a senior male medium would be 'father' and a senior woman medium 'mother' to the initiand, as among neighbouring peoples. There seem to have been local variations, but in every case the initiand is placed in the dependent position of a young child, which is demonstrated by the medium's feeding or even symbolically suckling the 'child'. A parallel is also drawn with the ritual of marriage, as in many other spirit possession cults (I. M. Lewis, 1971: 59ff.). Marriage and the birth of children was a symbolic theme of considerable importance in the Triad ritual though it is less striking in that of the Masons. But it can be seen even there: the initiand is shut up in a 'cave' which, as appears to be the case in other rituals, is both a tomb and a womb, and then emerges through an opening into the light like a new-born child. It seems that the relative stress placed on this feature varies according to whether the ritual is believed first and foremost to endow the initiate with new powers, like those of life itself, or whether the emphasis lies on submission to authority.

The second link with the two cases examined in the last chapter lies in the presence, in all but the Nyoro rituals, of oaths of allegiance. In all the examples so far, and indeed wherever formal oaths are a part of initiation, actions accompany the oath-taking: in the Triad rites the initiand swears to forfeit his life if he is not true to the oath. The ashes of the paper on which the oaths are written are dissolved into the liquid he drinks to seal the oath. The novice Mason drinks water which, by means of a trick, is made to seem like the poison that will affect him if he is untrue. The initiate's actions seem to incorporate the power of the oath into his or her body. The initiations into the organization known as Mau Mau were seen as oath-taking ceremonies by most people who wrote of them. The Nyoro rituals while lacking oaths each contain an element which resembles them. They demonstrate to the initiators that the candidate has been transformed by the ritual.

There are also a number of symbolic themes which underline the belief that the ritual confers a new social status with special obligations and duties towards people with whom the initiate[7] was hitherto unconnected. In return the actions of the mediums stress the closeness and intimacy of their relations with her and her inclusion into a group set apart from ordinary people.

Mediums stress the difference between themselves and ordinary people and their appearance seems designed to produce this effect. What Grant described as 'beads, bells, brass and curiosities' give them a weird exotic look. Traditionally they would arrive in a group to initiate a new *mbandwa* but during the 1950s when such activities were forbidden they assembled secretly at night and then donned their regalia. Their difference from ordinary people is also shown in prohibitions on their eating certain sorts of food. In this they resemble other persons with ritual power like the Mukama himself.

At the house of the initiand, foods that they may eat, finger millet, meat and beer, all traditional among the Nyoro, have been prepared for them and the initiand and her kin are waiting. The first thing the mediums do is to take her outside and strip her naked. Her whole body is then anointed with medicine nine times, the auspicious number in Nyoro culture. The empty potsherd which held the medicine is put on the ground and a black berry called *ngusuru* is placed in it. The initiand must raise her left foot and stamp it down on the shard, saying: 'May all the badness which was in me depart from me; I have trodden this under with my left foot and so shall I tread on evil in future.' Nyoro think that to be an intermediary between men and spirits is good but the spirits are believed to be strong and may destroy someone of bad character who attempts to be a medium. The moral evil of the initiand's former life is removed from her in the ritual washing and she repudiates it again by crushing it with the left, the inauspicious, foot.

The initiand is brought into the house and clothed in the traditional barkcloth, now only used for ritual purposes. The fire has been made up with wood which burns particularly brightly, and sweet-smelling herbs and grass have been strewn on the floor. These give further protection, and the novice may be purified again by the mediums' blowing smoke over her from their clay pipes. She is given a branch of the plant associated with the *mbandwa* cult to hold, and is ready to receive the spirit. Songs are sung which recount the advantages and pleasures of membership.[8] Everyone present joins in the choruses. After some hours without the novice's being possessed the mediums get impatient, start singing songs which criticize her, and then take her outside. There she is subjected to questioning which, in the version given by Beattie, suggests that possession may be simulated and that the techniques of inducing it are learned and do not all come at once. All Beattie's informants mentioned the criticism, removal and questioning of the novice, which indicates that it is part of the ritual, rather than evidence of its failure. It clearly provides an interval during which the initiand may be told what to do next.

They return to the house and the seance continues, but this time the initiand, following her instructions, shakes her wand more and more strongly, indicating that the spirit has entered her. The mediums surround her and she falls, or is pushed, down to the ground. They express their satisfaction by characteristic grunting noises and they may then bind her body with the grass swathes that tie a body for burial, three for a woman, four for a man.

The chief initiator demands payment from the initiand's kin for 'raising her up', and when he receives it, the mediums loosen her bonds and raise her carefully so that the palms of her hands do not touch the floor, until she is sitting again near the brightly burning fire. She is raised up as a woman must rise when her suitor comes to her home with the initial formal gifts of betrothal, but the spirit is believed to be in her head and now it is the spirit not the novice that is addressed. Her kin may ask the spirit what caused it to afflict the patient and what must be done. If it replies it will be in the special *mbandwa* language which must always be used by mediums, but usually the novice stays silent and the kin merely ask the spirit for its blessing. This is given by the novice spitting in her hands, in the character of the spirit, and then rubbing her hands over her own body. More singing and shaking of the mediums' rattles may continue to raise other spirits, in the mediums or other people present, but finally the mediums take the initiand outside to 'greet the dawn'.

After this a meal of the traditional millet porridge is prepared and the initiating mediums feed the novice, putting little bits of porridge into her mouth as a mother does for her child. They spit on the morsels before they put them into her mouth thus conveying their blessings. This way of feeding also occurs in the making of blood-brotherhood; it signifies the closest attachment, that of mother and child. The rest of the day is spent in making the appropriate regalia and charms for the new medium. The charms resemble sorcery medicines and are considered very powerful; they may enable the initiand to receive spirit messages in dreams, but they may turn and kill her if she neglects the spirit or breaks the rule of the cult, particularly that which enjoins respect for senior members.

When the regalia are ready the main fees will be demanded and shared between the chief medium and the assistants. The payment, which is substantial, is sometimes referred to as bridewealth, thus further emphasizing the analogy with marriage. On the second night there is further singing and spirits are 'raised into the head' of the novice and those of the mediums who are present. Next morning, attended only by members of the cult, the novice is symbolically reborn. One of the mediums, usually an old woman who has been chosen to be the novice's ritual mother, stands with her legs wide apart while the initiand lies on the ground behind her. Another medium, the 'midwife', seizes the initiate through the legs of her colleague and, helped by others, pulls her through the legs while the 'mother' groans like a woman in labour. The initiate must then cry like a new-born baby, is placed on her 'mother's' lap and must put her mouth to the breast. As in the real situation of birth, the 'mother' then ritually curses the 'baby' and immediately retracts the curse, a magical action which was believed to ward off evil, for in the negating of the curse all the possible evils that have been uttered in it are prevented from happening.

The theme of this first set of rites is clear: the initiand is purified to enable her to contain the power of the spirit, which is then induced to enter her so that its wishes may be discovered. The initiand is a 'bride' while the spirit is her bridegroom. Lewis has suggested that this very use of marriage to symbolize the relation between spirit and medium is appropriate because becoming a medium implies an alliance, a contract between different partners similar to that between spouses at marriage. The Nyoro ritual suggests that it is more than this, for it is the conjunction of powerful spirit and the medium's body which is believed to heal the affliction for which the seance has been called. The union also precedes the birth of the initiate herself as a medium. As Nyoro believe that it is the potency of a man's semen that causes a woman to conceive, so here the ritual seems to imply that it is the potency of the spirit that creates a new medium and generates health and good fortune. The power of sexual intercourse appears again in different form in the second set of rites.

Although the spirit has been induced to enter the body of the patient, she is not a medium until she has been initiated into the local group of mediums; this is what the second set of rites achieves. These rites are secret and take place in the bush away from settlements, and so, in a sense, outside normal society. They may follow immediately after the rebirth rite or they may be delayed for a day or two. The first rite consists of a curse which places the initiate in a state of dangerous pollution; this is said to be done in the 'black bush' with its connotations of evil.[9] Subsequent rites in the 'white bush' purify the initiate and enable her to resume normal social life.

The chosen place in the 'black bush' is marked by a heap of regalia, including that of the novice, piled up with the male initiators' spears thrust into the middle, blades upwards. The initiate must sit with her legs apart, supported from behind by one of her 'mothers'. The senior male medium, the *musegu*, then submits her to a severe and formal curse. He stands in front of her, dressed only in a loincloth and with his back to her. Then, bending forward, he thrusts his buttocks towards her face and, holding his gourd rattle with both hands, he passes it between his legs and touches her on the mouth. Then he pronounces a conditional curse, saying that if ever she reveals the secrets of the cult she will suffer various terrifying penalties. This obscene act (and it was obscene to Beattie's informants too) is the means of enveloping the initiand in *mahano* (mystical danger) so that she will be vulnerable to the next ritual, known as 'grasping' the secrets of the cult.[10] It is the curse and the obscene action which accompanies it that generate the dangerous power which will pollute the novice for several more days until it is lifted by a normal sexual act.

A further rite follows, which is designed to produce physical fear in the novice. I quote the verbatim report of an informant from Beattie's account of the ritual.

> The *musegu* [senior medium] withdrew his spear from the ground in front of me and told the 'mother' who was supporting me to hold me firmly so that he might kill me. My 'mother' did as she was told; she uncovered my chest, and tapping my breast-bone with her finger she said to the *musegu*, 'I have prepared her properly, here is her breast-bone, pierce her there.' The *musegu* stepped back a few paces and then rushed right at me with his spear poised to kill me. But he stopped at the last moment and said, 'Eh! I have a bad grip of the spear.' He did this twice; on the third occasion he brought the point of the spear right up to my chest as though he were really going to pierce me but he did not. I wept. When they [i.e. all the mediums present] saw that I was weeping they cheered loudly and grunted. They said, 'Now she has taken hold of [literally 'caught'] the secrets of the *babandwa*: others have undergone the same experience, now she will become a *mubandwa* like other *babandwa*.'

She was then asked to choose the regalia she liked from the pile. If she chose an item that had been made for her, she was praised; if she failed to identify it, and picked up someone else's regalia, she was slapped and beaten. The head-dress was then ceremoniously placed on her head nine times, to endow her with its properties.

During this period in the 'black bush' the initiate may get from her instructors some teaching of the *mbandwa* language which must be used between initiates and in possession. This 'language' has a Nyoro grammar, but the vocabulary consists partly of loan words from other languages and partly of obsolete words or ordinary words used with a different meaning. It is quite extensive in scope and one session would not teach all of it, so the initiate will acquire it gradually while attending subsequent seances. After the rites in the 'black bush' are complete, the party returns to the homestead, where some handfuls of thatch are taken from the roof over the front and back doors of the hut. These are burned in the courtyard and their white ash is smeared on the novice's throat and face. White, a pure colour in Nyoro ritual, is used to protect the initiate while she is still filled with *mahano*.

The next day a visit to the 'white bush' is made to enable the *musegu* to withdraw the curse. The initiate is warned not to disclose the secrets of the cult, nor to neglect the spirits whose medium she now is. It is significant that prominent among her instructions are those which enjoin her to treat her seniors in the cult, particularly those who initiated her, with special respect. She must never refuse a request from them and must share anything she has with them. If a senior male medium wishes to sleep with her she should not refuse him. She may receive more instruction in the *mbandwa* language and be given her regalia and a special bag in which to keep them.

There follow tests to show whether the rites have been effective. If the signs show that they have, then the power is removed by sexual intercourse between the senior male medium and the initiate. The sacrifice of a male goat follows; its blood is smeared on the faces of all present but none of the flesh is eaten. The body is left in the bush, in contrast to the procedure at other Nyoro sacrifices. Possibly it retains the evil powers of the rites and so purifies the participants. The party returns to the homestead where the initiate is once more bathed, her head is shaved and she is dressed in new barkcloth. The initiators return home but the initiate, like a bride,[11] must observe a period of seclusion.

The second set of rites sheds further light on the whole ritual, for they are an inverted form of the first. In the first there are symbolic references to marriage, while the second mimes perverted sexual intercourse; symbolic childbirth then follows in the first rite, while in the inverted version symbolic death ensues. If the first rites demonstrate the healing, life-giving powers of the mediums, the second series would seem to manifest the control of evil and dangerous forces. In both cases power is projected on to the novice, but in the first instance she 'dies' or becomes merely the vessel which contains her spirit. In the second the influence of the power which envelops her comes out in a spontaneous reaction (tears) which is welcomed as a sign that the ritual has taken effect. She is now enveloped in *mahano*, a Nyoro concept which links the spirit possession cult with the wider society.

The Mukama is believed to be the direct heir of the Cwezi heroes. His mystical power, also known as *mahano*, derives from his birth as the direct descendant in the patrilineal line from a former Mukama as well as from the ritual which installs him in office and is regularly performed throughout his reign to keep his *mahano* strong. The Mukama himself must keep food, and other taboos, in order to protect his *mahano*, for its strength directly affects the prosperity of his people and the productivity of the land. The natural and social orders are inextricably intertwined in the person of the king. Any political subordinate holds legitimate authority only if the royal *mahano* has been ritually conferred on him. Thus one meaning of the word *mahano* was the essence of royal authority stemming from the Cwezi, manifest as white *mbandwa* spirits in their modern guise. White spirits are not themselves *mahano* and the distinction between kingly authority and these forces for good is maintained by the taboo on royal participation in spirit possession cults.

Mahano can also refer to the power believed to be in unnatural, because unpredictable, events. Death and the birth of twins cause a state of dangerous *mahano* which must be removed from those affected by the events that caused it, or it will harm them and all those who come into contact with them. *Mahano* thus has two aspects, one royal and beneficent which must be protected by ritual, the other haphazard and evil which must be removed by ritual. The greatest *mahano* of all is caused by the Mukama's death, which affects the whole country and its people; but in a looser Nyoro usage any strange event may be a manifestation of *mahano*. It is *mahano*, as the antithesis of the qualities of kingship, that is mobilized by the senior medium to strike fear into the novice, and further to infect her with *mahano*, which completes her transformation into a medium.

Thus initiation rituals, like the rituals of kingship, are occasions for the manifestation and control of spiritual powers which, in Nyoro thought, lie behind authority. It was characteristic of the traditional state, as it was of China and the Europe of early Freemasonry, that the spiritual authority which supported kingship was morally good, while that exercised by those with no established claims to rule was seen by outsiders as at best, dangerous, and at worst, evil.

The effects of the ritual are judged by the acts of the initiand. In the first set of rites she is taken outside, given the information that possession may be feigned and then led inside to put this into practice, to obey her instructors. In doing this she demonstrates her acceptance of their right to command. If she refuses, the ritual cannot proceed. In the second ritual, a clearly spontaneous reaction follows the senior medium's acts and is taken as a sign that the person of the initiand is transformed. The individual has been 'caught' by the ritual and is committed as a medium.

The powers used by spirit mediums were conceived of as dangerous and unnatural, although they could be used to heal. Unless a newly initiated medium had been purified, she could sleep with no man who was not a medium, not even her husband, for her *mahano* was too dangerous to them both. Members of the royal clan were forbidden close contact with the cult but there is clear evidence that spirit mediums might use their powers to legitimize rebellions, and mobilize their supporters as a political force. Spirit possession, with its emphasis on individual powers and on the haphazard choice of mediums by the spirits among ordinary people, was an alternative source of authority and a challenge to the constitution of the Nyoro polity.

In Mau Mau we have an example of a secret society which was in direct conflict with authority, not merely a potential threat. A striking feature which was much emphasized at the time was the remarkable effect of its initiation rituals centring on the taking of oaths. The ritual was binding even if undergone, as it often was, as the result of coercion. Some Kikuyu, particularly those who were devout Christians, did break their oaths by informing on those who forcibly initiated them, but the government was sufficiently worried about the power of the oaths to set up rehabilitation camps and institute public cleansing ceremonies claiming to release people from the power of the oaths. Their success was very limited. This was a case in which initiation generated powerful loyalties, interpreted both by supporters and opponents of the movement as the effects of the ritual.

Mau Mau was a secret society and a guerrilla organization which kept Kenya in turmoil for four years.[12] It was largely confined to the Kikuyu-speaking peoples and their related neighbours, the Embu and Meru, although at its height it does appear to have spread to the neighbouring Kamba, a distinct people with a tradition of intermittent hostility to the Kikuyu. It was highly secret and spread rapidly so that when it reached full-scale insurgency the colonial government and the public were surprised and shocked at the extent of its organizational network. The Emergency declared in 1952 was to last until 1960 but individual groups of guerrillas lingered on in the forests for much longer, in spite of the newly installed President Kenyatta's two appeals to them to come out of the forests and settle down as honoured heroes of the Independence struggle. By the end of the Emergency, which cost Britain millions of pounds and resulted in the deaths of several thousand Kikuyu (over 10,000 of them Mau Mau members), deep and bitter divisions had been created among the Kikuyu people, but the organization itself had fragmented into numbers of small groups, most of them operating in the forests of Mount Kenya or the Aberdares range. It was never clear to what extent there was an overall organization responsible for co-ordinating the activities of different regional subdivisions. Both Waruhiu Itote (the self-styled 'General China') and Josiah Kariuki describe in their books an elaborate bureaucratic organization, the first modelled on army organization and the second on the pattern of the colonial administration, but their accounts contain differences which are hard to reconcile. There is much more evidence[13] for a rather loosely co-ordinated proliferation of small cells, responding to the direction of those leaders of the movement whose reputations gave them wider influence. (See Rosberg and Nottingham, 1966.)

The bitterness which was evoked on both sides has made evidence on the initiation rituals of Mau Mau liable to distortion. Both sides have represented their struggle as one of good versus evil, but the members of Mau Mau faced the opposition of their fellow Kikuyu as well. Indeed it was this opposition which became one of the deciding factors in the military action. As a result, and because of the need to heal the wounds in the body politic in the years immediately preceding and following Kenya's Independence in 1963, Kikuyu writers have represented the oaths of allegiance as being closer to Kikuyu tradition than perhaps they were, emphasizing both the African and the liberationist character of the movement. Christians and whites, on the other hand, largely took the view that Mau Mau was a reversion to primitive savagery. Stories of bestial rites and orgies were retailed very widely and found their way into such writings as Corfield's *History and Origins of Mau Mau*. Corfield's sources seem largely to have been rumour and the accounts, often second-hand, of confessions obtained from captured guerrillas. These have been denied as spurious by many Kikuyu, as the Templar Jacques de Molay also claimed of his 'confession'. It is also clear that the movement attracted to itself men of unstable personality as do most violent organizations. The isolated guerrilla life in the forests may have driven some men to abnormal behaviour.[14]

The government forces were not innocent of savagery either but atrocities are mentioned here to underline the fact that we do not have the sort of evidence on Mau Mau initiation ceremonies that is available for the other cases. In the bitterness and fear on both sides, more fear and horror was engendered by the stories each told of their opponents.

As in many other of the secret societies I have described, there were grades within Mau Mau, each with its own rite of admission. Forest fighters underwent two rituals, but some of the more influential leaders were said to have taken many more. The first rite, referred to by Kikuyu writers as the 'Oath of Unity', conferred membership of the society and was used to obtain mass support. There were reports of large numbers of people undergoing the ritual together. Undoubtedly people were sometimes forced to go through the ritual and some were beaten or even killed if they refused; as Barnett and Njama put it in *Mau Mau from Within* (1966: 60):

> Since the society was proscribed and membership in it carried the threat of a long prison sentence, it was necessary to ensure that would-be initiates brought to an oathing ceremony became, in fact, members of the Movement who felt themselves bound by the vows of secrecy.

As I have already indicated, extremes of loyalty are by no means peculiar to Mau Mau. Initiation rituals are almost always irreversible; an insider cannot reverse the process and become an outsider again.

Knowledge once acquired cannot be unlearned and since secret societies are organized around secret knowledge it is intelligible that they cannot provide for resignations. This is not to say that all initiates must play an active part in a society; it is clear that only a minority are either interested enough or able to reach the higher ranks. Many Masons do not go often to Lodge meetings; many Mende men who are initiated into the Poro society play no further part in its activities; and Stanton writes that in Hong Kong men joined the Triad to protect their families and businesses from depredations by the society, not in order to play an active part in it. Beattie notes that most Nyoro families have one member at least who has been initiated, but it is also clear that active mediums are relatively few in number and form a sort of professional inner circle of adepts (their experience makes them experts, unlike the majority of members, who undergo initiation as a means of alleviating personal problems). However, the political difficulties that the Kenya government faced with the involuntary initiates of Mau Mau focus attention on the fact that the initiation rituals of secret societies seem to induce a permanent change in the individuals who undergo them.

It is the second (and subsequent) rituals of Mau Mau that evoked the greatest European horror and the greatest Kikuyu defensiveness because of the bestiality and bloodshed they were alleged to include. These were known as *Batuni* (from the English word platoon), and endowed those who went through them with the status of forest fighter, thus distinguishing between what the government referred to as the 'active' and the 'passive' wings, although the latter term was probably a misnomer, for many of these people played a considerable part in providing the support and information needed by the forest groups. The account below is of a first initiation and is taken from the book by Barnett and Njama; it is cited by the authors as typical of many others although they, like most sources, point out that there were local variations. There were probably variations over time as well. (See Buijtenhuijs, 1982.)

The man who gave this description conveys in it the impression that, although he had expressed interest in Mau Mau, he had no warning that he was to become a member. He was visiting a girl-friend when he joined a gathering from which he and some others were called out for the rituals. I give the informant's description of his acts and feelings verbatim, but I have paraphrased and condensed his descriptions of ritual objects and added my comments.

He and other recruits were led under guard to a deserted hut.

As we approached the door, I saw a dim light and heard people whispering. But as we entered the light went out and there was complete silence. We were all frightened at this point and entered with some reluctance on the insistence of the guards. It was pitch dark inside and I could hear the whispered voices of many people who soon began asking us, in turn, who we were and other questions about ourselves.

All accounts of Mau Mau and its rituals emphasize the use of personal knowledge as a means of vetting the recruits for security purposes. However, the questioning may also have been used to frighten the initiates, since the man I am quoting here records being 'held round the neck and arms by three or four people'.

Lights were lit, and showed the ritual paraphernalia already in place. The door was bolted and there was a congregation of some thirty people beside seven men to be initiated. The informant recognized most of them and he records that he lost his fear at this point. The main ritual construction was an arch made of banana leaves, guarded by men with traditional Kikuyu swords. The arch has potent meaning for Kikuyu for initiands traditionally passed through one during the rites of passage from boyhood to warriorhood. Initiation into Mau Mau was thus identified with becoming an adult member of Kikuyu society. The ritual was not, however, entirely constructed from traditional symbols but was syncretistic.

The initiands were ordered to take off their shoes and remove any coins, watches or other metal objects from their pockets. This feature is an invariable element and is interpreted as a rejection of objects associated with colonial society, although some writers point to the similarity with Masonic initiation rituals. There is no evidence to show whether there might have been direct borrowing from Freemasonry, but readers will already recognize the recurrence of common symbols of separation in rituals in very different places.

The initiator then addressed the novices, telling them of the reason for the formation of Mau Mau. Then he announced that anyone who refused to take the oath would be killed and buried then and there. In spite of the threat one of the novices objected. He was not killed but was struck in the face and thereafter complied. The account then returns to a description of the arch, which was decorated with the major crops of the Kikuyu, maize and sugar-cane, and with other significant plants, as is the arch of initiation into adulthood. Hung from the top of the arch were objects with traditional ritual meaning and uses which also feature significantly in most accounts of rituals.

As at many traditional Kikuyu rituals, a goat had been slaughtered and roasted. The meat from the chest was removed and hung on the arch together with the bone called *ngata* in Kikuyu. The *ngata* is described as 'a bone which connects the head and the spinal column', and contains seven holes. It is clear from this and other accounts that it is the seven holes which are of most significance, seven being a ritually powerful number. The strongest oath administered by the elders in settling disputes traditionally involved *githathi*, a ritual object of great power described by Middleton and Kershaw (1965: 45) as made of clay or stone and containing seven holes. The eyes of the goat were also significant; in Kikuyu traditional thought they seem to have been regarded as the seat of the animal's life, which was present in the fluid in the eyeball itself. In this ritual the eyes were removed and fixed with thorns to a container for a liquid mixture of the goat's blood, soil and crushed grains mixed with the other Kikuyu staple, beans. The container, made of a hollowed-out banana stalk, was also decorated with two fruits that figured in other Kikuyu rituals. Finally, twisted strips of the goat's hide were made into nooses for each initiand to wear around his neck, and into arm-bands, which were distributed later. Each initiand was also given a ball of damp soil which he held against his stomach throughout the ritual. The ritual paraphernalia thus clearly referred to Kikuyu traditional ritual and also symbolized the land and crops which were vital to them and for which they were fighting.

The account continues:

> Standing before the arch, I passed through it seven times while the oath administrator uttered and I repeated the following vows:
>
> 1. If I am called upon at any time of the day or night to assist in the work of this association, I will respond without hesitation; and if I fail to do so may this oath kill me.
> 2. If I am required to raise subscriptions for this organization, I will do so; and if I do not obey may this oath kill me.
> 3. I shall never decline to help a member of this organization, who is in need of assistance; and if I refuse such aid may this oath kill me.
> 4. I will never reveal the existence or secrets of the association to Government or to any person who is not himself a member; and if I violate this trust may this oath kill me.

Following this, and repeating these vows again on each occasion, I was instructed to take seven sips of liquid from the banana-stalk container, seven small bites of the goat's thorax (meat) and – performing each act seven times – to prick the eyes of the dead goat and insert a piece of reed into the seven holes of the *ngata*. The administrator then had me take a bite of sugar-cane, poured cold water over my feet and made a cross on my forehead with the blood and grain mixture. When this was completed, I was surrounded by a number of spectators who took hold of the skin ring round my neck and started counting. Reaching the number seven, they all pulled, breaking the ring and saying: 'May you be destroyed like this ring if you violate any of these vows.' The rest of the people repeated this curse in unison.

The rites ended with a communal meal in another hut, uniting the new initiates with those who had been previously initiated, who had been witnesses of this initiation.

Other accounts include more symbols drawn from outside the Kikuyu ritual system. The similarity with Masonry, which also occurs in the 'noose' round the neck which is removed, though not as in Masonic ritual, has been noted. The cross on the forehead is a Christian symbol of baptism, and Christian symbolism is noticeable in other accounts. Waruhiu Itote, 'General China', reports that in what he calls the Action Oath, the administrator holds a gourd of goat's blood to the initiand's lips, saying, 'This is blood and whether it be of man or beast, make it a cup of love and drink you all from it.' The echoes of the Christian communion are very clear in this sentence.

Barnett and Njama comment that this was essentially an elaborate initiation ceremony, but compared with the others described here it is not very elaborate, and the tripartite structure is not very clear, although it is still possible to discern separation (the silent dark), a marginal stage (the Oath-taking), and integration (the communal meal) in this account. What is clear is that no commentator has found it possible to explain the significance of the symbolic objects without reference to Kikuyu culture. But it is not like any single Kikuyu ritual of traditional times for it mingles elements drawn from many of them. It also includes, as symbols with powerful significance, the cross and the notion of communion; the Kikuyu people had been mission-taught for many years and Christianity was no strange system of thought to many who joined Mau Mau. Moreover, just as 'first communion' is initiation into the Catholic Church and its repetition regularly affirms the faith of members and strengthens their membership of it, so the rituals of Mau Mau were repeated periodically to strengthen the dedication of fighters living in the forests. Overtly, however, the rituals express Kikuyu custom as the charter for the group, in opposition to modern society under colonial rule.

The central feature of the ritual is the oath-taking; indeed it is usual to find the rites referred to as Oath-taking, rather than initiations. The Kikuyu traditional system of government depended heavily on the use of oaths which invoked spiritual powers, usually the ancestors but the more distant creator god as well, to mete out justice in disputes or to seal peace-making. The Mau Mau rituals make use of the *ngata*, the oath on a goat's bone with its repetition of the mystical number seven, as well as the ritual *thenge*, a purificatory rite in which a goat was killed. The traditional rite of taking an oath included the two elements found in Mau Mau rites – a verbal promise and an action. Together the two elements are binding on the individual, even if he is coerced into performing them.

The actions associated with the verbal oath are of two kinds: they involve ingesting a ritually prepared substance or they place the novice in contact with powerful objects, in this case the goat's eyes and the *ngata's* seven holes. Drinking the mixture and eating the goat's meat are means of incorporating powerful substances into the very body of the initiate, where they will act against him if he violates the oath. Contact with the goat's eyes is, I have suggested, a contact with the life of the goat which is a powerful activating ingredient in the ritual. (It is also present in the goat's blood which is drunk.) The *ngata* which is pierced with a reed is also an abstract representation of life, for it stands for the sexual act, the creation of life itself, which the action of the reed also mimes. The mixture which is drunk also contains the life of the beast, the soil and the seeds of food plants. All these objects together do not merely embody the hidden powers of natural life or act as symbols of natural powers; they are the means by which the ritual is given its force.

In all the other initiations into secret societies the rules of membership are made explicit to the new initiate. He is, however, committed to them in different ways: in the Triad society the written rules are burned and mixed into the liquid that he drinks, but the newly initiated Nyoro medium merely has the rules recited to her formally by the senior medium. Among these four examples only Freemasons and the Mau Mau use the spoken word.

Anthropologists have paid much attention to the verbal formulae that accompany rituals of all sorts. Malinowski pointed out that in the Trobriand Islands the compelling part of a magical spell[15] lay in the verbal formula which activated the ingredients. This is not true of all magic in all societies but the words can be seen as vessels of power in the same way as other ingredients, such as the ones discussed above. Maurice Bloch, in discussing the use of language in ritual among the Merina of Madagascar, has demonstrated convincingly that the effectiveness of such language lies in its extreme formalization. Participants are not free to say what they like and if certain phrases are used, there are only certain other phrases which can follow. Such language is not like ordinary language which conveys information; formal language has only symbolic force. He shows that prayers, chants and songs, uttered by the elders who officiate at initiation ceremonies, represent authority which is derived from the ancestors for whom, and as whom, they use this ritual language.

However, the stereotyped formula of an oath is used here, not by the authoritative initiator but by the new recruit, who has the least powerful position of all. What authority can he have? If we consider what really happens in detail the picture is rather different. An oath is always administered; that is, the person who swears is led through the oath by a superior. In fact the account of the Mau Mau ritual quoted above says 'the oath administrator *uttered and I repeated* the following vows' (my italics). The oath is thus not, as is usually imagined, the point at which the candidate freely pledges himself to the society, it is a point which tests the candidate's acceptance of its authority over him. By repeating the words that are said to him the candidate, whatever else is also involved, is demonstrating obedience to his instructor. He simply repeats what he is told. I do not wish to imply by this that the candidate may not be deeply committed by his words; the sufferings of members of many secret societies from earliest times give the lie to that statement. It is both an acceptance of authority and a personal commitment to the group.

Perhaps this may seem clearer if we consider the equivalent ritual in the Nyoro rituals described earlier in this chapter. The rites in the black bush are designed to terrify the initiand so that she is receptive to, and 'takes hold of', the secrets of the *babandwa*. The senior medium works to obtain a reaction; the source of this account says, 'I wept. When they saw I was weeping they cheered and grunted ...' In both rituals fear is the dominant emotion, fear of the unknown; in all initiation rituals those who are going to be initiated do not know what is going to happen next. They are ignorant outsiders being given knowledge as they progress through the ritual. The tears of the Nyoro novice medium and the sevenfold repetition of the vows by a Mau Mau recruit both serve as a demonstration of their receptiveness to the ritual change that is being effected.

The active participation of other members is also necessary; listening to the repetition of vows they have made or watching reactions that 'others have undergone', they too are subjected to the authority of the words and their dedication is strengthened. In a more practical sense the congregation as witnesses are of significance too. Membership of the group implies relations with other members, not merely submission to the group's leaders. Moreover, in the case of the Mau Mau, as in other secret societies, the penalties for breaking the oath were in many cases inflicted by fellow-initiates on the traitor. The group is both the source of strength of the organization and the means by which it controls its members. They are also the visible reminder of the effects of past rituals. Thus in all the initiation rituals the participation of a congregation of initiated members is essentially a demonstration of the effects of the initiation: that it creates a loyal group, a cohesive social force.

NOTES TO CHAPTER III

1. For a full discussion of the sociological significance of spirit possession, see I. M. Lewis, *Ecstatic Religion* (Penguin, 1971).
2. The source of my information on the Nyoro is the rich and detailed ethnography of J. M. Beattie. The titles of the various publications I have referred to will be found in the Bibliography. I am also indebted to him for an interesting discussion of a draft of this chapter, which was most helpful. He does not, however, agree with all my conclusions, for which I must take responsibility.
3. The Nyoro believed that the motive for suppressing the *mbandwa* cult was the extinction of the Nyoro people, for denying them access to their clan Cwezi would affect their ability to produce children, and so they would die out. Beattie comments that their population has not shown the tendency to rise that other African peoples have experienced in the twentieth century, so that it appears that responsibility for a real and perceived lack of fertility was attributed to the cult's being abandoned.
4. 'The cult was not proscribed as such. It was taken as falling under the Witchcraft Ordinance' (Beattie, 1969: 49). 'In the 1950s people were certainly being prosecuted in the Native Courts for being in possession of the paraphernalia of the cult' (J. Beattie, personal communication).
5. Nyoro also believe in a variety of other causes of misfortune: witchcraft, sorcery and breaches of important social obligations may all result in sickness or other misfortunes. A spirit is thus only one of a number of possible mystical forces.
6. Grant, J. A., *A Walk Across Africa*, Blackwood, 1864, pp. 292–3.
7. Since most initiates are women, I shall follow Beattie in writing of the initiate as a woman.
8. Traditionally, drums would have been beaten in a distinctive, quick rhythm, but in the 1950s drumming was too dangerously revealing, so it was dropped.
9. It is not clear whether the 'black bush' and the 'white bush' are two different places in the bush or merely aspects of the bush which designate the nature of the rites.
10. Beattie, 1957.
11. The medium emerges on the fourth day to plant a small barkcloth tree and a creeper of the kind special to her initiation; a bride emerges on the fourth day to make a similar symbolic planting of different types of foodstuffs. In both cases these acts end the final seclusion.
12. The name itself was imposed by outsiders and never accepted as legitimate by members but it has continued to be used, even by some who object to it.
13. Kariuki's account of his activities shows how informal the organization was in 1953, when it was already well-established. He writes: 'I had no official position in the other movement [the Kenya African Union, a political organization that was not proscribed until 1953] but Muthee, who had taken the *Batuni* oath with me, had by now gone to fight in the forest and had spread the news that I was a reliable person. So groups from the forest in need of help would visit me from time to time. Once a party came from the Aberdares ... and I was

happy to be able to assist them with money, boots and safe quarters for the night. Some sympathizers on the railway staff provided me with a railway guard's uniform and I had no difficulty in travelling freely in this way to Eldoret and Kisumu in the guard's van. This enabled me to help in the development of our communications system and to act as a liaison officer between groups in these areas' (1963: 40). He clearly acted on his own initiative in these matters rather than under orders from a higher authority.

14. The famous Dedan Kimathi seems to have been mad by the time he was captured, and Kariuki admits that the movement had problems with some of their allies. He describes a category of people who were not part of the forest fighting units, the *Momerara* – those who are awake when they are thought to be sleeping – in these terms: 'They fought everyone, including civilians, and they did not have the skill to make their own guns nor could they fight a pure battle. This group was composed of weaker characters and lacked discipline and control, nor was it responsible to any higher authority ... The *Momerara* did very much as they pleased. Although the number of atrocities committed by our fighters has been exaggerated and played up, there is no doubt that some bad things were done' (1963: 96).

15. Some of what Malinowski described as magic we might now refer to as ritual.

CHAPTER IV SPIRITUAL
POWERS

An important feature of the secret society is that members commit themselves to it as individuals. A new recruit to Freemasonry is sponsored at initiation by a man who is described as 'a stranger'; this indicates that his desire to join does not derive from ties of kinship or friendship with other Masons but is a personal wish. Lord Ampthill, in his Introduction to Banner's book on the Masons, writes approvingly that 'the fact that King Edward VII was initiated in Sweden is sufficient proof that he was drawn to Freemasonry by his own disposition and a favourable opinion preconceived of the Order rather than by some sense of public duty towards the popular institutions of England'. In Bunyoro it is believed that the *mbandwa* spirits themselves select those whom they wish to have initiated into their cult. Some of Beattie's informants described how they resisted the spirit's demands but were finally forced to submit.[1] Even in the domestic cult of the white Cwezi, the spirits chose their mediums for their qualities of character rather than their position in the household. Such beliefs also indicate that individuals are singled out, whether by personality or circumstances, to join the cult; their participation is not dependent on membership of any category or group, or on other social roles.

Nowhere is the voluntary commitment of the individual to the organization more important than in groups dedicated to violent revolutionary change, such as Mau Mau. But in all our examples a sociological pattern can be perceived; members are not a random assortment of individuals. F. Furedi, in his analysis of Mau Mau groups in the European-settled areas of Kenya, has shown that the most likely to join were those who had achieved least under the colonial regime: the 'squatters', as they were called.

Squatters were tenants on European farms who, in exchange for a small amount of land to cultivate and pasture for their animals, contracted to work a specified number of days for the owner of the land. They were paid for the work but their security of tenure depended entirely on the landowner who could evict them whenever he chose to do so. Most Kikuyu squatters had little or no land in their homeland. They were tenants in the customary system of landholding who had held rights to cultivation from Kikuyu landowners. Some were younger sons who had received insufficient land from their inheritance, for Kikuyu inheritance rules, though sharing land, did favour the eldest son. Where land was short, younger sons might have to find land for themselves. In the past, they had done this by expanding the fringes of Kikuyu territory, carving out farms from the forest or encroaching on the territory of the Kamba and Masai. The creation of fixed tribal boundaries and the allocation of large tracts of land to Europeans under British rule precluded this traditional solution.

Within Kikuyuland itself, Mau Mau was the organization of the unsuccessful, the landless and those who had not been able to find employment or support themselves in occupations other than agriculture. The rich, the educated, and the chiefly families generally saw no advantage in joining or feared that they would lose their positions. One author (Holman, 1964: 26) notes the enthusiasm of Kikuyu women for the organization. He writes: 'It was remarkable how strongly Mau Mau appealed to the women, who were consistently more wholehearted in their support of it than the men.' Josiah Kariuki, in his book *Mau Mau Detainee*, writes: 'There is no doubt that ninety per cent of the women of the Kikuyu tribe supported the fight for Freedom and Independence with their minds, their bodies and their souls.'[2] The colonial system weighed heavily on Kikuyu women as their status was still closely tied to their traditional role as providers of food. Few of them had any alternative to farming, since they were not educated and such jobs as there were, even in domestic service, went to men (Tamarkin, 1973; Leakey, 1952).

Organizations such as the Triad and the *mbandwa* cult also seem to attract the politically weak, the unsuccessful and marginal members of society. For such people, joining an association has much to recommend it. It offers support and practical assistance and another way of obtaining the power and esteem that they are denied by their social position. The structure and activities of the group rest on philosophies which are opposed to those of the main body of society and question their validity. The Taoist and Buddhist symbolism of the Triad distinguishes its beliefs from those of Chinese society in general, for which worship of the ancestors and Confucianism formed the official cults. Freemasons questioned the unique status of Christianity and in the eighteenth century were often persecuted as heretics and free-thinkers. Mau Mau used traditional Kikuyu symbolism in an entirely modern emphasis on indigenous nationalism. They were no mere conservatives trying to reverse historical trends, but radicals attempting to infuse African organization with a moral authority equal to, but different from, Christianity, which was identified with white rule. It is important to recognize that, while the explicit emphasis is on difference, the difference itself must imply, and thus depend on, the main institutions for contrast.

It might seem that secret societies are always illegitimate in the sense of being opposed to the main structure of recognized authority. This is not to say that they have not been extremely powerful at times in their history. Even the Nyoro spirit cult, although closely associated with the most sacred institution of the kingship (through the cult of the white *mbandwa*, the Cwezi spirits), represented a potential threat to the chiefly hierarchy and even to the king himself, since it provided an alternative spiritual mandate to justify rebellion. It is more accurate to say that secret societies may provide an alternative, rather than a totally illegitimate, source of authority.

Secret associations are the central institutions among some peoples and their beliefs part of the accepted cosmology. Their secrecy is thus not a product of their opposition to established authority. New Guinean secret cults have already been mentioned; in this chapter I shall discuss two similar examples from other parts of the world, the Hopi of the southwestern United States and the Mende of Sierra Leone in West Africa. Among both these peoples the political institutions of the society consist of a series of interlocking cult groups; among the Mende, one of these, the Poro, is of paramount importance and it co-exists with a secular hierarchy of chiefs which is not the case among the Hopi. Despite other important differences between them, the two peoples have in common the fact that their initiation rituals transform individuals, not only into members of a group owning secret knowledge, but also into adults. The initiations are dual-purpose.

The rituals in these two societies resemble those of the *mbandwa* cult more than any of the others that have been discussed; they do not lay stress on any verbal formula which the initiand must repeat. Instead an important element is the endurance of hardship and pain, which in the Mende case constitutes a long-drawn-out and often severe ordeal. In both cases, too, the groups claim to possess ritual techniques which control non-human powers but, unlike the Nyoro rites, those of the Hopi and Mende do not endow initiates with these powers, but merely reveal how they may be acquired. All the initiates learn is that what they had previously believed as non-initiates was untrue. However, great stress is laid on the esoteric nature of the knowledge possessed by the group; its strength lies in secrecy. The Zuni, who live near the Hopi and resemble them in many ways, make this quite explicit. To them, secret knowledge is power and they say: 'Power told is power lost.' Among the Mende as well as the Hopi the ritual knowledge controlled by esoteric cults is believed to maintain the natural as well as the social order.

I shall concentrate on showing how ritual displays important social concepts, using space as a symbolic code. The intiation rituals of the Triad society and the Masons represent the marginal phase as a journey. The effect is to separate members and non-members in terms of distance travelled. In those rituals, performed within a 'temple' or a 'lodge', the actual space used is minimal. Those of the Mende and Hopi are not confined within a building; their candidates for initiation are taken into the forest away from the village, or down into the sacred chamber underground. Distance and location emphasize the separation of the novices from ordinary life. The three phases of the ritual each involve movements through space and so the changes in place represent the transformation in the individuals that occurs in the rites.

The tripartite structure of an initiation is a pair of states, separated by a margin, a boundary. Crossing a boundary at initiation thus emphasizes an opposition between members and non-members. In the rituals considered here and in the rest of the book, other ideas are associated with these opposed states. Initiation rituals at maturity can be expected to contrast child with adult, boy with man, girl with woman, but as I shall hope to show, oppositions which have a much wider significance, such as human/spirit, wild/cultivated, and other pairs of abstract ideas, are also represented. It is as though the ritual provided a mould into which many meanings can be poured.

In Hopi and Mende rituals, the marginal area is the place of contact between human beings and spiritual powers. The Hopi *kiva*, situated underground, is the meeting-place of the living and the dead; the Poro camp lies between the sacred bush of the spirits and the village. Such occasions are dangerous; they are controlled by those whose greater knowledge permits them to use spiritual powers. Here the spiritual powers are not separate from, or opposed to, the general organization of society; they are a part of it. The rituals are concerned with a universal transition – from child to adult – as well as with membership of an organization owning secret knowledge. All Hopi children are initiated and very few Mende are not. The ideas and symbols displayed represent orthodoxy and evoke the moral order on which the society is based. In order to interpret them we must refer more extensively to the social context than was necessary in previous discussion.

The Hopi are one of a number of similar peoples known as Pueblo Indians[3] who live in the arid area of North America which is now Arizona and New Mexico. Differences of language among them indicate that they probably have several origins but the differences are not of recent date, for their cultures are very similar and archaeological evidence suggests that they have been living in the same area for many centuries. The main Hopi village of Old Oraibi seems to have been occupied continuously since at least the sixth century A D; the Spaniard, Coronado, who entered the area in the sixteenth century encountered Hopi villages in much the same places as they are today. Since then the Pueblo peoples have suffered under the hands of alien conquerors, but they have retained their original culture to a remarkable degree. In recent years, as elsewhere among American Indian peoples, there has been evidence of a movement to revive ancient tradition. Ceremonies which, in the 1950s, were performed by a mere handful of individuals, now draw large numbers of participants, including young people, who take part in them as much to show loyalty to an Indian identity as to act on traditional beliefs, for two hundred years of American rule have changed the nature of their society and its religion in fundamental ways.

Traditionally the Hopi were agriculturalists, growing a variety of crops such as maize, beans and squash, all dependent on rainfall, which was sparse and irregular. Rain is assured, they believe,[4] by the regular performance of periodic rituals which mark and regulate the cycle of the seasons and link them with that of human existence. The rituals are linked in a complex manner with the organization of society. All Hopi are related in a variety of ways, as members of clans, cult groups and ritual associations, so that each such group is embedded in the social fabric by the fact that its individual members are also members of a range of different other groups. Rituals are the responsibility of the various religious associations whose knowledge is revealed only to initiates. The correct performance of the ritual cycle therefore depends on the entire village; as the rituals progressively unfold they dramatize both the nature and interdependence of the secret societies and the Hopi's relation to nature.

Land and houses are owned by matrilineal clans, each identified by reference to a totem which a myth associates with the founder of the clan. The totems refer to the natural environment and its denizens: bear, snake, dove, crow and rabbit are some important animal totems; cactus, reed, tobacco and squash figure among the vegetables; while fog, snow and cloud have different but still natural connotations. Others have names which refer to the beings of the Hopi creation myths. The clans are linked in groups, which seem to combine or divide according to the size and power of the constituent clans, so that the associations of clans are not the same in each village. However, the Hopi feel that there is some significant relationship between the totems which makes the linkage between the clans more than mere historical accident.

The significant groups in daily life are the clan-segments or lineages which own the houses, built densely packed together on the rocky mesas. Houses contain a resident core of women who are grandmothers, mothers and daughters. The male residents fluctuate, since men move out to live with their wives at marriage, although as most marriages take place within the village, a man keeps a strong link with his mother's household and frequently drops in there. Titiev, whose book *Old Oraibi* is a major source of information on the Hopi, says that when a man says 'my house' he usually means his mother's house, not the one where he lives with his wife. In the houses are kept the sacred paraphernalia for the rituals which · are 'owned' by various clans so that the older women, although excluded from office in most ritual associations, are important as custodians of these vital objects. However, women are under the authority of men, their brothers and mothers' brothers, who are the senior men of the lineage and have jurisdiction over its younger men as well, for a man's heir is his sister's son.

An important feature of all Hopi villages are the *kivas*, rectangular underground rooms, where secret rituals are held; they are also club-houses where men may spend their leisure or sleep. There are several *kivas* in a village, each easily identifiable by the ladder which projects from the opening in its roof that gives access to the interior. Uninitiated people should keep away from the *kivas*, particularly when an emblem is attached to the entrance showing that ritual is being performed. Today tourists, like myself, who visit Pueblo villages are very carefully watched to make sure they do not approach too close to a *kiva*. In Acoma village, lived in by a people related to the Hopi, teenagers acted as guides to the tourists, and one was not allowed out of the central square without a guide.[5]

However, the lay-out of a *kiva* is known, for abandoned *kivas* have been described: it consists of a single room, part of the floor of which is raised as a sort of dais. This is the less sacred area, to the south, where spectators may sit; the ritual is performed in the lower, northern half, where there is a scooped-out fireplace flanked on each side by stone benches which are containers for the most sacred objects. At the northern end is an altar and in the middle of the floor a cavity (the *sipapu*) which is covered with a stone plug when no ritual is in progress.

Ritual associations and matrilineal clans form the two pillars of Hopi society; the ritual calendar links them in a complex pattern. There are four associations to which all men, but only men, belong. Two, the Ahl and Kwan, are concerned with defensive magic, war and death; the others, Wuwutcim and Tao, with various aspects of fertility. In addition there are three women's societies, of which the main one, Marau, is said to be sister to Wuwutcim association. Minor societies have responsibilities for parts of more important rituals. Associations are 'owned' by clans and their rites performed in particular *kivas* which are also 'owned' by clans, in principle the clan that dug out the *kiva* and so created it. The term 'ownership' here means dominant control, not exclusive membership, for men of many different clans are members of the four societies and the *kivas*. Moreover, the clan which 'owns' the ritual of a ceremony is not always the same as that which 'owns' the *kiva* where it is performed. The *kiva* is usually called by the name of the association which uses it but it also has a name given it by the clan which 'owns' it. In the case of both *kivas* and associations, the controlling clan has the responsibility to maintain the ritual objects in its care, provide officiants, and ensure the initiation of new members,* particularly those who may be future officers. The rituals take place in a fixed order and focus in each case on the clans controlling the association and the *kiva*. The pattern is different in every Hopi village, although the ritual calendar remains essentially the same. In all villages, too, the main associations are those concerned with the ritual referred to as the Tribal Initiation, a secondary initiation of boys only, which follows the first initiation of all children. Both types of initiation are embedded in a series of other rituals; they are not separate occasions.

Any Hopi ritual has both a secret and a public aspect; in the public performance masked men represent the spirits (Kachinas[6]) in dances and dramas accompanied by singing. The latter is essential to the success of the former; the performance of the drama and the sustained effort of dancers over long periods infuse the secret rituals with further power to make them doubly effective. A myth recounts how, when the Hopi climbed out of the underworld on to the earth, they brought the spirits with them but how events drove the spirits back into the underworld so that now they must be represented by men and approached through ritual. (The Cwezi spirits left the techniques of spirit possession to the Nyoro when they departed.)

The Kachinas are also the dead and are associated with the clouds and rainfall, the source of agricultural life. Certain Kachinas are associated with particular clans and may be impersonated only by men of that clan, and the masks by which they are represented may not be changed. These Kachinas are *wuyu*, a Hopi term which means 'partner' rather than 'ancestor', although they are associated with the dead of the clan. They are spirits of clan totems and are perhaps best described as spirit patrons, as they are approached through clan rituals, and officials and clansmen have a specially close relationship with them. Other lesser Kachinas may be represented by non-clansmen and their costumes and masks may be changed by their owners. The Hopi hold that the power used by the experts lies in the masks, and the uninitiated are expected to believe that the masked figures *are* the spirits. Among the Hopi, girls and boys are initiated, so that it is only small children who are said to be deceived.

This account is severely simplified, since the rites are numerous and the symbolic system is so complex that it deserves a book to itself. The essential elements seem to be as follows. First is a drama of the recreation of the world, for the hole in the floor, which represents the original hole through which the first Hopi and the spirits climbed out of the underworld, is uncovered to open communication with the spirits; impersonations of them, the Kachinas, then appear. Secondly, the spirits are equated with the Hopi dead and both are seen to be the source of power which can be drawn on by human beings. Finally, children are identified with the dead and the underworld is shown as identical to that in which the Hopi live. The Hopi dead are born into the underworld as children are born into the upper world; Hopi funerary practices make this clear, for the corpse and the new-born baby are ritually treated in the same way. Initiation is the pivot of the system, for only initiated children may have a place in the underworld and so join the dead.

Children are initiated during the Powamu ceremonies, which are held every year in February, midway through the ceremonial cycle, but with special rites in those years when there are initiations. Strictly speaking, the initiates are only completely adult when the next set of children have also been through the rituals so that they are promoted from the position of newly initiated. Subsequently both boys and girls will become members of secret associations, which are largely single-sex groups although they may have officiants of the other sex. The preliminary initiation serves only to differentiate adults from children; it does not emphasize the division between the sexes which occurs at the later stage, but even then the fact that boys and girls are initiated into *kivas* weakens the effect of their separation by gender. As in many associations, the first initiation confers secrets upon the initiate, which serve to mark off the ignorant uninitiated to whom the secrets must not be told. The secret is that the beings who appear in rituals are not spirits but men who impersonate them. The sacred truth is that power lies with the masks and the ritual which controls the spirits. The rituals also set out a cosmology which makes life and death mirror-images, giving a new meaning to the life cycle.

The Powamu association in Old Oraibi holds its own initiations before the general ones which take place on the sixth day of rituals. The initiands are purified by being made to abstain from eating salt and meat, as the male participants in ritual do. The altar in each *kiva* is prepared; elaborate sacred pictures are made from an intricate combination of coloured earths, and medicine is prepared from spring water infused with powerful magic substances. The altar itself has two parts. A series of upright slabs set in the floor is painted with symbolic and naturalistic representations of sacred objects: maize, cloud and culture heroes. On the floor in front of the slabs are placed effigies of the various spirits and the mythical beings with other sacred objects, including a bowl of the medicine. This is placed on a low mound of sand, and from it are drawn six lines of cornmeal, which stand for the cardinal points, fundamental elements in Hopi symbolism. Each is associated with a colour, and an ear of corn of the appropriate colour is placed on each line: north is yellow; south, red; east, white; west, blue or green; above, black; and below, multi-coloured.[7]

The rites are conducted by the head of the Powamu association dressed to represent Muyingwa, the spirit of germination and growth. Each initiand has a ceremonial sponsor of the same sex as himself or herself, who is known as 'father' or 'mother'. Like sponsors in the Masonic ritual, they must not be kin, but the ceremonial link lasts much longer than the rituals and is seen as one of lasting closeness like the ties between kin. The sponsors take the initiands into the *kiva*. Titiev describes what follows:

> After a few preliminaries, the Kachina initiates hear a long recital by the Powamu chief ... He tells them much of the tribe's sacred lore about the Kachinas, describes their home in the San Francisco mountains and at other shrines, and then takes his departure. Immediately, a member of the Powamu society who has been keeping a look-out while seated on a high roof nearby, stands up as a signal to three Kachina impersonators who promptly head towards the *kiva* on the run ... With loud cries and frequent beating on the *kiva* hatch with the long yucca whips that they carry, they circle the *kiva* four times, then enter hurriedly and take up positions north of the fireplace. One after another, regardless of sex, the candidates are placed on a sand painting by their ceremonial parents to receive four severe lashes ... The boys are naked and hold one hand aloft while they clasp the genital organs with the other to prevent their being struck: the girls wear their dresses and lift both hands high above their heads.

The Kachinas then whip each other, and the Kachina chief dismisses them with gifts and they leave the *kiva*. The initiates are warned never to betray the secrets they have just learned, on pain of fearful punishment at the hands of the Kachinas. They are then removed from the *kiva*.

At the end of the Powamu rituals the initiates are allowed for the first time to witness a dance in the *kiva* at night. They are placed on the bench to the east of the altar, where they must sit motionless with their knees drawn up to their chins. This position is enjoined on all initiands into secret associations as well; it resembles that of the foetus in the womb, although neither the ethnographers nor the Hopi themselves seem to remark on this. The Powamu Kachinas arrive at the *kiva* hatch and announce themselves. They throw several ears of baked corn down to the novices, calling on them to eat, but the initiands, warned by their sponsors, do not move. Then they begin to come down the ladder, one of their number standing at its foot and calling out jokes at the expense of each man as he comes down. As each performer appears the initiates can see he is unmasked and that fact, together with the personal jokes, makes it vividly explicit that the Kachinas who appeared in the first ceremony were in fact merely impersonated by men whom they recognize as kin and fellow-villagers. The dances, which involve groups from all the *kiva* who visit each *kiva* in turn, go on most of the night. The performers give gifts to the unmarried maidens and receive in return packages of special food. At the end of the dancing the groups gather in their own *kivas* to feast on what they have collected during the night. The new initiates are taken to their sponsors' home where their heads are washed with suds from the yucca plant. They are given new ceremonial names, which will be used in the *kiva*, and take part in a celebratory feast.

Full initiation into a ritual association takes place some years later and follows much the same pattern, although the Kwan rituals are said to be different from those of the three other male societies. The rites in the *kiva* are so sacred that when Titiev published his account no outsider had ever seen them, so that the discussion which follows is based on information given to anthropologists, not on observation.

Full initiation, which in the case of boys is referred to as Tribal Initiation, takes place, as does the preliminary rite, in the context of ceremonies held by the four major associations. Although each of them conducts its own rites, there is also a joint ritual on the fourth night. The pattern of the rituals resembles that of the preliminary initiation although it is more complex, the main difference being that initiates are segregated by sex as they join different associations. The symbolism of birth is perhaps more pronounced in the Tribal Initiation, for not only do the initiands have to adopt the same cramped posture they took up in the preliminary initiation, but they must maintain it for four days, during which time they act as fledgeling birds, are fed by their sponsors and must use bird-like calls to announce their wants. Moreover, as a preliminary to the joint rites they are carried out of the *kiva* like babies, on the backs of their sponsors, helped to walk to a shrine of the association's Kachina and then allowed to walk back without help: during the ritual they 'grow' from babyhood to the first walking of a child and then to maturity. During the most secret rites on the last night, the dead are represented and it seems that the novices may be ritually 'killed' by the officers of the Kwan association, the association concerned with warfare and death, in order to bring them to life again as men.[8]

Certain themes appear in both rituals: the initiands are taken out of the village, and rites take place underground with its double connotation of the underworld and the dead. Hopi believe that the *kiva* is between the human world and the underworld; men enter it by the ladder from the upper world and the spirits enter it from the lower world through the *sipapu*. The concept of the above and below as two parts of a single circle appears in many contexts in Hopi cosmology. Human beings are born into the underworld when they die, to re-emerge ultimately when they are reborn on the earth as later generations of Hopi. The sun is said to descend into its western *kiva* (or house) at night and travel in the underworld to re-emerge from its eastern *kiva* at dawn. New-born babies are presented to the rising sun, while the dead go westwards to the underworld. The change from summer to winter can also be fitted into this cyclical model of life and death. All the different cycles depend on the correct performance of the rituals for if they are not performed the seasons will not follow in due course, crops will not be produced nor babies born. The Tribal Initiations are the pivot of the whole system for they enable initiates to have a place in the underworld, where they take part in the shadow rituals which in their turn assist in maintaining the cycle. It seems possible that, as is so often the case elsewhere, the natural cycle is seen as dependent on the human one; in one myth, Coyote, who brought death into the world by closing the *sipapu* through which men and spirits once passed freely between the two worlds, says: 'It is only by [*sic*] somebody dying every day, morning, noon and evening that will make the sun move every day' (Parsons, 1939: 171).

In both Poro and Hopi rituals contact with the spirit world is an ordeal; or rather the ordeal is the manifestation of the contact. For the Hopi there is a very clear association between the power of the spirits, controlled by the ritual experts, and the ordeal. Each Hopi association is believed to control a disease or bodily affliction which is known as its 'whip';[9] the whip may be used by the association's spirit partners to punish members who reveal its secrets or to afflict non-members with the disease. Like the *mbandwa* spirits which possess individuals, Hopi spirits indicate that the afflicted should become members of the association, for the curing rituals can only be performed for members. Thus the whipping that takes place at the first initiation has two levels of meaning: it is a very real foretaste of what will happen if the secrets are not kept, and it also represents the powers of the association which are controlled by its members.

The two-stage initiation of the Hopi must be seen in the context of the whole social system. Traditionally there was virtually no distinction between secular office and ritual powers. The village leader was the head of the clan which was credited with having first arrived in the village; this clan was also the 'owner' of important rituals. The village chief was thus *primus inter pares*, one of a number of heads of clans and associations all of whom co-operated to perform the rituals of the annual cycle. Although each clan had the right to certain rituals, was pre-eminent in certain associations and might be the 'owners' of a *kiva*, the stress in the system seems to have lain on the division of powers between such groups. The overlapping membership of associations meant that clan loyalties were counteracted by association memberships. It is important to remark here that, unlike clans among the Chinese, Nyoro or Kikuyu, the Hopi clan depends on the children of its female members for continuity, since it is matrilineal; that is, Hopi belong to their mother's clan.[10] Thus by a further division of labour, while women maintain clan continuity, men's ritual activities assure the proper placing of the dead in relation to the living to maintain the natural cycle. Yet the division between men and women is not highly stressed, for women's associations also have a specialist part to play: what is stressed is the ultimate authority of the spirits and the dead, the Kachinas.

Among the Mende, by contrast, there is a clear distinction between chiefship, which is a hereditary secular office, and ritual powers, dependent on knowledge that is, in principle, open to anyone to acquire. There are degrees of secret knowledge, possession of which enables the holders to move upwards through a hierarchy of ranks. The secrets of the Poro which are revealed at initiation are that there are more and more powerful truths yet to be learned. Among the Hopi, however, knowledge only differentiates clearly between small children and the rest of the community. The ritual of first initiation shows that children believe a lie: the spirits do not appear at rituals, they are impersonated by human beings. Once that is revealed, however, all the initiated may observe the rituals performed in the *kiva*, although it is the most senior men who undertake the ritual preparations, allocate the tasks involved to their juniors and know the meaning of the symbolism. Complete knowledge and the right to use it are thus dependent on position within the clan; legitimate authority is an attribute of seniority, of age and genealogical position, with the dead as the most powerful beings of all. Within any Hopi association, clan membership and position within the clan are crucial, for they determine what powers a member may claim. Those who are members of the clan which 'owns' the association may succeed in time to the ritual knowledge connected with its ritual objects, prayers and other religious observances; those who join an association to make use of its powers of healing or good fortune may not. Then among clan members there are distinctions of seniority which rank them in an order, so that greater knowledge is acquired as a consequence of progress through the life cycle.

Apart from the revelation of the truth about the Kachinas, two main features of the ritual deserve comment. In the first part of the ceremony the initiands are whipped by the masked impersonators of the Kachinas; this does not seem to be a test of courage because nowhere is it recorded that the children are expected to be brave. Later, they are expected to endure the discomfort of sitting still in a cramped position for a long time; this, like the tears of the newly initiated medium in the *mbandwa* cult, seems to be the proof that the ritual performed over them has had its effect, and they are able to pass this test. The whipping is too early in the ritual for this and it is interpreted by ethnographers of the Hopi as a demonstration of the power of the Kachinas, who whip each other before they leave. It seems possible to interpret it also as a means of making the novice receptive to the change he or she is undergoing, creating a vivid personal experience like that suffered by the novice medium when she is threatened with death by the initiator. The theme of suffering physical ordeals occurs again in the next instance discussed. It is central to the initiation rituals of the Gisu described in Chapter VI where, since I draw on my own field data, I can venture more interpretation than I can with the Hopi case where the ethnographies give few hints as to the meaning for the Hopi of this element of the ritual.

Hopi initiations take place in the context of other rites which are performed whether there are to be initiations or not, as part of a ritual calendar which orders the natural and social world. These rituals stress the division of powers between clans and associations, and their mutual interdependence. The first initiation of children is of boys and girls together; they are separated only when they become full members of associations at the second stage, but this separation is a consequence of their joining men's or women's associations so that the distinction between the sexes is assimilated to the division of labour which makes groups interdependent. By contrast the Mende make the initiation of boys the major focus of ritual activity, and boys and girls are segregated at initiation. Hierarchy, not interdependence, is the theme of the Poro.

The Poro, which is known by a variety of names, is an institution among most of the peoples of southern Liberia, Sierra Leone and the Ivory Coast. As an organization it is not confined to a single people, nor even a single linguistic or cultural region, but provides a network of connections over a wide area. The name, which is used by the Kpelle, Mende and Temne of Sierra Leone, is taken from the term for the council of members in session, the 'poro'. Reliable records of its existence go back to the sixteenth and seventeenth centuries and some writers have even suggested that the place name *purrus campus*, which was taken by medieval map-makers from Ptolemy's maps of Africa, refers to the area dominated by the Poro. With one or two notable exceptions among officiants, the Poro is restricted to men, but there is a parallel women's organization known as the Sande. Among the Mende the Poro is one among several secret societies, but it is by far the most powerful and its membership is very numerous and widespread. Indeed, most men and women are members of the Poro and the Sande (MacCormack, 1979), although children of poor parents who cannot afford the fees may have to join later than normal. As in the other secret societies discussed in earlier chapters, there is a hierarchy of ranks within the Poro and the society's activities are controlled by a small number of members, the highest ranked; most members do not progress beyond the first grade and take little part in the Poro's activities, although they are subject to its authority. Among the Vai people the elaboration of grades is the most extensive and there are said to be ninety-nine degrees of membership; the southern Liberian people and the Mende, whom I shall be discussing here, seem to have fewer, about thirty. All ranks above the lowest are symbolized by masks, in each of which reposes a spirit, whose power is acquired and controlled by the mask's owner. In principle, any member is eligible to rise through the various grades, so that as in the Triad and Freemason societies the emphasis is placed on the acquisition of leadership by merit or learning, rather than inheritance or selection from above. The comparison with Freemasonry is made explicitly both by some authors who have written on the Poro and by some Poro members. Dr Schwab who studied the Poro in Liberia (1947) quotes an educated Liberian as saying to him; 'It is a pity you are not a Mason, for then I could tell you more. The Poro is just like Freemasonry.' Indeed, it seems likely that when the Creoles in Freetown became interested in Freemasonry, it was in part because it provided them with a secret society like the Poro, of which the citizens of Sierra Leone who were full tribesmen could become members, while the Creoles could not (Cohen, 1971, 1981).

However, in many aspects of its organization the Poro is not at all like Freemasonry. It is, and has been for a long time, an integral part of the established political system. A Mende ruler and his subordinate chiefs were both supported and, on occasion, overruled by the Poro whose authority, being derived from the spirits they controlled, was held to be higher than that of the chiefs. Thus the Poro might declare that a chief's action angered the spirits and he would have to make an offering to them through the Poro. Or it might demand community action, usually ritual offerings, with which the chiefs would have to comply. Chiefs were Poro members themselves but they might not hold office in the organization and so were always subordinate to its senior officials in matters involving the spirits. Since the Mende made no clear distinction between religious and secular affairs, the jurisdiction of the Poro was potentially very wide. In principle, chiefs and Poro officials represented two distinct types of authority, secular and religious; generally they worked in harmony but most students of the Poro point out that, in any conflict, it was believed to have the gods on its side. Since the identity of Poro officials and their activities were closely guarded secrets, there is little evidence to indicate what did happen in actual cases of conflict, but we have seen how, in the case of China, military success could prevail over the mandate of Heaven and be the basis for claiming divine approval. So it seems likely that chiefs and Poro leaders might well have competed for power, with success going to one or the other according to the particular circumstances in each case, or the balance of power at that time.

In any one tribe there was a series of local Poro groups, usually called 'Lodges' in the literature by analogy with the organization of Freemasonry. These Lodges were linked into wider areas through the association of the higher-ranking members, who were relatively few in number. The initiation rites admitting members to the higher grade drew candidates from a wider area, since there were relatively few members who were entitled to carry them out. It seems to have been believed (as many believed of Mau Mau) that there was a single powerful inner council for the whole intertribal institution, but again there is really no evidence that such a council existed, or that there was any widespread Poro organization, although powerful Poro leaders from different communities undoubtedly maintained personal contacts and co-operated in various ways. In addition the ranks were similar over wide areas and a man from one kingdom or district would probably be accepted into the Poro organization in another territory at the grade he held in his own. Indeed, the network of interpersonal ties between members of Lodges in different localities provided members of the Poro with useful contacts and hospitality over whole regions, a fact of significance where long-distance trade was an important activity. Probably, as in other secret societies, the ties between Poro members might be useful in a variety of different ways: as a link between traders, as a network for providing information or as a source of political support.

According to Professor Little, whose work on the Mende has provided me with the account of Poro initiation I shall discuss below,[11] Mende boys entered the Poro about the age of puberty, although adults might also be initiated. Some boys might be marked out as destined for high position in the Poro at an early age. The position of *zo*, a ritual expert, was a hereditary one; the heir to such a position might be told some of the secrets of the Poro before his initiation. Boys might also manifest symptoms of what Mende, like many other peoples, interpreted as signs of possession by a spirit (I. M. Lewis, 1971: 66 ff.). Chronic illness, particularly if there were fainting fits or seizures, mental or emotional disturbances, were believed to be signs that a spirit wished the boy to become a *zo*. The cure was to identify the spirit and induce it to possess a mask which became the boy's property. Like the heirs to established masks, these boys went through an abbreviated version of initiation and were subject to less arduous ordeals, since their suitability for Poro membership was guaranteed by the possession of exceptional qualities, in the one case by inheritance, in the other through the spirit's own choice.

The manifest aim of the Poro is to control the spirits and ensure that their intervention in the affairs of men is beneficial. The special position of hereditary experts or those possessed by a spirit is consistent with this actors' view of the organization. We can also see it in a broader, comparative perspective as a modification of the principle of individual achievement which normally governs the selection both of members and officers within a secret society. The modification can be attributed to the incorporation of the Poro into the main structure of Mende life where inheritance is highly significant. Initiation into the Poro is general; even hereditary chiefs and their sons are members of the Poro, unlike the royal house of Bunyoro which is kept out of the *mbandwa* cult. Mervyn Jones has drawn attention to the fact that as Freemasonry became more widespread in England it also became 'more respectable'; that is, it became accepted as part of the normal structure of society. When this happened the leading offices of Freemasonry began to be occupied by individuals of noble birth: dukes and members of the royal family, even Edward V II when Prince of Wales. Similarly, the Poro, while ostensibly based on a principle of achievement by individuals, the antithesis of the hereditary principle on which chiefs were selected, showed the effect of its institutionalization.

Initiation into the Poro has become, among the Mende, a necessary stage in the individual's becoming accepted as adult. The social change is marked by physical changes, scars on the back. The parallel initiation for girls involves excision of the clitoris as a part of the ritual changing girls into women and making them members of the Sande. Circumcision was not part of the boys' ritual, although it was a necessary preliminary to it among some of the peoples where the Poro existed, though not all. Among the Mende, boys would be circumcised before entering the Poro and if, for some reason, they had not been, they would be operated on immediately by Poro officials.

Mende, like many other peoples in the world, associate the spirits with the uncultivated areas of their territory, the forest or bush. In general, the bush is the home of spiritual beings while the villages and cultivated fields are the home of human beings, the lesser powers. Parts of the forest are particularly associated with the spirits belonging to the various secret societies and only initiated members may go into them. In former times, if a woman or uninitiated boy wandered into the area by mistake and was seen, he or she would have been killed. The spirits, though attached to areas in the bush, are mobile and diffuse, unlike human beings who are settled in permanent villages. The period of the initiation ritual is described as the visit of the main Poro spirit, Gbende, to the world of men; his stay usually lasts a full dry season, from November to May. During it peace must be maintained in the whole region lest Gbende be offended and bring down disasters on the communities concerned. His camp is located in the bush, but away from the area sacred to the Poro for it will be inhabited by uninitiated boys. The place where initiation takes place is thus between the world of the spirits and that of human beings, like the Hopi *kiva*, although it is a temporary place, unmarked by a permanent building. The Mende ritual moves back and forth between bush and village in a complex fashion as the change accomplished in the marginal camp is slowly achieved.

The three locations also exemplify gradations of knowledge. The uninitiated, women as well as children, are told that the Poro spirit swallows the initiands and they remain in his belly until he gives birth to them as men. In swallowing them, the spirit marks the boys with its teeth and the initiates' backs are scarred as 'proof' of this. The initiates learn that this story is not true: the masked figures are men, not spirits, their backs are scarred with knife cuts, not Gbende's teeth. They are told that the spirits are incorporeal beings but their power resides in the masks; still greater knowledge is required before the initiates will be able to perform the rites which control these powers. The initiands are not allowed to witness these rites which are performed in the sacred bush, to which they will be admitted later. Initiation into the higher grades of membership takes place there but initiands of the first grade must keep away. They are thus between the secular life of the village ruled by chiefs and inhabited by the ignorant, and the sacred life of the spirit bush ruled by Poro officials, who represent the greatest mystical knowledge.

The initiands are removed from their homes with a show of force from the spirits; men concealed in long raffia skirts and masks rush into the village and seize the boys. Although their fathers will have arranged their initiation in advance and paid the fees, the act dramatizes a sudden separation from the familiarity of childhood life. They are carried into the bush where they will spend several weeks in seclusion. Women and children are warned off by signs on the paths leading to the camp, since they must not go near it. The division between the bush and the village assumes a further significance because the bush is associated with men, the village with women (and their children). The camp's intermediate location is appropriate to the boys' status: not yet men but no longer children.

Initiation into the Poro involves a marginal period which is much longer than the rituals discussed so far. The boys are naked except for the

reddish netting that is the mark of Gbende; their parents send food to the
bush 'for the spirit' but even so the boys may go hungry as everything
must be shared, and the initiators may take what they please from it. Since
the boys are outside normal life they are not bound by its rules so they
may also steal food from the fields, as long as they are not seen, particularly
by women and children. The ordeal is a severe one and occasionally a boy
may even die. In such a case his name may not be mentioned, nor his
absence be remarked upon when the initiates are finally presented formally to the village. His death is announced to his parents by a Poro
official, who goes to visit them and announces: 'I am sorry to tell you that
the pot that you gave me to fire is broken.' Whatever private feelings his
family may have, publicly it is as if he never existed.

The length of the marginal period is partly to give the cuts on the
initiands' backs time to heal, partly, it is said, because the initiators
instruct the boys in skills and social rules; there are privations and ordeals
in addition to the cuts made on the boys' backs with a knife at the
beginning of the phase. As well as being a mixture of preparation and
testing for manhood, the prolonged seclusion of the initiates emphasizes
the divisions between the pairs of concepts associated with bush and
village. These distinctions – between secular and spiritual authority, bush
and village, men and women, knowledge and ignorance – underlie the
major values of the Mende moral code; they are given special prominence
in the ritual.

Only the initiated men may pass between the separate worlds created
by the ritual; the rites emphasize their mediatory role, for throughout the
initiation period ritual action expresses, not only the distance between the
categories it has established, but their interdependence. Movements
between village and bush link the two as complementary parts of a whole,
culminating with two rites of integration, one in the sacred bush and one
in the village, to mark the emergence of the newly initiated men.

During the marginal period the 'spirits' emerge from the bush to visit
the village and dance there but the initiands remain hidden in their camp.
The end of the phase is marked by three visits to the village on which the
masked dancers are accompanied by the boys. When women and the
uninitiated hear the sounds which announce the group's arrival they
must shut themselves indoors, on pain of death should they catch sight
of anyone. On the third visit, Gbende and the initiands enter the house in
the village where Poro meetings take place and stay there. The women
and children emerge and join in the dancing which lasts till dawn when
they retire again. The 'birth' of the initiates is then mimed and the ritual
party leaves the village.

Gbende is said to 'fly away' after having given birth to the initiates, and the initiates are taken, not back to camp, but into the sacred bush for the first time. They undergo the ritual of integration into the Poro, making them full members. When they retun to the village, they are unaccompanied by guardians and mentors; they are received in the reception hall of the village, which is used for visitors, and treated as honoured guests. The initiates are given new names to mark their new status and there is public feasting and gift-giving to celebrate their arrival. The initiates still do not rejoin their families and their heads are still bound, to cover the wounds they are supposed to have suffered when they were 'born'. For four days, until these wounds have 'healed', they remain as guests in the village. A final visit to the spirits in the sacred bush, for which they depart publicly, is necessary to remove the headcloths and enable them to return to their homes. They then cease to be referred to as 'goats', mere domestic animals; they are now *so hinga*, those who procreate: future heads of families.

The movements of actors during the Mende ritual relate the significant oppositions which are established by their association with separate places. The initiated men belong to both the village and the bush; they move freely between the two and, significantly, the newly initiated represent their status as men by a visit to the village and from thence to the spirits in the bush. The Hopi rites make symbolic use of the vertical dimension, associating spirits with the underworld beneath the *kiva*. In all initiations there is symbolic meaning in the placing and movements of the actors, although what is expressed in this way varies with the social context of the rites.

Both Mende and Hopi rituals demonstrate the fact, remarked on by Van Gennep, that transition rites may elaborate one particular phase so that it becomes a miniature transition within a major one, with its own separation, marginal state and integration. The integrative phases of these two initiations are elaborated into several stages. In the Mende example there are, in effect, two rituals of integration, each in a different place, but both Mende and Hopi distinguish between the achievement of adult status and membership of the group to which initiates are admitted. Since adulthood is achieved once and for all but, in both societies, people are allowed and even expected to join more than one group during their lives,[12] such a distinction is intelligible.

Initiation into adulthood, which can be distinguished by the term 'maturity ritual', marks a change of much wider social significance than joining a secret society. While membership of the Masons, the Triad or the Poro may be an important sourcc of assistance in business or political life, it is an added, optional dimension to other relationships and social roles. By contrast maturity rites transform all the relationships of individuals;

the Mende boys, for example, must leave behind everything pertaining to their former lives and may not take anything back afterwards. It is the whole person that is changed. It is perhaps in the light of this that we can interpret the prominence of physical ordeals which occur in these rituals and not in the others. The experience of pain is common in rituals of maturity, often accompanied by the teasing or terrorizing of initiands. The suffering is a necessary part of the ritual and may be seen as a means of transforming the individuals or as a test of their fortitude or as both. Ordeals play the same part in the rites as the oath-taking in the initiation of secret-society members, demonstrating submission to the authority of officials and individual commitment to the group. In the *mbandwa* rites, the two elements are separated: the novice simulates possession on the instructions of the initiating mediums and later shows by her tears[13] that the ritual has been successful.

Physical mutilations which leave permanent marks as a badge of adult status are most common in maturity rituals, although they do not invariably form part of them. The commonest is some operation on the genitals, symbolizing sexual as well as social maturity; it is this feature as well as the different sociological implications that has led to maturity rituals being considered in isolation. There is a large body of work concerned with them that disregards any similarity with other kinds of initiation. It has, therefore, been largely disregarded so far in this book. However, as we have seen, Mende and Hopi rituals distinguish between access to maturity and joining a religious association; in other societies, where there are no such groups, initiation involves only a transition to adult status. It is necessary therefore to consider whether such maturity rites can be explained separately, or alternatively whether the attempt to explain these initiation rites can offer a general understanding of them all.

NOTES TO CHAPTER IV

1. This common feature is discussed by I. M. Lewis (1971: 70).
2. This sentence occurs in a paragraph which poses a question that Kariuki does not answer: why Kikuyu women changed their allegiance during the Emergency, so that by the end of it the majority was aiding the Government against the gangs? It seems to me that women (and their children) suffered most from the turmoil and were perhaps quicker to perceive when a cessation of hostilities was vital.
3. So-called because they live in compact settlements like Spanish towns (*pueblos*) (see Dozier, 1970). Eggan (1950) describes their social organization.

4. I use the 'ethnographic present' which refers to information collected at various times over the first half of the twentieth century – see the Bibliography.

5. Our guide took pains to explain to us the cruelty of the first Spanish priests to live in Acoma under the protection of Spanish arms. His account of the forced labour by which the church was built, and of other Spanish exactions, was so vivid that it was hard to realize that it had all happened in the sixteenth century. Our guide told us that all Acoma young people had to do some work for the community; many of them preferred carrying water the long journey up from the plain to the mountain top on which Acoma is built, to contact with tourists. Indeed, some water-carriers we passed shouted at our guide in jeering tones, which obviously made him uncomfortable; he would not translate what was said.

6. The term for the spirits or gods, as the word is translated by some authorities, is spelt in a variety of ways. This is the most common, modern spelling.

7. The corn grown by American Indians is brightly and variously coloured, unlike the sweetcorn eaten by non-Indians in North America and, increasingly, in Europe, or the maize which is a staple in Africa. Titiev describes the ear of corn on the 'below' direction as 'speckled', which I have interpreted as a mixture of colours, given the Hopi belief that the origin of everything was in the underworld, so that the mixture of colours could be said to mean every colour.

8. I could find no description of this ritual and it seems likely that no outsider has witnessed it, in recent times, anyway.

9. Cf. The double meaning of 'scourge' in English.

10. In this respect the fact that boys must be sponsored by 'ceremonial fathers' who are not kinsmen has a double significance: first, they are outside the clan (a father being the closest kinsman who is not a clansman), but secondly, they are only metaphorical kin, they belong to the wider world outside the household.

11. See Harley (1941).

12. There are fewer secret societies among the Mende and no link between them and clan membership.

13. We might also compare the popular belief that a baby should cry when the cross is marked on its forehead with holy water at baptism; the cries 'let the devil out', showing that the child has been purified.

CHAPTER V **PROBLEMS**
OF
INTERPRETATION

The rituals described in the last chapter are initiations in both senses of the word: they serve not only to admit novices to groups defined by powerful secrets but also to transform children. This latter transformation is usually referred to as becoming an adult, although in many societies it is marriage rather than initiation which confers full adult status on the young individual. Such dual-purpose initiations are found in many parts of the world, notably Melanesia. Allen, whose work on initiation rituals was mentioned in Chapter I, goes so far as to define as initiation only those rituals which also admit initiates to secret, single-sex groups. His usage is difficult to accept since, in other parts of the world there are large-scale, complex ceremonies which are clearly *rites de passage*, but which do not act as a means of admitting new members to secret groups. The term 'initiation' has long been accepted for them. Even in Melanesia admission to secret societies is not a universal feature, and Allen is forced to relax his definition in order to consider the rites of some peoples which would otherwise be excluded from his study.

The classification of *rites de passage* into subclasses, based on social significance and function, distinguished between these initiations, which I shall also refer to as maturity rites, and rites such as those of the Triad society and others described in the first part of the book. However, the two types are not empirically distinct as these examples show, and they also share many common features: the tripartite form of the ritual, which is common to all *rites de passage*, the symbolism of death and rebirth, and the existence of oaths and ordeals. The element of secret knowledge transmitted is important in both types of initiation too; it is on the basis of the significance of secret knowledge that Allen admits the rites of two peoples, excluded on other grounds, to his study. Earlier writers on maturity rituals described them as 'schools' of initiation, by analogy with western institutions, and sought to show their educative functions. However, as I have indicated in connection with the Masons, the Triad society or the spirit cults of Bunyoro, the information which is received in the ritual is minimal and must be supplemented later by instruction, explanation and further experience of performances of the ritual. As far as maturity rituals are concerned, the 'instruction' given in adult roles is barely more than symbolic of adult tasks, with which the initiates are already familiar from daily life. Richards points out that Bemba girls do not actually see much of their own initiation rituals as they spend much time with their heads covered; the words of the songs, the meanings of the actions or the objects used, are not explained to them (Richards, 1956: 125–9). What is conferred in both cases is experience of the ritual.

There are also significant differences between the two types of initiation. First, and most important, maturity rituals are normally mandatory, in that all individuals must go through them; it is not a matter of choice, as is joining a secret society. Among the Hopi or Mende, to be adult is to be initiated, although there is some choice as to which secret society initiates will join. Among the Gisu of Uganda, where I did field-work in the 1950s, no man, however old he might be, was considered adult, and therefore entitled to drink beer on equal terms with other men, unless he were initiated. An uninitiated man, even married and a father, would be referred to contemptuously as a boy. Traditionally[1] Bemba believed that their *chisungu* rituals were essential for girls to become real women; uninitiated girls were 'rubbish'. These cases are examples of the general fact that among those peoples who perform rituals at maturity, the identity of initiates is a matter of public knowledge and concern, not a secret. Those individuals who escape initiation are known and, usually, despised. Since initiation into maturity is a central institution it is not surprising to find that the symbols employed in the rites refer to the central, most deeply held values of the society concerned. The recognized authorities of the community, village chiefs and headmen or the office-holders of kinship groups, lineage heads and elders or their ritual officers, priests and officiants at ancestral shrines, conduct these initiations. The right to hold them, sponsor them or officiate at them may be an important index of political authority. The Ndembu of Zambia have been mentioned in this connection; the same is true of peoples as far apart as the Barasana of Amazonia (Hugh-Jones) and New Guinea (Herdt).

The public significance of such initiations contrasts with the privacy of the secret society, by which a minority is marked off from the rest of society. The contrast between insiders and outsiders may include a dramatic opposition to the wider society and its values, which is emphasized by the regular repetition of initiation and other secret rites. It is consistent with this that membership of such societies may be secret and that members and officers are often drawn from sections of the population which have little access to power or prestige.

The existence of dual-purpose initiations, like those of the Mende and the Hopi, suggests that such differences are not fundamental. The members of a secret group may be a large section of the community. The differences concern the social setting of the rituals and not the ritual itself. There are, as the next chapters will show, other common symbolic themes as well as an emphasis on mysterious knowledge, which are common to initiation at maturity and initiation into secret societies. Both types of ritual establish boundaries between different categories of person. The rites show that maturity is a social status, not merely a matter of physical growth. The social distinctions involved are established by the ritual, not given in nature, although this is how members of these societies may think about them. One of the sources of confusion in thinking about such rites is failure to distinguish adequately between the social categories involved and biological differences (between male and female, old and young).

The transformation of individuals, by the ritual which transfers them from one social state to another, is a demonstration of the power of ritual knowledge, experienced by the initiates and other participants alike; it supports the position of those in authority, the officiants, whether these are secret-society officials or traditional leaders. The individuals are, to this extent, objects used in the ritual, rather than its central focus through which the ritual is to be explained. Initiation rituals cannot be understood simply as a means of changing the status of individuals.

Failure to recognize that initiation rituals are 'for' those already initiated, as much as for the novices, and that explanations of them must include all the participants, has been a handicap in analysis. As I have already pointed out, the concern with social function has altered the original intention of the term *rites de passage* from a description of a sequence of ritual to an emphasis on its purpose. The (perhaps unintended) result of breaking down this unitary category into a number of subdivisions was to ignore the similarities between them in favour of the distinctions established, between rites classed as concerned with natural and those concerned with human transitions, and to focus attention on the individuals whose status was changed, rather than on the ritual. All that seems to have remained of Van Gennep's attention to the rites themselves was a concern with defining, ever more narrowly, classes and subclasses of ritual.

The establishment of a class of life-crisis rites directed attention to human development. Initiation between infancy and marriage was considered a key element in the transformation of the raw material of childhood into the fully social adult. Particularly in America, where cultural anthropology was centrally concerned both with socialization as the process by which culture was transmitted and with the relationship between culture and personality, initiation has attracted much scholarly attention. The bulk of what was written shows the strong influence of psychology and psychoanalytic theory; the rituals are no longer of central concern but elements, such as genital mutilation and other ordeals, may be taken as characteristics of initiation as such, despite much evidence that many initiations do not include operations on the genitals. They will be discussed in some detail for, although I do not find them convincing, they have been influential on general thinking on initiation. They illustrate the failings of theories which apply insights into the workings of western society uncritically to the explanation of other, quite different societies.

Reik was one of the earliest to use Freudian theory to explain initiation rites; from then onwards, many scholars have used a version of Oedipal theory and castration anxiety as a basis for their explanation. Reik saw circumcision and the symbolic killing which is often enacted in initiation rites as punishments, or rather threats of punishment, for the sins of parricide and incest with the mother. Circumcision is a representation in symbolic form of castration which inhibits incest; symbolic killing is the sanction against parricide. The ritual is imposed on young men by their elders to control them and punish their secret desires, ensuring their obedience and maintaining the taboos. This crude sketch shows the basic elements of separation from the mother and of the power of the father. It also represents the ritual as a means of frustrating feelings which are engendered in childhood.

Whiting, the earliest of the cultural anthropologists to attempt a universal theory of initiation, used a modification of this approach. His article, written with Kluckholn and Anthony, advances the theory that male initiation is necessary where practices of child-rearing associate boys with their mothers in an exclusive bond, thus generating hostility between father and son; the trauma of initiation breaks this tie and separates boys from their mothers, incorporating them into the male world and preventing a revolt against parental (paternal) authority. Whiting later modified his theory to emphasize conflict in sexual identity rather than the frustration of unacceptable desires by hostile fathers. He has also included change of residence at puberty as a functional alternative to initiation, to account for those societies who show the social prerequisites for initiation but do not have initiation rites.

Whiting's innovation was to seek to demonstrate the universal validity of his hypothesis. Rather than argue from general principles or a few select cases, he attempted a statistical test. Using material from the Yale Human Relations Area Files he demonstrated correlations between the variables he selected to show the strength of the mother–child tie, paternal authority and the existence of initiation rites. The results appeared to confirm his hypothesis, but as others have pointed out (Young, 1962) a statistical association does not by itself show why the variables are asso-ciated (they could be dependent on the same underlying cause) or which of them is cause and which effect. In addition, several authors have pointed to errors in the ethnography. I will not repeat Allen's criticism in detail here; he cites a formidable list of objections made by Norbeck, Walker and Cohen. The most telling, to my mind, is the lack of evidence either for the emotional states which are said to generate the need for initiation ritual, or for the effect of the rites.

Critics of Whiting and his associates have put forward alternative hypotheses using institutional arrangements, rather than emotions such as dependence and hostility. Thus Young has argued that the existence of cohesive male groups and a dramatization of the male sex-role are the significant variables. Cohen's thesis is somewhat similar but it refers to the extrusion of children of both sexes from the family and their incorporation in other groups as adults. Both Young and Cohen use a similar statistical method and both see initiation rites as a product of other institutions. All these writers are interested in the presence or absence of rituals, not in their details. They all treat as significant two major distinctions: between the sexes and between the generations. While they formulate these divisions in emotional terms rather than conceptualizing them as socially significant, they are, in effect, rephrasing Van Gennep's statement that initiation rituals transferred initiates from association with women as children, to association with men as adults.

Modifications of Whiting's original thesis tend to a more sociological interpretation, arguing that the existence of institutional arrangements which structure relations between generations of males are more likely to be significant in relation to male initiation than emotions engendered in early childhood. Thus Cohen argues cogently that institutional arrange-ments 'do not arise out of personality or out of conflict as such' (1964: 532). In his view, initiation establishes a social identity, a 'sense of social–emotional anchorage for the growing individual'. He associates the rites with puberty and with the establishment of membership of a descent group and subordination to elders, other than fathers. He points out that Young had demonstrated the association of male initiation rites with the existence of exclusively male cohesive groups, often descent groups. Both these authors, while criticizing Whiting for an approach which was too psychoanalytically oriented, themselves also focus on the growth of the young individual and the socialization process. It is as though none of the other actors in what are often long, complex series of rites, engaging the energies of large numbers of people, are affected. Van Gennep's thesis that these are transition rites concerned with a change of status is accepted but reduced, under the influence of cultural anthropology and psychology (including psychoanalytic theory here), to a matter of bringing up children. As I indicated, most of these studies are concerned with male initiation.

Cohen includes the initiation of girls in his book (1964a), which covers a wider field than the article just cited, and Judith Brown has contributed an article of the Whiting school on girls' initiation. Her conclusions introduce a slightly different focus but some of the concerns of this whole school are shown clearly, which makes consideration of her article an opportunity to discuss them.

The first problem which is encountered in the attempt to explain the distribution of initiation rites, classified as life-crisis rituals, is to define them clearly. Obviously this is a necessary preliminary to the tabulation of instances. The effect of varying definitions can be seen dramatically if one compares the work of Cohen and Brown on the distribution of male and female rites. Both these authors use the same source of data, but their definitions of initiation produce radically different pictures of the relative frequency of initiation rites for girls and boys.

In his book, *The Transition from Childhood to Adolescence*, Yehudi Cohen (1964a) defines initiation as mandatory for all individuals and concerned with sets of initiands rather than single persons. Using the Yale Human Relations Area Files he extracts 65 societies which have the data necessary for his study. Of these I exclude 5 which relate either to America or Europe but in an ill-defined way, which makes them not strictly comparable with the others. Of the remaining 60 societies, initiation rituals exist in 19, of which 13 are only for boys. (A further 2 societies formerly initiated boys only but Cohen counts them as not having initiation rituals.) Another 4 societies initiate both boys and girls, and only 2 have initiation rites for girls and not boys. Thus only 6 societies, 10 per cent of his sample, initiate girls, while 17 societies, 28 per cent, initiate boys; there are nearly three times as many cases of male initiation as there are of female initiation. Moreover, in two-thirds of the societies who initiate girls, both sexes are initiated, so that it is even more rare to find cases where girls are initiated and not boys.

Judith Brown takes a much more inclusive definition of initiation using the age of initiands rather than their association in sets. Girls' initiations are, she considers, 'one or more ceremonial events, mandatory for all girls of a given society, and celebrated between their eighth and twentieth year. The rite may be a cultural elaboration of menarche but it should not include betrothal or marriage customs' (1963: 838). Her sample includes 75 societies, of which I exclude 2 on the same basis of exclusion as I used for Cohen's data and 3 because they seem to me to be wrongly classified; there are insufficient data on 12 societies, leaving a total of 58. On her definition the opposite conclusion of relative frequency must be drawn: more than half the societies (34) initiate girls, while only 23, less than half, initiate boys. The table below compares the results of Cohen's classification with Brown's.

Relative Frequency by Male and Female Initiation

	Cohen (60 cases)		Brown (58 cases)	
Initiation for boys and girls	4		11	
boys only	13		12	
boys (all cases)		17		23
girls only	2		23	
girls (all cases)		6		34
No initiation	41		12	

Too much weight must not be placed on the actual figures, since the two authors have used rather different samples from the Human Relations Area Files, rather than attempting a world-wide coverage. However, the comparison makes clear that the rarity or otherwise of initiation and the relative frequency of male or female initiation rites depend heavily on the initial definition of initiation. It also indicates that using the criterion of rituals concerned with groups of individuals allows more cases of male than female rituals to be defined as initiation. The life cycle of women thus seems to be more likely to be punctuated, between childhood and marriage, by ritual treatment of separate individuals.

Brown's explanation of female initiation is closely related to Whiting's modification of his original hypothesis. In it he takes conflict in sexual identity as the key to initiation, arguing that a change of residence at puberty has a similar function to initiation rites, in clarifying sexual identity for the adolescent. Brown's argument is that a similar conflict of identity for girls is related, not to female initiation generally, but a particular form of it, considered later. Female initiation is related to post-marital residence and the contribution of female labour to the economy. Since in non-industrial societies girls marry early, a change of post-marital residence is equivalent to a change of residence at puberty. According to Brown this change of residence has the effect of separating the adolescent from the natal family and resolving the emotional problems which are generated in early childhood. If there is no change in a girl's residence at marriage, initiation rites separate her from her mother and establish her adult identity. Initiation rites thus distinguish between the generations. Further, Brown argues that such a distinction is of significance only where women contribute significantly to subsistence; that is, where the division of labour according to sex makes the female role one of economic importance.

The control of women, the devaluation of their role in the production of children, and their subordination to men, are all elements that have been used in feminist explanations of the initiation of girls. These authors have concentrated their attention on the more dramatic aspects of female initiation, painful mutilations which, as Brown remarks, are very rare. The concern of most recent writing on this subject has been the abolition of such operations and the explanations are asserted rather than argued (Maclean, 1980). Nevertheless, there is some truth in the assertions, although it should not be forgotten that genital mutilations are more often performed on boys than on girls and that where girls undergo painful operations at initiation it is usual that boys must suffer equally.[2]

The consideration of female initiation separately from male rites is based on an unexamined assumption that the 'natural', i.e. biological, differences between the sexes influence the ritual. Moreover, societies like the Hopi where boys and girls are initiated together are rare; most initiation rites are for one sex only, and where both sexes undergo initiation, usually the rites are separate (see Chapter VIII). Where girls are concerned the ritual attention paid to the onset of menstruation, which is very common, raises the question of the relation between puberty, as a stage of biological maturation, and initiation. Since among boys there is no single dramatic bodily change which can serve as a sign of maturity the question seems less significant for male initiation. Whiting assumes that initiation and puberty coincide, although Van Gennep has pointed out, on the basis of evidence from many societies, that initiation rites are concerned with social rather than physical maturity. The rites may be performed on small children, as among the Merina of Madagascar (Bloch, 1974), or on young men, as among the Gisu of Uganda (see Chapter VI). Commonly male initiation rites are performed for sets of boys together, and in such a case, even where there is a notional connection with physical puberty, not all candidates for initiation will have reached the same stage of physical maturation. Young points out that the most elaborate ceremonies, which he would term initiation, occur when sets of candidates are initiated. Most writers on male initiation accept, either implicitly or explicitly, that initiation involves sets of individuals. They thus ignore the question of its relation to puberty. If one uses this social criterion, as we have seen already, many fewer of the rites for girls qualify for inclusion as initiation rites.

Brown, however, includes the widest possible range of rituals within her definition of initiation rites for girls. Using an arbitrary age-range, eight to twenty years, she specifically includes the rituals associated with first menstruation. However, the two types are not mutually exclusive; in societies such as the Bemba, girls undergo individual menstrual or puberty rites when they reach menarche, and later are initiated in a distinct ritual which usually involves more than one individual. In still other societies it is a matter of concern, as it is with the Nayar of South India, that initiation be complete well before puberty since it is thought sinful or polluting if an uninitiated girl menstruates. In societies like those of the Berba or Pokot, both discussed in Chapter VIII, it is pregnancy which may not occur until after initiation. In both cases, the ritual events are clearly disconnected from the physical process of maturation by the insistence that changes in social status must precede specific stages of physical growth. This is not dissimilar to the prohibition which prohibits an uninitiated youth from having sexual affairs or fathering a legitimate child. Indeed the people of Wogeo Island, discussed in the next chapter, like other New Guinean peoples, assert that it is the rituals that cause the subsequent physical changes. Of course, an explicit disassociation between initiation and physical events permits the performance of regular initiations of sets of individuals. This seems to be more likely where boys are initiated; girls are more often the subject of individual rites.

Many societies which (on any but the most inclusive definition) do not initiate girls mark the onset of menstruation with ritual. Of necessity these are simple affairs, as they cannot be planned. However, Hogbin points out that on Wogeo Island parents might turn a blind eye if their daughter's first menses was very inconveniently timed, so as to be able to celebrate suitably at a subsequent date. Such a practice, if openly followed, would rapidly destroy the association of ritual with natural events. As it is, it is kept quiet, which suggests that, unlike initiation, the link between ritual and physiological markers in rites of first menstruation is intentional and significant.

This difference supports the distinction made between puberty rites for individuals and initiation for sets of girls (Richards, 1956). Defining male and female initiation in the same terms also makes it possible to compare them. Puberty ritual effects a change of status; like initiation, it is a transition rite, although, as the Bemba case shows, the two are not merely functional alternatives. It is mistaken to think that female initiation is less common because the onset of menstruation provides a natural marker of female maturity, needing only ritual celebration to make it the equivalent of male initiation. The two are transition rites of different kinds.

In some societies, people do see a parallel between menstruation and what happens in male initiation (see Chapter VI). The connection does not constitute an explanation of the ritual, nor is it universal, but it has been made the basis of an influential theory explaining, not male initiation, but circumcision. At this point we must consider the nature of the physical ordeals suffered in maturity rituals which are often very different from those which admission to a secret society entails, since they may involve permanent changes to the body.

Circumcision is so widely distributed as a feature of rituals of maturity for boys that the term 'circumcision rituals' may be used as a synonym for them. The comparable operation for girls is excision of the clitoris, clitoridectomy, which is sometimes called 'female circumcision'. The use of the terms is somewhat misleading, though. Not all operations on the genitals are circumcisions or clitoridectomies; various operations, some more severe and others less so, are reported from different parts of the world. Operations on the genitals are not the only painful initiatory ordeals: Mende boys are scarified. It is these scars which identify the initiate rather than the circumcision which generally precedes the ritual. Hopi children are whipped and made to sit in a cramped position for hours, and similar ordeals are imposed in many other initiation rituals. In parts of New Guinea blood-letting, either from the penis, or the nose, is the main physical ordeal,[3] while the Nuer of the Sudan mark initiates with scars on their foreheads. However, circumcision, particularly the male form, is sufficiently common for many writers to seek to explain its wide geographical distribution in many different societies. Most attempts to do so focus on male circumcision, which shows much variation: it is performed on Jewish babies, on small boys among the Muslims of the East African coast (Caplan, 1976) and in Madagascar, or as an ordeal of manhood among boys at about the age of puberty in Australia and southern Africa. Among the Gisu of Uganda and a few other peoples it is even performed on men well past the age of puberty. Except in western society, circumcision is always performed as part of a ritual, a fact which must be stressed. Nowhere, except in the secular hospitals of western Europe and America, is it performed simply as surgery necessary for practical reasons. While many peoples may justify its practice in hygienic or cosmetic terms, as is the case in the West, everywhere else it is part of a ritual of transition and therefore such reasons do not explain it.

The ritual surrounding circumcision itself may vary, from the private, family affair to large-scale, national events of deep emotional significance, so that a unitary explanation is hard to find unless the social and ritual significance is ignored. This, indeed, is what most of those who take the explanation of circumcision as their central problem largely do; they account for its occurrence either in terms of local rationalizations or from within psychoanalytic theory. Some of the latter present some interesting suggestions about the interpretation of symbolism, although they do not to my mind offer convincing explanations of the institution of circumcision, let alone of initiation rituals. Their ideas are worth considering in more detail, because they are by no means at variance with the ideas of social anthropology.

Bettelheim, in his book on Australian initiation, *Symbolic Wounds* (1954), attacks Freudian orthodoxy for regarding initiation as imposed on initiates and concerned with fears of castration. He points out that there is evidence that young men desire to be circumcised and, further, that many myths explaining the origin of circumcision attribute it, as indeed the Gisu do, to a practice instituted by women. Allen points out that among the Möwehafen of New Britain a woman circumcises high-ranking boys (1967: 18). Bettelheim goes on to argue that circumcision, far from being the threat of male impotence, is designed to increase male powers by an imitation of menstruation, designed to acquire female reproductive powers for men. He derived his insights from the study of some of his patients. These were a set of seriously disturbed adolescent boys and girls who planned to make the boys bleed from their genitals in the belief that menstrual blood contained magical powers, related to the female childbearing capacity, and that male bleeding would generate equal powers in them. This belief in the power of menstrual blood does have many parallels in the beliefs of many other societies, although menstrual blood is commonly also feared as dangerous. Bettelheim draws on Reik's discovery that envy of women's capacity to have children is a powerful motivating force in men, as well as his study of these young patients, to argue that circumcision is an attempt to show that men can bear children. In the Australian rites he analysed, the boys are snatched away from their mothers and reborn as men. The imitation of birth and the insistence on rebirth are the means by which men assert that they do have the ability to create life.

Anthropologists do not accept the assumption that the institutions of any society can be identified with the fantasies of disordered adolescents. Behaviour in non-Western societies cannot be explained by comparing them with children, let alone psychotic children. Nor can the obligatory formalized actions of a ritual, which is not created anew each generation but forms part of a long tradition, be convincingly explained as springing from individual fantasies. There are many other questions which Bettelheim's work leaves untouched: why should circumcision not occur in all societies, if male envy of childbearing is found in such widely differing social contexts as industrialized cities in America and among Australian Aboriginals? Why should similar rites exist which do not include circumcision? And why should girls, the source of male envy, themselves suffer genital mutilations? However, to reject Bettelheim's work altogether, as some anthropologists have tended to do, is to throw the baby out with the bath-water. Bettelheim's thesis has drawn attention to the fact, now well attested in many parts of the world, that male initiation, particularly where blood flows, is explicitly compared by some people who practise it with menstruation (see below). Menstrual taboos, which Bettelheim associates with male envy of female powers, and others such as Allen with male sexual anxiety, are usually believed by the people who hold them to be protective measures, guarding vulnerable persons, often young children or babies or potent men, from the dangers associated with a powerful yet dangerous substance. The central idea is the control of natural powers to make them beneficial not harmful.

The explanations for circumcision advanced by anthropologists have mostly stressed its symbolic significance. Van Gennep pointed out that clitoridectomy removes from the female organ those features which most resemble the male. Discussing this, Gluckman remarked that he might also have suggested that circumcision removes from the penis features which resemble the labia. The circumcised penis, like the erect penis which it resembles, is unequivocally male. Indeed the Ndembu of Zambia make this idea quite explicit (Turner, 1962: 191–2). Circumcision and clitoridectomy may thus be seen as intensifying masculinity and femininity by removing those anatomical features of each sex which resemble those of the opposite. They also create distinctions between mature and immature individuals of each sex, so that social and physical differences coincide. Such interpretations do receive support from the ideas of people who practise these ritual operations. In parts of East Africa it is believed that an uncircumcised girl cannot conceive or that if she does her baby will not survive. The Gisu connect failure to circumcise youths with the begetting of children who die, and their neighbours the Sebei argue that uncircumcised girls are not real women. Yet, even though these anthropological interpretations may be valid, they cannot be used to explain all the different ordeals which are characteristic of initiation rituals, and so they are of limited usefulness.

In considering circumcision and clitoridectomy together with other operations on the body, what becomes clear is that the ritual is both seen by others of the society, and experienced by the initiates, as a permanent change, affecting their capacities in every social role they may hold. If we consider each living member of any society as having many different roles, such as son/father/neighbour/workmate[4] and so on, then as an individual he is a living body, a personality, and the sum total of his social positions. The body is often used to represent this individuality so that what happens to the body affects all aspects of the person whose material form it is. The bodily transformations which may be made in initiations thus manifest a radical change in the individual; but they are more than mere symbols of social changes.

It should be realized that the physical changes that take place in initiation rituals may be quite severe tests of the initiate's capacity to survive. Exhaustion, cold, shock and loss of blood are debilitating; wounds may become infected or fail to heal. In considering the symbolic meaning of these operations, we must not forget that they are more than that: they may risk the health or even the lives of the initiates. Those who conduct the ritual are accepting serious responsibilities and a successful outcome tests qualities in the initiators as well as in the initiates. During 1954 when I was studying Gisu initiation, two boys died; many peoples, like the Mende, have developed stereotyped formulae to announce such a death. There is often a quite practical sense in which such a ritual may be described as successful or not.

However, not all ordeals are of this severity. Many resemble the tests described in the discussion of Masonic ritual. Considerable importance is placed on the candidates passing them. When Audrey Richards asked what would happen if the girls failed to perform their tests successfully, the Bemba women told her, 'We do not *let* them fail.' She noted considerable anxiety among the women; the mothers of the girls felt that they, as mothers, might be at fault if their daughters failed, and the mistress of ceremonies that her skill might be impugned. It seems that oaths and ordeals are demonstrations of the effectiveness of the ritual, whether what is at issue is an administered oath, a test of skill which may be easy or difficult, or even taking risks with the lives of initiates. The operations, whether on the genitals, or on some other part of the body, which are thought to distinguish initiation rituals, are less distinctive than they seem at first sight. They do not, as some have thought, mark out a class of rites distinct from all others which would require a separate explanation. They share in this general characteristic; they are both tests and guarantees of the efficacy of the ritual.

Maturity rituals seem to share a distinctive concern with adult sexuality, with puberty rites and marriage. It was for this reason that Frazer termed them fertility rites and Van Gennep pointed out that fertility ritual accompanies them. Fortes has remarked that since adult status normally involves the rights and responsibilities of parenthood it is not surprising that rituals of adult status should be directed to ensuring the ability to procreate. As we saw, Mende initiates are referred to as 'those who procreate'. The overt concern of many initiation rituals marking adult status is adult sexuality, and the rituals imply the particular ideas about human reproduction held by the people who perform them.

Sexual symbolism also appears in rites like those discussed earlier, which create members of a distinct social entity and are not concerned with maturity, whether social or physical. The account of these rituals has shown how birth can be seen as a means of dramatizing and enacting the separation of individuals from normal life and the transformation which takes place in the initiands. This interpretation goes back to Van Gennep and was given further elaboration by Mircea Eliade. Sexual symbolism is not confined to enactments of birth, however; more direct representation of the sexual act can also be seen in such rituals, even where there is little or no use made of the analogy with birth. The clearest example of this comes from the ritual of induction into Mau Mau. There the action of the reed placed in the holes of the *ngata* is a mime of the sexual act, although the *ngata*, the bone from a goat's vertebral column, is chosen for its association with the sacred stone on which oaths were sworn. The sexual act itself may even be part of the ritual, as it is alleged to be in the spirit cult of the Nyoro. The meaning of these acts cannot easily be accounted for solely by their perceived link with birth or fertility. Sexual symbolism is widely found in transition rites but it has generally been interpreted with reference to the particular rites under discussion. Thus Bettelheim regards its referent as the procreative capacities of women, regarding the male mime of childbirth as a claim to equality with women. Eliade gives a more metaphorical interpretation, arguing that sexual symbolism represents the transcendence of the spirit over the facts of physical death. In a more recent collection, concerned like Eliade with funerals, Bloch and Parry argue in a similar vein that funerals establish social continuity despite the mortality of human beings. They associate sexuality with the biological,[5] as distinct from the social, element in the individual and stress the funeral as 'a device for the creation of ideology and political domination' (1982: 42). The common element in these interpretations is that sexual symbolism refers to generation, and whether this is interpreted more or less literally varies with the occasion for the rituals under analysis. The problem of explaining the presence of sexual symbolism in rituals which are concerned neither with maturity nor death, and are explicitly opposed to the central system of authority, remains unresolved.

In his book on symbolism, Leach has drawn attention to the common use of the phallus to represent ideas of mystical power (1976: 39). Male potency and the power of the gods are analogous and mysterious forces, conceptualizations of a causality underlying all events, including birth and death. The very general attribution of powerful qualities to the blood shed at menstruation and during childbirth has already been mentioned; female reproductive functions are widely considered to embody qualities which, like those of the male, manifest hidden powers of generation. Sexual intercourse, in creating new life, mobilizes mystical power; the miming of sexual acts or their performance in ritual contexts is therefore to be understood as a means by which the ritual action is infused with potency and generative force. Sexual symbolism is not so much a referent to human sexuality and fertility as an attempt to harness immaterial powers to social purposes. Its appearance in the rites of initiation into groups which do not depend for their continuity on the children of their members, is intelligible in these terms, as the mobilization of the causal force manifest in the process of reproduction. Even in maturity rites, which seem overtly concerned with adult sexuality, such symbolism should be interpreted as part of actions aimed at inducing change, rather than as referring solely to human physiology.

Initiation rites establish a distinction between childhood and adult status which is a matter not of physiological development but of social definition. This distinction and the related one of gender, the social roles designated by the terms 'man' and 'woman', which is also constructed by initiation, are fundamental to the organization of society. They are thus of significance to all who participate, not merely to those being initiated. The transformation of the initiands from human raw material into socially responsible persons displays the difference between these basic states of being. The purpose of the ritual action is achieved through the mobilization of power by those whose knowledge entitles them to do it. As the next chapters will show, the success of the performance demonstrates the efficacy of these techniques and hence manifests the powers of traditional authorities.

NOTES TO CHAPTER V

1. Even in 1931, when Richards watched a performance of *chisungu*, not all Bemba girls were initiated. The older people regretted this and girls who had 'had their *chisungu* danced' were valued above their peers.

2. I am not arguing for the retention of clitoridectomy, which has long-lasting consequences, for the individual, of a painful and even dangerous nature. However, the practice has to be understood in its social and ritual context, before the social problems involved in any change can be considered.

3. A Freudian interpretation might identify the nose as a symbol for the phallus; I do not know if such an interpretation is made by the people concerned. Other New Guinean rituals include painful deprivations, terrorizing, fellatio and such intimidation of the novices that the initiators may be worried about it (see Porter Poole, 1982: 123, 137).

4. Or daughter/mother/neighbour/workmate.

5. Bloch and Parry also make a distinction between sexuality and fertility, which is not quite clear to me, but which relates to their emphasis on distinctions of gender and male domination.

CHAPTER VI

**MALE
AND
FEMALE**

All maturity rites proclaim a fundamental distinction between male and female, which is imbued with social significance. It cannot, however, be assumed that the anatomical and physiological differences between the sexes are understood or interpreted in the same way in all cultures. The concepts of 'man' and 'woman' are constructed and justified by references to what is selected for emphasis by the society in question. The inhabitants of Wogeo Island off the north coast of New Guinea, who form one of the two societies considered in this chapter, consider that contact between the sexes weakens both men and women, an idea directly related to their maturity rites for boys and girls. Ideas about the relative capacities of each sex for withstanding pain are linked with initiation for boys and the superiority of the male sex among the Gisu. Sexual identity is an important aspect of adult status in all societies, and the allocation of social roles to men and women is everywhere explained and justified by reference to ideas concerning their natures. Western society has been made aware of this by the writings of women in support of their liberation from the social constraints imposed on them in this way, but in all societies there is a division of labour based on gender[1]. In societies which lack a complex social organization based on class, caste or hereditary rank, the sexual division of labour has greater importance. The tracing of descent, either in the male or female line, may provide the basis for the significant residential and political groups in a society, giving a further dimension to the meaning of gender. The association of initiation with organization based on descent, which was remarked on in the last chapter, indicates that sexual identity is likely to be a key concept in understanding it.

Maturity rituals are usually dramatic reinforcements of sexual distinctions, designed to underline the separation between the genders. Only rarely are boys and girls initiated together, as they are among the Hopi; even there, the subsequent rituals separate them. The Gisu, who only initiate males, think their neighbours, the Sebei, barbarous to initiate girls, while the Sebei think it equally barbarous not to, since they believe that both sexes must be ritually inducted into adult sexual roles. The Mende and the Wogeo islanders initiate both sexes but, like the Sebei, keep the rites for each sex secret from the other. Among the Mende there are some roles for women in the rituals of boys' initiation into the Poro, and some male roles in the girls' rites of entry into the Sande, but membership in each society is restricted to one sex. Still other societies initiate girls only, like the Bemba and the Nayar of India (Gough, 1955). The link between initiation and the allocation of roles is not a simple matter. The rites form part of a complex cosmological and social order, in which the opposition between male and female is linked to other dualisms in mutual reinforcement. The relation between sexual polarity and the other conceptual pairs is a matter of debate, but it is arguable that male and female are symbols of more abstract notions, rather than that the main symbolic focus is the definition of men and women by the attribution to them of additional qualities.

Maturity rituals are overtly concerned with affirming adult status in terms of the opposed categories of gender. The ritual division established in them resembles the opposition created in rites of admission to secret societies: insiders and outsiders are separated. However, the distinction between male and female, while based on a similar conceptual boundary, relates to the main structure of society in a different way. While Masons and members of the Triad society are set apart from the wider society in terms of their opposition to its ideals, the members can remain recognizable only to each other. Sexual identity is public, recognized by all, and cannot be segregated from the individual's other social roles. The women from whom Mende boys are snatched to inaugurate their initiation are their mothers and sisters, who cook for them, and for whom they work at tasks which women do not perform. The separation between men and women in ritual sustains a social division of labour which makes the sexes socially indispensable to one another. Men may define themselves in opposition to women by virtue of the secret knowledge which they alone possess, but they are intimately associated with women in joint domestic enterprises; members of secret societies do not depend on outsiders in the same way.

The social division by gender may imply complementarity but it usually implies asymmetry as well. The ideas associated with maleness are represented as superior. Thus the ritual which marks the division of the sexes also produces the justification for male domination of society, even in societies where descent is reckoned through women and only women are initiated. The hierarchy displayed in the initiation rituals of secret societies does not relate to society at large but only to a small segment of it, just as the relations of authority revealed in girls' initiation rites refer usually to female society. Women may be defined in terms of ideas which oppose or reverse those of the wider society, thus associating 'normality' firmly with men and male domination.

The initiation rites of the Gisu[2] of Uganda rest on a conscious, stressed difference between men and women but the people draw a parallel between male initiation and childbirth, both of which make adults of immature individuals. Youths undergo a single initiation which has, as its focal act, the operation of circumcision, which is emphasized as a trial of courage. Girls, on the other hand, undergo ritual when they first menstruate, when they are married, and at each childbirth. Women's ritual marks out events affecting individuals and thus does not, according to the definition used here, constitute initiation. Gisu consider that women are incapable of suffering the pain of the knife, which is what initiation means to them. More significantly, they think that if women were to be initiated they would not submit to male authority. Initiation confers this on men through their voluntary undergoing of the ordeal involved. The pain inflicted by circumcision is compared with that suffered in childbirth and the accepted dogma is that the latter is less significant for it is not deliberately undergone. (Gisu women publicly accept the social evaluation which gives them a lesser place; privately they may dispute it or add that since childbirth happens many times in a woman's life, the cumulative suffering is greater. But they agree that women do not choose to submit themselves to the pain; they merely cannot avoid it.)

Gisu initiation is thus overtly concerned with the testing and enhancing of male powers which have already developed but which are intensified by the ritual. The rites are also the major public ritual of Gisu society, a biennial festival which involves the whole society and mobilizes its most important social symbols (La Fontaine, 1969). Sixty years of incorporation into the wider society of Uganda, first under colonial rule and then in an independent state, have altered, but not diminished, the significance of initiation for the Gisu. Yet it incorporates initiates into no secret group and the transmission of secret knowledge is not a central concern. It focuses on the ordeal of submitting to circumcision, without flinching and in full public view.

Most Gisu youths start to press their fathers to allow them to be initiated when they feel themselves old enough to marry and become independent householders. Rich men may have already allocated land and the cattle for bridewealth to their sons before their initiation, but all men should do so to their initiated sons. Initiands are thus well past the age of puberty; they may be in their twenties and even thirties, but between eighteen and twenty-five was the usual age in 1954 when I observed the rites. Preparations for the ritual take several months, interspersed with agricultural activities, but the rites themselves are held after the harvest when food is plentiful and work at a minimum. Traditionally they took much longer to complete, but in modern times the whole country has circumcised its youths in a period of three weeks.[3]

The initiands, who are referred to as *basinde*, 'boys', no matter what their age, prepare for initiation in a way that immediately brings them to the attention of the community. They begin to perform the songs and dances of initiation, wearing the distinctive dress of initiands: a head-dress of colobus-monkeyskin, and bells on their thighs. Other ornaments are added to give a gay and festive air. The fashion for these may change slightly but what is important, and lends a youth prestige, is that he should wear women's adornments which have been given him by his father's sisters and his 'sisters'[4], not necessarily his close kin but cousins and other women who are kin, of his own and his father's generation. These are bead girdles, like the ones which all women wear round their loins; it is said these tokens of affection will give him strength to endure his ordeal. He wears them diagonally crossed over his chest.[5] The number of the strings indicates the number of his female kin and their affection. In 1954 youths wore also the kerchiefs that women tie on their heads and, in a manner shocking to their elders, were wearing tokens from lovers as well as kin. Older Gisu said that the tokens should be of affection, with no connotations of sexuality; they found the display of sexual ties shocking and a sign of the degeneracy of modern youth! The observer can see in the beads, which are associated with an intimate part of a woman's body and subject to a number of rules of etiquette in sexual life,[6] an identification of the initiand with the women of his group.

The primary group of Gisu society is a patrilineal group descended from a single male ancestor. The idea of common descent is used to identify all groups which are of political, ritual or cultural significance, up to the whole Gisu people, who can be spoken of as the descendants of one man. Women are transferred to the jural authority of their husband and his lineage at marriage but never completely lose their lineage identity. Their fertility, as evidenced in the children, and especially sons, that they bear for men of other groups[7] is a matter of lineage pride, a sign of the strength of the lineage and the power of its ancestors. The dress of an initiand therefore carries a whole range of meanings which identifies him with women in general and with female kin in particular, and with the reproductive power of his lineage which gives him strength. He seems an individual with both male and female attributes, a brother/sister composite which represents both male and female aspects of his lineage and yet also a child, undifferentiated by adult sexuality.

The dancing continues through the season of agricultural work and begins to intensify as the harvest approaches. By the time the millet is harvested, the groups of initiands are dancing and singing most of the day and well into the night, visiting their kin to inform them of the approaching events. Preparations are made by the seniors: the ancestral groves are cleaned and the shrines repaired, beer is brewed by the women, and animals are selected for slaughter. A hut, slightly removed from other houses, is prepared as a convalescent hut for the boys of each neighbourhood; the site where they will be circumcised is chosen. The youths, still wearing the distinctive garb of initiands, with its iron bells strapped to the thigh and head-dress with plumes of colobus skin, have been dancing more and more. They visit the homes of their kin, where they are given gifts and homilies about the seriousness of their undertaking, and lavishly fed. In return they dance to honour their host and indicate their commitment. These visits ensure that the whole countryside is made aware of the impending rituals, and gradually more and more people join the dancing. The novices are followed around, both by younger members of the community and by older initiated 'brothers'. Married women may return to their natal homes for the occasion and there is an air of carnival. People dress themselves up; some of the costumes burlesque the physical features, gait and dancing of the opposite sex, others refer to the traditional dress or accoutrements of the past. Even older women who are 'mothers' and 'fathers' sisters' to the initiands, will eventually join in. No one who is able to participate should be absent; there is much beer, little sleep and not much cooking. As one married man wrily said: 'Everyone suffers during initiation.' Only the senior men do not dance. They are concerned with the ritual preparations: cleaning the ancestral shrines and making preparatory offerings. Their seriousness contrasts with the noise and excitement of the crowds.

The preparatory singing and dancing are not incidental but an essential part of the proceedings, for they are believed to strengthen the novices for their ordeal. In 1954, when I was there, old men were grumbling that boys who went to school no longer took the preliminaries seriously and, as a result, more of them took fright and ran away before they were circumcised, shaming their kin. One could argue that they were right, for the additional meat and the constant exercise did seem to bring the novices to a peak of physical fitness. However, the participation of the community was also important, to encourage the novices; the atmosphere was certainly that of feverish excitement. More seriously, the goodwill and blessings of kin, particularly the mother's brother,[8] are also important in that they give support and help to ensure a successful outcome. A sign of their support is the white yeast paste with which the candidates' bodies may be smeared by their senior kin, to bless and protect them.

To be initiated successfully is to stand absolutely motionless in front of a critical audience of men while the lengthy operation is performed. It requires, Gisu believe, both strength of purpose to conquer fear[9] and strength of body to maintain self-control. These qualities are not clearly distinguished as aspects of 'strength' but the dancing affects both. Heald (1982) has reported that the period of preparation does seem to strengthen the resolve of initiands; at the time of her field-work there was somewhat greater emphasis on the degree of responsibility shouldered by the youths themselves than I noted earlier. It was repeated on many occasions that they had chosen to be initiated and that no one had forced them into it. However, even earlier it was clear that Gisu feel that boys must show, by their determination and willingness to undergo the preparatory dancing, that they are ready for adult status. Their suitability is finally tested in the ordeal itself.

A second but equally important quality, which is evinced in the period leading to the central events on the day of circumcision itself, is also thought to be intensified by the singing and dancing. This is the violent emotion, characteristic of men, called *litima*,[10] which is regarded with a certain ambivalence. It is the origin of quarrels and the cause of violence; but it is also the basis for the independence and competitiveness that Gisu admire in men, and in this context it is the source of eagerness to undergo initiation. The recognized end of the preparatory activities is that the initiands should be in a state of high emotion. The combination of continuous exercise, better than normal food, lack of sleep, and general excitement, induces a condition in the novices which resembles a state of trance or disassociation; they speak in a special yodel and appear not to understand what is said to them. Older 'brothers', already initiated, accompany them, protecting bystanders from their wild behaviour and the novices from blundering into things. Gisu see this as evidence of a single-minded violent drive to be initiated, but they also describe the novices as wild, and the novices are not held accountable for things they may do in this state.[11] To the observer they appear to be giving an impression of untamed humanity, outside normal society; they are powerful but asocial.

At this point the formal rites begin. The three main rituals may be varied slightly in different parts of the country: they concern relations between the ancestors and the living members of the lineage, the relation of novices to senior members of the lineage, and that between the lineage and the land. The first is an ancestral sacrifice, an offering of meat and beer to ensure the benevolent presence of the ancestors at the rituals. It is performed in the ancestral groves and at the shrines built for the ancestors in the homesteads of elders. The congregation at the groves represents all sections of the lineage, but women, children and uninitiated men are excluded from the sacrifice. Afterwards, the elders take in their mouths beer that has been offered to the ancestors and spray it in blessing, first on the initiands, then on other members of the lineage, particularly the young. This will enhance their fertility and strength. Kin who are related to lineage members through their mothers may also be blessed.

The second ritual consists of a formal admonishment and blessing of each initiand at the homestead where he will be circumcised, usually that of his father's elder brother or father's father. An animal is slaughtered for the ancestors and the entrails inspected to see whether the omens are good. After offering the sacred portions to the ancestors, the sacrificing elder takes chyme (the stomach contents of the beast) and smears it on the initiand, on his forehead, chest and legs. While he does so he makes a formal speech, over the initiand, rather than to him. The words refer to the purpose of initiation and contain the command which Gisu blessings always include: 'Beget sons.' The speech also states that the ancestors must not be forgotten, that guests should be treated well and the good name of the lineage protected. The initiate stands in silence; he is not expected to speak, for this is not a swearing-in like the administration of the oath in the initiation rituals of the secret societies that have been examined. It is a magical preparation of the novice. The authority of the elder, fresh from contact with the ancestors, infuses his words with power; the chyme from an ancestral sacrifice also conveys the same effect. Words and substance are the medium through which the effect is created: the youth's successful passage is (almost) assured.

The final ritual contact with the ancestors usually takes place immediately before circumcision.[12] The initiands, with their following and the elders, run to various sacred spots where there is a swamp or stream. Here they must jump into the mud with force so that they are thoroughly spattered. The assistants take handfuls of the mud and smear it over the youth's body. This is the final purification and the whole group then hastens back to the site where the circumcision is to take place, taking another path. Gisu say that this change of route is to prevent ill-wishers placing sorcery on the path to harm the initiands; we can also see it as a way of showing there is no going back now.

Gisu youths are circumcised in small groups of related boys, never more than four or five together. They stand in a line surrounded by men, with the women at a little distance, all watching. The circumciser emerges from where he has been hidden. He is an outsider; he does not live in the community and people speak as though a circumciser just appears from nowhere at the right time. In fact, arrangements are made beforehand with the fathers and senior kinsmen of the initiands, but the effect created is of strangers swooping down on the boys. The circumcisers and their apprentice-assistants hold themselves aloof; they operate and move on to the next homestead at a run. Many of them affect dress which immediately marks them off as distinctive: a leopard-skin tunic or, occasionally nowadays, white clothes with a red cross, recalling hospital attendants.

The boys must stand quite motionless until all have been circumcised; the circumciser starts with the most senior, going down the line in order of seniority.

During the operation, an older woman representing the initiands' mothers must be inside the hut, outside which the initiands stand. She may be the real mother of one of them and her part is to take up the position that Gisu women adopt during labour. She stands or squats near the centre-pole of the hut, which is associated with the lineage ancestors, clasping it in her hands. Her actions, like most others in the ritual, are said to give the initiands strength to endure their ordeal and show courage. They can also be seen as symbolic of the rebirth of the initiates and equate the pain of childbirth with that of initiation. The initiands are being closely watched for any signs of weakness by all the assembled men, who shout loudly both in acclamation when the foreskin is severed and while the rest of the operation is performed. The women and girls, standing back from the men, ululate shrilly. The noise is deafening but the watchers are not distracted. I was constantly surprised by comments on the twitching of eyelids, movements of the toes, or other slight departures from the ideal of complete motionless rigidity, which I had not noticed, but which never escaped the attention of at least one onlooker. The performance of each youth as well as the skill of the circumcisers was the topic of conversation for several days. It is important to convey the very public, very critical, evaluation of performance in the ordeal. In this the women are not merely permitted to be spectators; they are necessary witnesses. One secondary schoolboy wrote inviting me to 'come and admire me at my initiation'. He was expressing the general view of the role of women in the rituals. They are there to be impressed with the strength and endurance of men.

After the initial bleeding has stopped, the initiates are led away to the hut where they are to be secluded in convalescence. Care is taken to dispose of the foreskin, other tissues and blood, so that they cannot be used in sorcery to prevent healing or cause infections. The day ends with a feast for the members of the lineage, but the initiates may not touch food with the hands or drink beer until they have been cleansed by the circumciser. They must use sticks to raise food to their mouths, like menstruating girls, and have liquid poured into their mouths. For the rest of their convalescence they must avoid contact with women; their food is brought to them by prepubertal children and they should not speak to or, formerly, even see women. During this period stoicism is not enjoined; indeed, the initiates are expected to dwell on the agonies they have endured, and are enduring. Several to whom I spoke appeared stunned by the experience and said that in spite of having seen older brothers initiated, they had not 'known' what it would be like. One or two said that they would not have had the courage to be initiated had they known. The source of their own courage was obviously somewhat mysterious to them. During this marginal state the newly circumcised also sing, which, it is said, reminds those living within earshot of their presence; the songs claim the honour due to their courage. At a later stage, when they are allowed to leave the hut and walk about, they may harass those who are now their inferiors, the uncircumcised and girls; they may still not approach adult women. The marginal period, with the taboos that symbolize it, is ended with a presentation to the initiates of the symbols of adult manhood. These were traditionally a spear and the skin worn by circumcised men;[13] in modern times new clothing was the usual gift. The presentation was followed by a feast for lineage members and kin; the initiate participated as an adult, drinking beer with the men.

The ritual as a whole sets out the major social categories, linking them in a structure which is the ideal form of Gisu society. The fundamental division is between adult men and women. Children of both sexes are identified with women and a number of symbols make this clear in the rites. However, the identification emphasizes particular qualities associated with the polarity of gender: weakness and strength, dependence and independence, ignorance and knowledge. These are abstract ideas which are made manifest in the persons of the participants, who thus become living symbols of basic concepts, the truths on which the moral order is founded. The association of the initiands with women thus becomes a representation of the mixture of weakness and strength; as time progresses, the singing and dancing increase the strength of the novices until they are 'wild', violent and barely under control. Circumcision demonstrates the control which is necessary for the ideal man; it is self-control but fortified by ritual support provided by lineage superiors and kin. The superior state to which the successful accede is symbolized by the initiated men: strength, which is responsible and independent.

The rite can thus be read not merely as a change of status for those who are initiated but as a demonstration of concepts in which the participants are both actors and audience. The very common insistence on the presence at initiation rituals of those who are neither being initiated nor acting as officiants thus becomes intelligible. They re-enact the moral order to which they are committed and thus regularly reaffirm its significance to them all. This approach also explains another common feature of initiation, which is less significant in the Gisu case, but very clear in the next case to be considered: that the initiands may not witness much of what is going on and cannot be considered to have been taught anything by the rites. If the whole process is seen as the expression of fundamental social values, then the novices are merely one category of the structured ensemble, not the focus of the rites, nor the recipients of any message the rites might be deemed to convey. Among the inhabitants of Wogeo Island, boys reach maturity through a series of rituals aimed at encouraging their development into men. The rituals resemble one another and as boys proceed through the series they learn by participating more and more fully in the rites concerned with their juniors. Thus the requirement, found among the Nyoro, for example, that the newly initiated assist with further initiations, indicates that it is learning by participation and experience that is significant; those who acquire understanding are those who have already obtained the right in earlier rites, not those who are in the process of being transformed.

Gisu initiation displays a further set of concepts of great social significance: those that support their traditional lineage organization. The congregation is defined in these terms; the subcounties who circumcise on one day are seen as lineages, divided into the smaller segments and subsegments who perform their independent rites at the places sacred to their separate ancestors. Even the novices, lined up in small groups for circumcision, are ordered in terms of genealogical seniority, the sons of senior brothers taking precedence. In addition, within each lineage members are ranked by generation. The adult women who, in terms of the ideal of exogamy, will marry out are replaced in the congregation by those married in, the mothers and sisters-in-law of the novices. These women thus stand for the connections between lineages, established by marriage, an idea focused on the important role of the mother's brother, representative of a novice's distinct maternal origin and the alliance between lineages that brought him into being. As dependants of their fathers, Gisu youths have no right to marry; their relationships with women are those of kinship with mothers and sisters. Hence the outrage of the elders at the wearing of tokens from sweethearts can be understood as concerned with the violation of the ideal order of society, ritually constituted in the initiation rites. The informal love affairs of individuals have no place in that order, which is concerned with social institutions, such as marriage, and domestic authority, the prerogative of adult men.

Among the societies found in New Guinea and its surrounding islands, the division between the sexes is a much more marked structural feature than it is among the Gisu. Although there are considerable differences between the languages and the social systems of the people who live in this area, in most of them the sexes are so segregated that men and women seem almost to be mutually hostile subgroups. In many Highland New Guinean villages, men and women live separately: men in communal houses, known as 'men's houses' in the literature, and women in smaller dwellings with their daughters, small sons and often the pigs as well. Boys' initiation permits them to enter the men's house which is the focus of male society and the place of ritual activity. Women and children are strictly excluded. The people of Wogeo Island do not practise such extremes of residential separation but in other ways they exemplify very clearly this basic division in New Guinean society (Hogbin, 1970).

The differences between men and women in Wogeo are summed up in the people's dictum: 'Men play flutes, women bear children.'[14] The flutes are played in a secret male cult, in which men impersonate spirit monsters, like the Poro spirits. These are creatures who were made by the culture heroes, the founders of the Wogeo world. They preside at important rituals, and seem to infuse power into the proceedings, although they may also be called out by the headman to add prestige to proceedings at which monsters are normally not present. Women are not supposed to know about the flutes for they must shut themselves into the houses with their children when their sounds are heard; they are said to believe that the flutes are the voices of the monsters, and that the masked dancers who impersonate them are the monsters themselves. However, Hogbin shows that there is considerable evidence that this is merely a fiction, for women's rituals display some parallels with those of men, and women make remarks which show some knowledge of what is happening.

However, the general statement indicates the respective spheres of men and women: women produce children and men exercise the magical powers which control the social and natural orders. Men and women are thought to be mutually attractive and interdependent, but sexual intercourse is a source of danger to both sexes. Close intimate contact with the opposite sex is weakening because of their different natures; before undertaking an important enterprise both men and women refrain from sleeping with a lover or spouse, so as not to endanger success. The success of many rituals demands that the officiants abstain from sex for particular periods of time. However, Wogeo believe that women rid themselves periodically of male pollution by menstruating; men have no such natural safeguard but resort to incision of the penis, which the people equate with menstruation. Boys are taught to do this separately from the series of rites which accompany their growth to manhood.

The parallel, but opposed, natures of men and women are displayed in pollution concepts. While menstruation cleanses women, the blood itself is polluting and a woman must not come into contact with people or property while she is in this condition, nor touch the food of her husband lest he die. She is secluded in her hut; must keep warm and observe food taboos; uses a hole in the wall or in the raised floor, not the usual door, when going out to urinate or defecate; wears a special skirt which proclaims her polluted status; and must use special instruments to eat or drink with. In this condition she is *rekareka*, the term also used to describe a man who has incised his penis or who has had contact with ritual paraphernalia such as the flutes; mourners and homicides who have been polluted by contact with death, are all *rekareka* and must observe similar restrictions until the pollution has passed. The restrictions, including the food taboos and the injunction to keep warm (pollution is 'cold'), actively help to rid the *rekareka* person of the pollution.

The blood spilt in childbirth is even more dangerous than menstrual blood for it represents nine months' accumulation of pollution. A newly delivered mother cannot be touched by anyone, so she must cut the cord and dispose of the afterbirth herself, wash herself and the baby and then go to a seclusion hut built outside the village. Food is brought to her, and the baby may be picked up, once it has been washed, but the mother herself is untouchable. Anyone who touches her then is, in principle, as polluted as she is and must suffer the same restrictions, which will last until the day after the next full moon.

Men are expected to 'menstruate' regularly[15] but since the pollution is considered greater, they observe the taboos of *rekareka*, fast in seclusion in the men's house for a few days and refrain from sexual intercourse until the next new moon. Men may also become *bwaruka*, the term used for the pollution incurred by childbirth; men become so by officiating at the initiation of boys. Like newly delivered mothers, they are secluded in a pollution hut outside the village, with their charges, but they observe longer fasts and more severe privations than the latter, who are only *rekareka*, not *bwaruka*, just as a new-born infant is less polluted than its mother.[16] All those who have been *bwaruka* must abstain from sexual intercourse after they have emerged from seclusion. In theory the ban lasts for nine months, in practice it may be relaxed sooner.[17] Thus the physical difference between men and women is linked with the idea of their different powers; contact between the powers, though essential, is dangerous. The rites, and the precautions surrounding pollution, protect male and female from contaminating and weakening each other; in so doing their distinctiveness is emphasized.

The parallel between the ritual bleeding of men and the natural bleeding at menstruation seems to be quite explicit among Wogeo islanders; it led Hogbin to call his book *The Island of Menstruating Men*. A boy bleeding from the tongue during initiation is *baras* and the same word is used to designate a girl at the celebration of her first menstruation. On Wogeo people say that the tongues of boys must be bled to rid them of the femaleness taken in during infancy with their mothers' milk. To an observer who is aware that the different bodily orifices may be symbolically identified, the act appears to be an artificial menstruation. Yet Wogeo islanders identify menstruation with penile bleeding, which is an adult male means of purification taught to youths at a much later stage in their development, but this may not be significant. Similar parallels between the natural events of the female life cycle and initiation can be found implicit in Gisu symbolism, although Gisu do not recognize them as such. Gisu initiates, like girls at their first menses, may not touch food with their hands until they have been ritually cleansed; other details seem to have symbolic reference to events in the development of women's reproductive powers (La Fontaine, 1972).[18] Bettelheim's thesis that the symbolism represents an attempt to replicate female physiology seems plausible if reinterpreted in cultural terms.

Gilbert Lewis, in his careful discussion of this question (1980: 111–12), has pointed out that for an action to be an imitation of another, there must be a prior classification which establishes them as different. One must be the 'real' action. For the Gisu, circumcision is not the same as menstruation; they use different words to describe the two events. By contrast, Wogeo islanders use the same words for both male and female bleeding. After considering Hogbin's account of their ideas, Lewis concludes: 'Their concept of menstruation differs from ours – men and women both "really" menstruate' (ibid: 112). What is essential in the Wogeo concept is that bleeding purifies the body from the weakening pollution of the opposite sex.[19] The Gnau, whom Lewis studied, did not respond to his suggestion that penis-bleeding in the male puberty rite was like menstruation; they merely said that they did not see it like that. It seems therefore that in these two cases, where the parallel seems most exact, there is no justification in interpreting their actions as an imitation of menstruation.

The Gisu do compare circumcision explicitly with an event in the female life cycle, but with childbirth, not menstruation. They may use the same verb to refer to excision of the foreskin as is used for the defloration of a virgin but it is not used exclusively in these contexts. It means, in a more general sense, to break or spoil something that is whole or complete. By implication, then, both men and women are children that are spoilt. But this is not an important idea. The main theme, as already indicated, is that enduring pain creates adults. What is relevant in the two events that are compared is the suffering entailed. The greater strength of men to sustain a single ordeal compares favourably with the weakness of women, whose step-by-step progress to womanhood is thought to be easier. Their endurance justifies male authority over women.

Women are also the subordinate sex on Wogeo island but Hogbin asserts that they are 'neither pawns nor slaves'. A woman has a weapon with which to retaliate for a beating or slight from her husband, for should she touch his food when she is menstruating, he will contract a fatal illness. Adultery is common, and in their ritual, women mock at male powers. The women appear to have a more nearly equal relationship with men than in many other New Guinean societies (Strathern, 1972). Unlike these other peoples, Wogeo islanders have family dwellings in which men live with their wives and children, although they sometimes sleep at the men's house, in the centre of the village.

Male and female also have structural significance in the organization of the basic social groups. A village is divided into halves, each led by a hereditary headman, who is the leader of a group of kin. Kin related through men are referred to as *dan*, a word which means water but is a euphemism for semen. Villagers also belong to two moieties, named 'hawk' and 'bat', membership of which is traced through the mother. Marriage within the moiety is forbidden so that husband and wife are members of different moieties, as are father and son. Those in one moiety call themselves 'one blood' and the group is referred to as *tina*, 'mother', but only when there are traceable links between them do they consider themselves kin. The headmen own the flutes and the masks for impersonating the spirits as well as the magic for weather, trading, fighting and making peace. Inheritance, through men, of exclusively male powers, is the source of the headman's authority.

The initiation of Wogeo boys takes place in a number of stages. All childen, girls and boys, have their ears pierced at the age of about three 'to assist their growth'. This is an informal event for a girl, but for a boy it is the first ritually assisted step on the road to manhood. At about nine or ten he will be formally taken from his mother and introduced into the men's clubhouse; about the age of puberty he undergoes a further ceremony designed to enable him to play the flutes; and then a final stage permits him to wear the head-dress which is the sign of an adult man. The purpose of all the rites, which can be seen as an extended initiation, is to ensure that the boys will grow into men; that is, natural growth is seen as weak and likely to fail unless strengthened by the rites. The suffering which the initiands undergo is viewed with sympathy but seen to be a necessary part of actions which are designed to prevent worse befalling them. Hogbin tells us that the initiands are not expected to demonstrate that stoical endurance of the ordeal which, as we saw earlier in the chapter, is an essential feature of Gisu initiation.

Wogeo initiation rituals, then, are actions designed to induce physical maturation. Their effect is to break up the continuous process of maturation into a series of stages, each separated by the appropriate rituals. The rituals are marked by feasts, by the appearance of the sacred monsters and by the opposition of men and women as participants and spectators. Each of them involves the purification of the initiands either by letting blood or washing in the sea. Several boys, roughly contemporary in age, go through the rituals together and become linked to one another by special ties of brotherhood which are said to be stronger than kinship itself. Wogeo girls undergo a ceremony at their first menstruation but since the ceremony is triggered off by the natural event, it concerns one girl only, although she is accompanied by two companions who have not yet menstruated, but who seem to benefit in a secondary fashion from their participation in the ritual. Elements in the boys' ritual appear also in that of girls'. In describing the rituals for boys I indicate some parallels for discussion later in the chapter.

The first ceremony, that of ear-piercing, involves minimal participation on the part of the initiands but sets out the ritual elements which recur in the later ceremonies: the presence of the monsters, the separation of men and women, a ritual fight, which demonstrates the opposition between the parents and the wider community, and purification of the initiand, who is much in contact with women. The ceremony is organized, and the feasts provided, by the fathers of the little boys, who choose a kinsman of the opposite moiety to perform the ear-piercing. Visitors from other villages come with gifts and pairs of flutes to honour the headman of the officiating village. The pigs and other foodstuffs provided for gifts and for feasting the visitors are displayed in decorated piles in front of the men's clubhouse, where the ceremony takes place. After the morning has been spent in preparations and the visitors have played their flutes in a secluded spot away from the village, everyone assembles in the village; at the sound of the approaching flutes, the women and children shut themselves indoors, thus demonstrating that the ritual is a male concern. The younger men form themselves into two groups, one representing the parents of the initiands, the others the community, although there seems to be no clear principle by which men choose which group to join. Locals and visitors are to be found in both groups. The ritual fight which follows is described by Hogbin in the following terms:

> One of the elders struck a sounding-board ('the *nibek*, monster's bond') and they rushed at each other with fists flying. They were without weapons, but one man grabbed a dog that was wandering down the street and slung it at the face of an opponent. A youth killed the frightened animal, and the carcass went on the pile of food, to be roasted with the pigs. The fracas continued for about 5 minutes, when the headmen and other elders present called loudly for order.

The fight is seen by the Wogeo as a means of releasing tensions and thereby ensuring peace. During it, all the rules of behaviour appropriate for different categories of people are suspended. Members of opposite moieties who must normally be on formal polite terms, brothers and brothers-in-law, may all, in the ritual fight, punch and strike each other. Blood may even be drawn. The crucial point lies in the explanation given the anthropologist that anger is vented, 'then a fresh start can be made'. The suspension of all social rules, even for five minutes, marks a break in the continuity of social life, marking the occasion as separate.

The operators then enter the houses where the little boys are sitting with their mothers, grasp them, blindfold them and push them outside among the men. Against a background of loud noise from the sounding-boards, slivers of bone are pushed through the lobe and top of each ear of the screaming children. Red cordyline leaves are inserted in the holes and the boys' bodies rubbed all over with crushed ginger, a magical preparation to give warmth to the body. The little boys are told: 'There, the monsters have bitten you; they've made their first mark and will come back later when they're ready to eat you up.' The boys are then sent back to their mothers where they are given the vegetable curry which is a magical specific for persons in a ritually dangerous condition. Thereafter they play no part in the ritual. The men light fires on the beach and feast the visitors who then leave, bearing with them as gifts the bulk of the supplies which were displayed. The women eat none of it, for the meats of initiation are considered fatal to women.

The admission of the boys to the men's club is described as their being swallowed and excreted by the monsters, much as the rituals of the Poro conceptualize the transition. The initiands' pierced ears show that the monster has 'bitten' them, although interestingly enough little girls have their ears pierced by their fathers with no ceremony and do not seem to be described as 'bitten by the monster'.

What should be pointed out is that the bulk of the activity is not concerned with the little boys. The two major oppositions are between the men, active in their ritual, and the women, secluded indoors and forbidden to participate in the feast. The boys, for the first time, are outside with the men; this and the experience of having their ears pierced is the means by which they are moved from one category to the other. Notice, too, that they are told that they have been bitten by the monster but no monster was visible. At the next stage the significance of this will be explained to the initiates, but it is *not* explained to girls, who are supposed to believe in the existence of monsters. Joking references to the monsters, made by women at the girls' rites, seem to me to indicate that they at least are not deceived.

The main events of the next ritual, which takes place some time later, can be briefly set out, as follows. Each boy is sponsored by a member of the opposite moiety who performs the ritual actions, visitors are invited from other villages, and the monsters are summoned but the flutes remain outside the village. At daybreak the sponsors enter the men's house, then the parents daub their son with red ochre and lead him to the foot of the ladder. Each sponsor descends, pushes the boy's mother away, giving him a sharp slap on the shoulder to expel female influence, and carries him into the clubhouse. The boys are terrified but are reassured that if they lie still on the broad shelf under the eaves where they are laid, it will not be too painful. The mothers run weeping to their houses and the ritual fight then takes place.

The men withdraw to the beach where a meal for all is prepared and the rest of the day is spent in playing the flutes, while the boys stay in the men's house. At dusk the main group of men returns from the beach to spend the night in the club, feasting and playing drums in the sweltering atmosphere produced by two fires and a crowd of occupants. In the morning several of the younger men, strangely decorated, come whooping to the men's house, seize the boys by the shoulders and ankles and carry them to the beach, pulling and stretching them to 'make them grow'. The guardians follow and point to the flutes, demonstrate how they are played and explain that there are no monsters. However, each initiand is led into the sea by his sponsor who scrubs him with sand and water 'to remove all traces of the gastric juices and excrement left from the monster's bowels'. Then a kinsman twists the blade of a spear in the boy's hair and hauls him ashore. This too is said to stretch the boy and promote growth.

Back in the men's house, the initiates are given a full explanation of the mysteries of the monsters and promised that after their next initiation ritual they will be taught to play the flutes, for without learning the flutes no Wogeo boy could hope to be a man. They are told a myth to point the fearful consequences of revealing the secrets. Then for the rest of the day, senior kinsmen weave rattan bands in complex patterns round the boys' wrists, upper arms, ankles, waists and necks. A girl celebrating her first menstruation also has these woven for her. The boys (and girls at the end of their initiation rites) are rubbed with oil and ochre to make their skins shine, decorated with ornaments, then paraded around the village in their finery.

They are still allowed only the magically warming vegetable food but they may leave the clubhouse and spend several days going about in their finery while the men of the village fish and smoke the catch in preparation for the feast of integration which allows the initiates to eat ordinary food again. After the feast, the initiates are taken to cleanse themselves ritually in a pool at the foot of a waterfall. They drink the waters in pairs, the action linking each pair as brothers, closer than siblings.[20] Hogbin calls this the bond of blood-brotherhood but it is water that unites the boys in this bond, not blood; as we have seen, the word for water, *dan*, also means semen and refers to the group of patrilineal kinsmen. It seems likely that the symbolism here is of spiritual kinship through men. Such bonds of male solidarity contrast with the kinship of 'blood', of the mother, which allocates boys to a family and their mother's moiety. The ritual also cleanses them of the pollution derived from living with women and they then incorporate masculinity. Henceforward they will sleep in the men's house.

The division between men and women is not the only opposition which is displayed in the ritual: the fight puts 'the parents' against 'the village', family against community. 'Family' is represented by the parents but in other contexts it is mothers, women, who do this, as the next ritual makes clear. The Wogeo islanders believe that boys will not grow into men unless they are separated from the contaminating influence of their mothers. The ritual makes clear that women/mothers also stand for the private concerns of the family; boys must be part of the wider community, which is symbolized by the men's house and by men. The second rite, more complex than the first, makes this quite explicit, for it emphasizes – by removing the boy into the men's house – where he now belongs. It underlines the irrevocable distance which the secret knowledge he has been given creates between himself and those who do not know what he knows: that there are no monsters.

In the next rite the initiates are finally cleansed from the pollution of women, by drawing blood from their tongues. The scarification which results enables them, in the Wogeo view, to learn to play the flutes and so to become mature men. The relation between flute-playing and the male part in reproduction is implicit in a number of ways: the statement of the tasks of men and women quoted earlier equates flute-playing with childbearing. Learning to play the flutes leads to maturity and sexual activity which requires regular purification. Men must refrain from sexual intercourse to remain pure when in contact with the flutes. Wogeo believe that it is the power of the flutes which ensures the success of magic to promote the boys' growth. We can see that the boys' growth demonstrates the power of men's ritual knowledge, just as the birth of children demonstrates the reproductive powers of women, also ritually protected.

The blood-letting ceremony requires the services of a hereditary ritual specialist, known as the 'headman of the beach' since the ceremony, and the isolation of initiates which follows, takes place on the beach. Both officiants and initiates are isolated and restricted much more severely in this ritual than any other, for the blood that drips from the initiates' tongues is believed to be deadly and severely polluting. The specialist chooses as his assistants a number of strong mature householders, unrelated to the boys, who will act as guardians.

A special hut is built, close to the beach and protected from the wind. Breadfruit and green coconuts[21] are provided in large quantities by the initiands' kin who must then withdraw to a distance. The specialist owns magic for the preparation of the coarse leaves he will use to draw blood, and for the ginger and red cordyline leaves he will also use. The spell cited by Hogbin opens with a statement: 'The pollution flows away with the blood.' It proceeds to command the winds to enter the tongues and give them the breath to blow the flutes. Then the specialist kindles several fires in a row, protecting each with magic and being careful to see that the smoke will rise straight up. Each boy is assigned a fire and then the specialist spits chewed ginger into their mouths 'to make them warm'. Then they must bite certain acrid roots which will bring the blood into the tongue. The assistants position each boy with his legs wide apart, head over the flames, tongue thrust out. The specialist then walks down the line, rubbing the tongues with coarse leaves until the blood is flowing steadily onto the fire. The assistants repeat warnings to the specialist and the boys for the blood is deadly: 'Legs right out of the way, heads on top of the fire, tongue as far out as you can manage and remember don't swallow' (Hogbin, 1970: 117). When the bleeding has eased, the tongue is wiped with soft leaves, but each initiand must spit into the fire in case there are particles of blood left in his mouth. The specialist drinks large amounts of green coconut juice to make him urinate freely and expel the dangerous pollution through his urine. He rubs his hands with a certain sap, which will make the skin peel off, to cleanse them.

Later the specialist prepares a mixture of red cordyline leaves and coconut juice which promotes healing; the boys swill out their mouths with it and spit into the fires. Then the participants go into the seclusion hut to remove the pollution. No one may sleep, eat or drink that night; the boys must keep their tongues out. The heaviest restrictions will last, for the initiates, until the third sunrise after the bleeding, although as time passes the restrictions are eased, and they may eat with a bone fork and drink through a straw, like menstruating women and others in the *rekareka* condition. However, the men have three extra days of fasting and privations, and in addition they must let blood every day to purify themselves.

On the seventh day, the monsters are summoned and the flutes are carried to the seclusion hut. The specialist makes a number of herbal potions which are thought to have magical efficacy and places them in holes in the ground lined with leaves. Each hole is named after a culture hero and is decorated with brightly coloured leaves, fruits and shell ornaments. The specialist dips a pair of flutes in each hole, in order; then calls the boys up in pairs (one from each moiety) to drink from the holes beginning with the one whose liquid contains ginger to promote bodily warmth. Some of the liquids are bitter or nauseating but the initiates must take deep draughts and the last to drink must drain the holes. The men then take the initiates to the forest where they make them pass through holes cut in the dense aerial roots of the ficus tree, to make them tall and smooth-skinned. Girls also do this and for the same reason.

The initiates and their guardians are secluded until the new moon, drinking further potions sent by neighbouring specialists, and practising the flutes. They also make gifts for their guardians. With the new moon, the monsters are 'sent away' and the boys enter the village in a procession. The specialist and his assistants face seclusion in the clubhouse for another month, during which they must have no contact at all with women. During the next few months their restrictions are gradually lifted.

Before the final stage of initiation, a youth is taught to incise his penis to remove the female taint he will incur in sexual intercourse. The instruction is a practical matter, not the occasion for ritual, but the teacher must be carefully chosen. He must be an outsider, usually from another village, and should not be either a close kinsman or a member of the same moiety. Both he and his pupil observe the pollution taboos incurred by letting blood but no more, underlining the distinction between secular teaching and the exercise of ritual powers which entails severe pollution. This occasion makes it clear that the idea of earlier writers that initiation involved learning about sexual matters was mistaken. Mende youths are said to receive instruction during their seclusion but it is clear that even there such learning is less significant than the whole experience of the rites, the secrets of the Poro.

The final step in the long transition of island boys to maturity takes place much later. It was characterized by the confinement of the youths' hair within the traditional conical head-dresses but even when Hogbin worked there it was becoming less common. Its importance lies in the fact that it marks the right to marry, become householders and parents. They will develop domestic interests, which may oppose them to other members of the men's house, and as married men they will sleep there only to maintain ritual purity.

On Wogeo, men and women are interdependent; each sex has its own powers, which are believed to be strongest when not diluted by contact with the other. Their separateness is underlined in the ritual, which is based on these ideas and aims to encourage male growth by removing femaleness. Male initiation rites everywhere include a separation rite, which has been interpreted variously as separation from the mother, from women in general or from childhood. Initiation is often followed, as it is on Wogeo, by a change of residence, either to a bachelor dwelling, a men's house, or to a new household established by marriage. Explanations of this resemble those concerned with the rite of separation and concentrate on the individuals whose status is changed. If they are not the focus of attention, a different interpretation is possible.

The categorical distinctions made by the Wogeo rites centre on the distinction between the family houses and the men's house. The latter is associated with ritual activities and sexual abstinence; the former with family life and sexuality. Men move between the two but women and children may not enter the men's house. There is thus an implicit association of the family houses with women, which in a variety of forms appears in many different societies all over the world. Some anthropologists have argued that women's association with the domestic world derives from their classification as 'closer to nature' because of their reproductive functions. The location of these functions being in the domestic sphere, they are doubly segregated from the public world of politics and ritual, which is thereby associated with men, whose dominance is thus made both legitimate and unassailable. The argument depends on a number of questionable assumptions which have been exposed by several critics (see Strathern, 1981; MacCormack, 1980). In the context of these rites it is apparent that the distinction between the sexes is used as a symbol for other, less clearly articulated, ideas. A cluster of these ideas concerns the incompatibility of ritual with sexual activity. Like men and women, these are similar but distinct powers which are strongest when kept apart. The parallelism is evinced by such ideas as the powers of 'water' and 'blood': the one male, concerned with patrilineal connections, the sacred flutes and purification; the other female, the basis of the moieties which are concerned with the regulation of marriage and with sexual contact.[22] It is thus intelligible that purification ritual aimed at countering pollution from the opposite sex should include a thorough scrubbing with water, and that the beach, cleansed regularly by the water of the sea, should be the place for it and for other rituals designed to emphasize separation between the sexes.

The polarity of male and female represents other opposed qualities with direct relevance to the organization of society. In the case of both the peoples discussed in this chapter, as in many others, the rites establish household and community as distinct categories, by the removal of the novice from one to the other. On Wogeo Island, this involves taking the boy from his parents' house into the men's house; among the Gisu, the 'world of men' has no particular location but is identified only by opposition to women. Both rituals assert the superiority of that world over the domestic, represented by women. Among both peoples, women are seen as limited in their concerns, quarrelsome and provocative of interhousehold conflict, which is divisive of the community. As Freedman has pointed out, the interests of men are not less bound up with their households, so that such statements are a means of denigrating such quarrels and maintaining the ideal of a united community (1970). In these rites, household concerns are subordinated to the world of ritual knowledge, controlled by men. This 'says' as much about the integration of separate domestic concerns into a wider social unit as it does about the 'place' of women and men. Moreover, on entering the masculine world the initiate discovers that, as in a secret society, he is subordinated to the authority of his seniors. It is that authority which permits him to exercise the privilege of full manhood by marrying and becoming the head of one of the community's dependent households.

NOTES TO CHAPTER VI

1. This term refers to the social aspect. I use it interchangeably with 'sexual identity' and both should be understood in social, not psychological, terms. See also Ortner (1974), Rosaldo and Lamphere (1974) and MacCormack (1980).
2. See La Fontaine (1959, 1972, 1977) and Heald (1982).
3. In 1954 the African Local Government issued a circular showing the date allocated to each subcounty (*gombolola*) for its ritual. Each was allowed one day and the whole cycle took some three weeks, with no initiation on Sundays!
4. These are more distant kin, classified by the Gisu under the same term as they use for women we would consider sisters. The use of single quotes indicates this classificatory usage.
5. These seem a common adornment for male initiands in many parts of the world; the resulting design may represent breasts but Gisu are not aware of this interpretation nor have I seen it made in any other ethnography so that it must remain speculation, although it is consistent with the Gisu view that uninitiated youths are like women.
6. For example, to break a woman's beads was considered rape, even if intercourse did not take place.
7. Gisu see the women of a lineage as extending its influence into the other lineages whose men they marry.
8. He is described as that particular brother who used his sister's bridewealth to obtain a wife for himself, thus underlining the inter-dependence of lineages in marriage; in practice it may be any man of the mother's lineage who accepts the role. Usually he is a full brother of the boy's mother. He must give formal permission and his blessing to the novice, for without this, Gisu say, the youth risks dying from the circumcision. The disapproval of the mother's brother is much more serious than that of the boy's own father, who can be circumvented

by getting another senior male kinsman to act as sponsor. But a mother's brother must give formal approval and, in the north, give certain charms to the novice to indicate this and act as magical strengtheners. Given the fact that novices do occasionally die or suffer serious mishaps from the operation, the role of senior kin is a powerful one. Heald (1982), writing of a time about ten years later, reports that a mother's brother must ask the novice just before circumcision if he is still determined; I did not hear of this anywhere in the country or see it done; it is consistent with the greater emphasis on personal responsibility for being initiated which she found, and is a good example of the way in which ritual details and interpretations may alter over time.

9. Women whose labour is prolonged may be urged, quite sharply, to get rid of their fear, which is believed to be making the childbirth difficult. 'Fear' is a poor translation of a word which also means lack of courage or determination, shyness. It is the opposite of strength, which is admired.

10. *Lirima* in the southern and central dialects.

11. Heald and I differ slightly in our interpretations of this state. I see it as irresponsible, asocial, because of the many times I was told that no one could sue a novice for damage done to crops or other possessions, or even take offence at anything said. I was also told of an initiand who hit his father's brother, an unthinkable act in normal circumstances, but the older man ignored it. However, my informant added, with typical Gisu realism, that it was unwise to rely on this immunity too heavily!

12. In parts of the north of Gisu country, this rite is replaced by another ancestral blessing, at a different place.

13. Formerly the uninitiated went naked; only initiated men wore the skin garment which was male dress. Some Gisu have taken over the view that long trousers indicate the adult man, shorts a mere (uninitiated) youth.

14. The flute is clearly a phallic symbol as it is elsewhere, in the Amazon Basin and in Mozart's *The Magic Flute*. Blowing the flutes is thus an allusion to the male role in sexual intercourse.

15. They are not expected to shed blood as often as women do, for this would mean permanent seclusion.

16. Two other ritual actions on behalf of the community also cause men to become *bwaruka*: the building of a new men's house and the ceremonial recognition of the headman's heir. After fulfilling their duties, officiants must be secluded. However, Wogeo recognize these states as not quite the same, metaphorical extensions of the term.

17. The taboo and the deprivations of fasting and seclusion are considered dangerous for the elderly, and are often inconvenient for those with family responsibilities, so that it is often difficult to find men who will undertake tasks which entail severe pollution.

18. In that article I was inclined to assume a Gisu concern with the definition of nature, but the evidence that Gisu do make any distinction between nature and culture, or nature and ritual, is rather weak. What follows here indicates my changed views.

19. Similar ideas are widespread in New Guinea. See the essays in Herdt, 1982.

20. The girls wash in the same stream but in a lower pool. A girl also contracts a close tie with the companions who drink with her. The association with a peer-group is made clear by the absence of married women at the girls' rite.

21. The ritual for tongue scarification needs a plentiful supply of bread-fruit, which grows wild, and not of the usual cultivated foods which are collected for feasting and giving gifts at the other rituals. If there is not enough breadfruit for the seclusion period, then bananas may be permitted, but these must be stolen from other villages. They are thus, like the breadfruit, not cultivated by anyone involved in the initiation; they are 'wild', not part of domestic life. As Hogbin remarks, and as was indicated in the discussion of Mende initiation, a suspension of normal morality is common to mark the marginal state.

22. In that it is the flow of blood which purifies from sexual contact, it is arguable that such blood contains the impurities concerned. But while the blood from tongue scarification and genital blood are highly polluting, not all blood has this quality. If someone cuts himself or herself the blood is wiped away by others, with no concern; but Gell, writing of the Sepik area, reports great concern with this kind of bleeding (Gell, 1979).

CHAPTER VII THE
AUTHORITY
OF
EXPERIENCE

Gisu initiation rituals seem to divide males into two distinct classes: the immature boys, whose lack of independent authority is indicated by their exclusion from public affairs, and the initiated; public affairs are the concern of the second class. This is the image projected by the ritual, which creates a clear distinction between those who have experienced circumcision and who have not. By contrast, Wogeo youths, like initiates into secret societies, enter a world where males are ranked in progressive stages, each associated with further knowledge, conveyed by successive experiences. For both, however, the final ritual transition establishes them as legitimate householders.

In other societies the ladder of ritual knowledge may be extended throughout adult life, as Barth has shown in his vivid account of the Baktaman of New Guinea. There each stage reveals the ignorance of the earlier one, changing and deepening the initiates' understanding of their world and its control by ritual. In the tiny Baktaman community, men are ranked in terms of their degree of knowledge and hence of ritual power. Seniors transmit this to juniors with reluctance and occasionally a man takes his knowledge with him to the grave without sharing it. The fewer the men who share a ritual secret, the more powerful it is, and the knowledge of the dead is ultimately the source of greatest power.[1] The effect is to place legitimate authority in the hands of those closest to the ancestors, the older men.

The Baktaman, like many other New Guinean peoples, initiate men into secret cults at maturity; like the secret societies described in earlier chapters, the male world is a hierarchy based on increments of knowledge. In secret societies which are unconnected with the conferring of adult status, individuals who are gifted or particularly ambitious may in theory rise through the hierarchy by their own efforts. Indeed, as I indicated, secret societies generally lay stress on individual ability and achievement, as opposed to the criteria of hereditary rank and other principles, which allocate authority in the world 'outside'. Among the peoples we are concerned with here, by contrast, the world of secrets is the only male world and its principles of authority relate directly to the way in which society is organized. The nature of the linkage affects, and is affected by, initiation ritual in ways which this chapter will explore. In every case, however, accumulated experience is equated with wisdom and knowledge, and this gives legitimate authority to those who are senior in age. The distribution of economic and political power may or may not coincide with the allocation of authority, and this is a fact which must be taken into account. This chapter, then, is concerned less with the symbolism and meaning of male initiation rites, and more with differing social contexts. The emphasis will be on the effects of the ritual.

In the most general sense, regular ritual, such as that of initiation, creates a social calendar. Any society's sense of the passage of time is based on the divisions which punctuate the flow of events. In traditional Gisu society, initiation took place biennially; the interval of a year between rites made a dividing line between the successive sets. Each set had a different name, which had usually emerged by general consensus by the time the new initiates were being reintegrated into the community. It referred to a notable event of the year or some distinctive feature of the rituals performed during it. In theory the names are not repeated. Certain events, which used to be more common than they are today, such as famine years or plagues of locusts, would be referred to in different ways so as not to duplicate a name. The set of 1936 was called 'Fences' because in that year the colonial administration, under pressure from the missionaries, ordered the Gisu to perform the circumcision operation within fenced enclosures; and 1954 is called 'Nambozo', the name conferred on me by the Gisu during the time I lived with them. Older men can remember a long list of age-set names which thus serve as a record, against which events can be dated. These chronologies are not always reliable[2] for although initiation should take place every other year, food shortages or warfare might prevent its celebrations, so that sets are not always two years apart; and of course memories may be faulty, especially when the sets were initiated long ago. Reference to written records gives the impression that lists from different Gisu men were pretty consistent and accurate as far back as the beginning of this century. They provided a historical framework for at least fifty years and possibly more.

For every Gisu man, his initiation marks a clear distinction between his childhood and his manhood. Those who were initiated in the same year are age-mates (ba-magoji). They are expected to have close ties to one another, especially if they have shared the same convalescent hut, when there are certain specific obligations marking the relationship. In particular, age-mates should be present at the initiation of each other's sons, when a special beast must be slaughtered to feed them. The rites thus have the additional effect of establishing sets of contemporaries, ordered by the time of their accession to manhood, and given recognition in the rites of the next generation.

In several East African societies, such as the Samburu, the ranking of men in sets defined by initiation is a basic element of the whole social system. In Gisu society, however, it is secondary to the organization based on kinship in general and descent in the male line in particular. The men of local communities are conceived of as descendants of a single male ancestor, members of a single lineage, whom Gisu therefore consider ranked as grandfathers, fathers and sons. Seniority of generation is accorded respect and the right to expect obedience from juniors. At initiation a Gisu man enters a masculine world in which his close associates are divided by generation. Some of his own generation will be his seniors, in having been initiated before him, but these differences are less important than the fact that they are considered brothers. In an important sense all adult – that is, initiated – men of a lineage are equal as householders. A man is expected to hand over to each of his sons, as they are initiated, the land on which to build a house and the bridewealth with which to acquire a wife. He thus diminishes his own resources and loses most of the power over his son by which his authority was backed. Friction between a man and his sons is not uncommon and it often focuses on the timing of the latter's initiation;[3] men have a strong incentive to delay the initiation of their sons, on the pretext of the expense involved, in order to keep control of them. A man retains throughout his life the power to curse his son, and senior men control access to the blessings of the ancestors which they can refuse to recalcitrant young men, but these spiritual powers must not be used lightly. The ancestors are believed to punish a man who curses his son (who is also their descendant) without serious cause, so that the paternal curse is a weapon of last resort rather than a common punishment.

In an important sense, then, a Gisu man, once initiated, is independent of his senior agnates. The traditional Gisu leaders were men who had achieved recognition of their pre-eminent position, through a judicious use of wealth to build up support. There was some significance in having inherited ritual powers or senior status, but political competition for pre-eminence was always an important part of the system. This could be seen most clearly in the position of the very old men; they were treated with deference and their knowledge of ritual was a source of respect, but they were not the effective political leaders; they might be ignored, and the most ineffectual were laughed at behind their backs. There were local variations in this pattern but, in general, Gisu society was characterized by a distinction between the formal authority of seniority and the exercise of power by a few men, usually rich men in late middle age.

The basis of wealth among the Gisu was land, for which members of a descent group were in competition with one another, although they also joined together to defend their territory against outsiders. Young men might be encouraged by the elders to encroach on neighbouring villages' land or push into the territory of adjoining peoples in order to deal with their demands for their own farms. However, this solution was not possible for all and population pressure seems always to have varied in different clan areas.[4] In the mid 1950s there was a clear relationship between the ages at which youths were initiated and the difficulty that their fathers would have in allocating them land to cultivate. Where land was in short supply the initiation of sons was delayed; on the fringes of Gisu territory, where Gisu were expanding into the relatively less settled area occupied by the Sebei or the peoples of the plains, the age was lower (La Fontaine, 1957). The time at which a young man was initiated was not merely a matter of a rule which was followed to a greater or lesser degree in particular instances. It was the product of pressures on father and son, generated by the former's economic circumstances and the Gisu ideal that an initiated man should establish his own household. To a certain extent, a youth's first adult achievement was to persuade his father to let him be initiated.

Gisu are widely known for their competitiveness and their assertive natures; their society rewards individual achievement. This is reflected in their concepts of personality and motivation, one of which, *litima*, has already been discussed (page 122). *Bunyali* is equally relevant to initiation, for it is this quality which is tested in the ordeal. The word can be roughly translated as 'ability', from the verb *ku-nyala*,[5] which means to be able or competent to do something. It is related to personality and strength of character and also carries the implication of surmounting obstacles.

Each individual has his or her share of *bunyali* and the successful show that they have more of it than others; men have, by nature, more *bunyali* than women since they are stronger. Accordingly, Gisu see a youth's behaviour during his initiation ordeal as a manifestation of his *bunyali*. Those who show any sign of weakness indicate an unmanly lack of it which may be remembered years after the event. The inefficiency of a local chief was once explained to me in terms of his display of a marked deficiency in this respect at his initiation years before. Ideally all candidates should come through the ordeal in the proper stoical manner but there is scope for some to manifest extra strength by singing and dancing after they have been circumcised, as one young man did when I was observing the ritual in 1954.

Before the operation it is the violent emotion, *litima*, which Gisu initiands display. This anti-social emotion must be held in check, although it is appropriate to this occasion. A rather similar interpretation of the behaviour of the youths is made by the Samburu of Kenya. In both societies the anger of youths is contrasted with the controlled behaviour thought proper for elders, but among the Samburu the division between elders and juniors is institutionalized in a manner which delays the final maturation of youths for years. This type of political system, usually called an age-set system, which is found among a number of East African peoples, like the Pokot discussed in the next chapter, is one in which generalized authority belongs to a group of older men by virtue of their ritually defined position as elders. We might call this the 'authority of experience' to distinguish it from the 'authority of birth' into a chiefly or aristocratic group, or the 'authority of achievement' of the successful, rich man with personal qualities of leadership.

Paul Spencer, who studied the Samburu, has suggested that, in some ways, it is appropriate to treat the whole period of young manhood there as the marginal phase of a long-drawn-out *rite de passage* which starts with a boy's circumcision at about the age of puberty and ends with his marriage and promotion to elderhood. Samburu men marry late, in their thirties, and their wives, who are initiated shortly before marriage, are fifteen to twenty years younger. As among the Gisu, marriage marks the start of a public career, with the essential difference that Samburu men do not obtain full control of all their resources until after their father's death. This fact, and the delay in conferring on young men the right to marry, seemed to Spencer to justify describing the system as a gerontocracy. Both Gisu and Samburu initiates enter a world which, like that of the secret society, reveals further distinctions of authority to which they are still subordinate; but the initiation itself is a long-drawn-out process in the Samburu system.

The existence of a series of rites which delay the initiates' entry into full manhood is not the cause of the late achievement of maturity. Wogeo boys must pass through a series of rituals which step by step increase their knowledge through experience. However, they seem to marry at about the same age as the Gisu, who have only one ritual dividing line between boys and men. What is critical is the age at which the series starts.

While Wogeo boys are first 'bitten by the monster' about the age of four or five, Samburu boys do not take the first ritual step till puberty or later. In those parts of Bugisu which lie next to the present Kenyan border, the Gisu also circumcise boys at about puberty, and in that area, despite the initiates' formal status of men, marriage takes place later, at about the same age as the rest of the country. In most of Bugisu, initiation confers the right to marry, and the senior generation has an incentive to delay the entry of its sons into manhood. (Young men have a corresponding incentive to demand of their fathers, as they often do, permission to undergo the ordeal which will prove their manhood.) Where initiation is a single rite, the age of entry can be varied more easily and most sets of initiates whom I saw varied in age, although there was still a greater difference between the average age in most of the country and that on the border.

The difference between the south-east and the rest of Bugisu, which contained the bulk of the population, lay in the fact that the south-easterners were included in an age-set system which is still characteristic of the Vugusu, a closely related and neighbouring people in Kenya. An age-set system divides the male population into a number of classes, by reference to their time of initiation. Each class recruits members for a number of years and those initiated in a single year may form a subgroup within the class; a period when there are no initiations may mark the division between classes. The characteristic of this system is that ranking by age-class gives all seniors authority over their juniors, and in principle a class moves through the stages of life, from young manhood to what is usually called retired elder status, as a group. In practice the rate of progress of different individuals varies, and not all men of an age-class will be political leaders when their class is said to be in power. The system is concerned with ranking and deference rather than the actual distribution of power; however, it ensures that only equals may be rivals and under-lines the division between the generations. While the south-eastern Gisu no longer organized themselves in this way in the 1950s, the age-ranking seemed to persist. Since no youth could be his father's political rival, the latter had no incentive to delay his son's initiation[6] and boys were initiated much younger than in the rest of Gisu society where an age-set system never existed.

In south-eastern Bugisu not only are the candidates for initiation younger but the emphasis that is placed on the ordeal of circumcision is less. In the heartland of Bugisu the operation is divided in two: first the foreskin is severed, and then, after an interval which may be as long as two hours, much of the subcutaneous tissue from the prepuce and the area surrounding the glans is removed. In the south-eastern areas, there is a single operation, quickly finished. A skilled circumciser is one who operates swiftly and with care. Far less attention is paid by the spectators to the minutiae of the initiand's posture and stillness during the operation. Gisu from other parts of the country told me that the characteristic stance in this area, where initiands grasp a stick laid across their shoulders, makes it easier for them to hold themselves immobile. Whether this is true or not, it seems that boys there do not have to demonstrate their fortitude to quite such an extent. It seems that, among the Gisu, the degree of emphasis on the ordeal and the age at initiation are both affected by the nature of the political system. Comparison with the Samburu supports this hypothesis; in that society, boys are circumcised in their early teens and then enter a long period when they are virtually segregated from adult society, until they finally are permitted to marry and assume the status of full adult at about thirty. While great emphasis is placed on not flinching during circumcision, this is a minimum requirement and there does not seem to be the close scrutiny of the novices that the Gisu give them; Samburu boys sit down while they are circumcised and are held by two men. Gisu would think little of this as an ordeal and indeed it does seem a less severe test.

The rituals of initiation that a boy undergoes in Wogeo are painful but they are not interpreted as an ordeal, testing the initiate. Their purpose is to purify, and strengthen; the blood which flows is dangerous because it contains the impurities of femaleness. The boys are not expected to be brave. Suffering is necessary, they are told; what is done to them will assist their growth by removing the evil effects of pollution. The truth of this, in Wogeo terms, is demonstrated by the growth of the boys in the intervals between rites. We cannot therefore explain all physical suffering, imposed in such rituals, an an ordeal or a test, unless it is interpreted as such in the society concerned. Even where there is a true ordeal, as there most emphatically is among the Gisu, there is a sense in which the pain is one element in the whole experience, impressing the initiates indelibly with the sense of their own transformation.

Tests and ordeals in the ritual of initiation into secret societies have been interpreted, earlier in this book, as a submission to the authority of the initiator, manifesting the helplessness of the initiated and, by contrast, the power of the initiators and what they represent. Among the Samburu the whole of the ritual directed at the novices during initiation seems designed to create this effect.

An age-set system justifies authority in terms of experience, the wisdom of older men. In Samburu this is called by the term *nkanyit*, which is glossed by Spencer as 'respect', the respect for elders, for social rules and for the ritual powers, which comes from understanding why rules should be kept. This is explicitly contrasted with the physical strength required for the tasks of younger men, which is summed up in the fact that they are often described as warriors. Although when Samburu or Vugusu communities were attacked by enemies, everyone would fight, including on rare occasions women, fighting was a proper occupation for young men between initiation and elderhood. The Samburu relied on them to protect the settlements and their herds and expected them to raid other people's too. However, the system also stressed the superiority of the powers of the elders, of wisdom over force, as the legitimate basis for authority.

The Samburu are a pastoral people living in the arid area in north-eastern Kenya, where they keep cattle, goats and sheep, on which they depend entirely for subsistence as they do not practise agriculture. This is not merely because the sparse rainfall makes it impracticable but also because the Samburu, like the Masai, despise cultivators. The Samburu language is a dialect of Masai and they resemble that rather better-known people in many ways. The people are divided into a number of clans and lineages based on patrilineal descent, which are dispersed over a fairly wide area and are not seen as occupying an exclusive territory or as 'owning' land. Although their ethnographer has emphasized the significance of their age-set system as the main framework of Samburu social life, initiation is a clan ritual, the officiants are senior members of the clan, and the context emphasizes relations between successive age-classes within the clan. The authority and power of a Samburu father last until his death, but the whole structure of the age-set system seems to draw attention away from this relationship. Such systems have been interpreted as designed to sustain a militaristic society (Mair, 1962: 81, 84), in which the role of young men as warriors is the crucial element, but they have persisted after the colonial imposition of peace. Spencer, like other modern authorities on such East African people, does not subscribe to this view. He uses the Samburu term, *moran*, for young men in the marginal position between boyhood and social maturity, instead of 'warrior', so I shall do the same.

The Samburu political system is based on a division of males into three main categories: uninitiated boys, *moran* and elders. Unlike the rituals of the Gisu, Samburu initiation does not admit initiates to full manhood. What this involves, essentially, is a distinction between sexual maturity[7] and social maturity. Initiation confers on *moran* the right to take mistresses among the unmarried but not to marry or to father children. (Girls are circumcised around puberty, shortly before they are married, and must not become pregnant before that, lest terrible misfortune ensue.) Elders are married, owners of herds and fathers of children, associated with the central settlements, as the *moran* are closely identified with the unsettled bush, the frontier between the Samburu and their enemies. It is the elders in whom power is vested, as Spencer has shown. The series of rituals which mark the transition from boyhood to elderhood have the effect of maintaining this gerontocracy, even in modern times when the role of warriors is largely in abeyance.

In the Samburu rites, there is a clear distinction between circumcision, which is the prerequisite for *moran*hood but does not admit those circumcised into the class of *moran*, and the characteristic rituals of the *moran*. The Samburu, however, draw attention to similarities, rather than differences, between them. A settlement where circumcisions are to be performed, or one where rituals for the *moran* will be celebrated, must be carefully laid out to show the genealogical relations of the participants. Huts are placed round the circular encampment in order of lineage segments and seniority within segments; Spencer also mentions 'ritual details', which are repeated and to which the elders draw attention (Spencer, 1970: 137–8). Yet there are clear contrasts between the two: circumcision is an ordeal in which the boy must preserve his honour and that of his lineage by remaining motionless, while in the rituals for *moran* it is common and expected that the *moran* will give way to their feelings so violently that they lose all consciousness of their surroundings. Circumcisions are performed at the family homestead and the circumcised are carried into their mothers' huts where they stay until they are healed. Their fathers are honoured in a rite which raises their status to that of 'fathers of the *moran*' and earns them added respect. By contrast, rituals involving *moran* are addressed to the *moran* as a group of peers, not as members of particular homesteads, and their fathers are not affected by them; a special enclosure is built for them outside the settlement as befits their marginal status. While circumcision is often the centre of the rite of initiation in which it is performed, among the Samburu it is only the initial rite of separation from boyhood.

A number of preliminary rituals are performed by the officiating class of elders, known as the 'firestick elders' from the kindling of fire which is their first ritual act. They decide when the circumcisions will be done, in the clan settlements which have been set up. The initiates may range from about thirteen to twenty; a timid boy will not be permitted to be circumcised until his father and the elders are reasonably certain he will withstand the physical ordeal, since their honour as well as that of the boy rests on his enduring the pain without flinching. The boys to be circumcised together are closely related through their fathers: they must be circumcised one at a time, in order of the seniority of their patriline. The circumcisers are Dorobo, not Samburu; as among the Gisu, the operators are outsiders, but in the Samburu case they are not even members of the same people. Each boy is circumcised sitting outside his mother's hut; two men hold him during the operation, during which time he must not move. After he has been circumcised the boy should sing the circumcision song (*lebarta*), which is held to be a powerful form of coercion. (Before circumcision, those who will be circumcised use the song to persuade others of their age to join them; later they use it to obtain gifts of sheep to slaughter for meat.) At this point *lebarta* is followed by the gift of a heifer from the boy's father.

The newly circumcised youth is then carried into his mother's hut and laid down on a specially prepared couch to convalesce. Later his father is blessed by the elders and his head is smeared by them with butter. This enhances his authority over his son who must now treat him with added respect, so that although the circumcision has started the advance of the youth towards maturity, it has also increased his father's authority over him so that the social distance between them is maintained. Sleeping in their mothers' huts and subject to a strengthened paternal authority, the newly circumcised are still children, partly at least, in a domestic world. Until they have undergone the first of the essential ceremonies of the *moran* they remain not quite children and not yet *moran*, in a marginal phase lasting about a month.

Circumcision is considered an ordeal; his conduct of himself during it reflects on the honour, not only of the boy himself, but of his whole lineage. Boys know nothing about the rituals they will undergo; all they know is that they must not flinch at circumcision or they will bring lasting shame on their lineage. Spencer describes how anxiety about their courage successfully builds up in the initiands, their fathers and brothers, so that the slightest incident may trigger off what seem like hysterical reactions. He describes one case in which a young initiand, in singing his vow to be brave and honourable, invoked the leading bull of his father's herd. His elder brother and father reacted strongly to what they perceived as a foolish pledge which might be dishonoured by the boy's performance at his ordeal. A fracas ensued which was blamed on these kinsmen who should not, said other Samburu, have showed their fear that the lad would shame them. In this case the boy successfully went through his ordeal without flinching, but if an initiate does flinch he is ostracized and neither he nor his close kin will live down the shame, which may cling to the line over more than a generation.[8]

During the marginal period which follows circumcision the newly circumcised visit each other to drink the mixture of blood and milk (*saroi*)[9] that is considered appropriate, and to eat meat. They may only eat mutton, but instead of using their hands as they normally do, they must use sticks; they may not wash or touch any knife or spear (the weapons of *moran*). While in this state they are also privileged; they may not be harmed even by the Samburu's enemies lest misfortune befall the spiller of their blood.[10] The boys may enter the homestead of any elder and sing *lebarta*; the elder must kill a sheep for them, cook and cut it up for them to eat, lest misfortune befall him, his wives or children. The boys also shoot small birds with bows and arrows that they have been given by the men who held them for circumcision, their ritual patrons. They use the feathers to make head-dresses to wear.[11] As they share things, and give each other gifts, the boys adopt various names referring to their common ties, and the use of these names will from then on mark out those who were circumcised at the same time. But they are not yet a group of *moran*.

The first ritual, which establishes the age-set and incorporates the circumcised boys into the *moran* group, refers back to this special phase; it is both the final (integrative) phase of the first period of initiation, and a rite of separation which will separate the new initiates from normal society for the entire period of their *moran*hood. It is also the first of a series of similar rites, known as *ilmugit*.

All *ilmugit* rituals pertain to the *moran*. They have the same constituents: the slaughter of cattle for a communal meal, an address and a blessing;[12] and no other ritual is known by that name. The officiants are the clan elders, largely the same as those who officiated at the circumcisions, and who will be in charge of the *moran* throughout the period of *moran*hood. They are two classes senior to their protégés and at least one class junior to the *moran*'s own fathers. At the *ilmugit* of the arrows they address the *moran* in the first of a series of harangues which are the central feature of all but one of the *ilmugit* rituals.

The *ilmugit* of the arrows is simple. Each initiate provides a beast, ideally an ox, for slaughter; the meat will be divided up among the residents of the settlement. Two ritual patrons are chosen for him among the senior class of *moran*. They slaughter his beast for him and use the fat in a ritual which makes them his ritual sponsors. They cook the beast and finally, amid shouting and encouragement, the initiate breaks the hip-bone of the beast with a blow from his knobkerrie. He should break it with one blow, just as the Turkana or Karimojong initiates should kill their beasts with one thrust of the spear. Then half of the bone is taken by the lad, led by his sponsors, and presented to his mother. This gift is a pledge to keep the most important food taboo of the *moran*: not to eat meat that has been seen by a married woman.[13] The meat-eating which accompanies the *ilmugit* of the arrows takes place, for the *moran*, in a special enclosure built outside the main settlement, and the shared feast seals the bonds of common membership of an age-set. Boys circumcised later will perform the same ceremonies, but on a smaller scale, as they are incorporated into the class.

About a month later the *ilmugit* of the roasting-sticks is held. During this ceremony the age-set is subdivided into two groups which are called 'right' and 'left'. 'Right' is the senior, and should two brothers be initiated together the elder must be in the right group and the younger in the left. The set is also divided into the fully-grown *chong'onopir*, and the younger boys. The age-set thus becomes two subsets, and further rituals may add one or two more subsets before the class is closed to further recruitment.

Subsequent *ilmugit* rites follow the pattern of the first. Each *moran* must provide a beast for slaughter, the meat being divided according to a set pattern, with the elders and all other members of the camp getting their prescribed share. The *moran* are also extensively harangued by the elders, led by the firestick elders. These emphasize the *moran*'s irresponsibility and misbehaviour, and threaten them with the elders' curse. The elders may pick on a particular *moran* to castigate and shame before his peers, or force the *moran* to admit their faults and promise to show more respect (*nkanyit*): finally the elders bless the *moran* and let them go. Elders other than the firestick elders join in the harangues which may last several hours; the elders may get so worked up that they are reduced to shouting 'Respect! Respect!' over and over again. These harangues may be repeated at any time but they are an indispensable feature of any *ilmugit* ceremony. The Samburu see them as the means by which the *moran* are taught the sense of respect that is a prerequisite of elderhood. They are followed by a blessing which is a dramatic example of the ritual powers of the elders.

Once incorporated into *moran*hood, the new initiates form part of a group which progresses through the various stages of development as a single unit. Each stage is opened by an *ilmugit* ritual and is marked by the relaxation or acquisition of prohibitions and privileges. The *ilmugit* of the arrows incorporates the circumcised into a group, as *moran*; from then until the next *ilmugit* they wear their hair long and smeared with red ochre in the characteristically spectacular hair-style of the *moran*. Throughout the period of *moran*hood they observe the taboo on eating meat which has been seen by a married woman, but after the *ilmugit* of the arrows they may eat meat other than mutton. The *ilmugit* of the name promotes the age-set to senior *moran*hood, permitting its members to act as the ritual sponsors of new initiates when the next age-set is initiated. At this *ilmugit*, which is actually a pair of rituals held a month apart, the ritual leader of the set is chosen and installed. At the *ilmugit* of the bull an age-class is closed to recruitment.

After the *ilmugit* of the bull the ritual leader of the senior class may marry. He must marry first of the class and his marriage is a symbolic abduction of the bride, in which he is helped by all the *moran* of his phratry (a group of related clans). This *ilmugit* marks the collective transition of the age-class to the next stage in seniority, but most will not marry yet. They should now begin to moderate their behaviour towards the restraint that will show their developing 'respect'. Many of the girls who have been associated with the class are now being circumcised and married; henceforth they must avoid *moran*. The *moran* start to shave off their distinctive ochre-smeared plaited hair and endeavour to make themselves acceptable as elders. At this stage tensions develop as the elders appear to block the advancement of the *moran*; the latter may not marry until their ritual leader marries, and his marriage may be delayed.

Yet finally, one by one, the *moran* marry and become elders. They leave *moran*hood individually. As each man marries, he calls the elders of his clan who live locally, to bless him and his wife, in order to lift the food restrictions which he still observes, even in respect of his own wife. However, a final ritual does mark the end of the class's *moran*hood. It is called the *ilmugit* of the milk and leaves. The *moran* bring milk and cowhides, and before the first oxen are killed for the feast, the elders and the *moran* go into the elders' enclosure from which the *moran* had been excluded before. The hides are placed round the inside in order of seniority, and the elders and former *moran* drink milk together as elders. This is the final, integrative ritual of the whole series.

There are no collective rituals for elders to mark their promotion. Or rather, their functions are linked to the initiation and progress of the linked age-class, their juniors. Thus the promotion of *moran* into junior elderhood means that the immediately senior age-class, the former junior elders, will be firestick elders to the next class to be initiated. They assume their duties when they perform the ritual acts which permit circumcisions, and kindle fire for the future *moran*. The whole system pivots on the initiation of boys into *moran*hood and their eventual emergence as elders; the elders themselves are differentiated according to their role in this. Among themselves they may compete for wealth and influence in the determining of public policy, but they are formally divided into those who are directly concerned with the current set of *moran*, the firestick elders, and those who participate in the rituals but are not in charge of them. This latter category includes both those who have recently been promoted to elderhood, junior elders, and those who are referred to as the fathers of the moran, more senior men who have already been active as firestick elders to the junior elders. A man's age-class is always relevant to his position in the community for it allocates him a rank within the total series of classes existing in it and determines his role in the *ilmugit* rituals.

Yet accession to elderhood is an individual affair. Once the ritual leader of the class has married, others of his class may do so. After the *ilmugit* of the bull, each *moran* has to prove himself worthy of elderhood and marriage, which are virtually synonymous. Elders may prevent his marrying if they do not consider him to have shown enough respect, and delay his becoming an elder, but the formal accession to elderhood of the class often comes after the individual rite, in which a man is blessed by his clan elders to remove the meat-eating taboo which defines him as a *moran*. The final group ritual, the *ilmugit* of the milk and leaves, is performed when most of its members have already become elders as individuals. The absence of any harangue in this rite, which makes it strikingly different from all the other ritual activity punctuating the period of *moran*hood, is therefore appropriate.

We can now see why it is that Spencer can interpret the whole period of *moran*hood as a prolonged transitional phase in the passage from boyhood to responsible maturity. The major contrast which all aspects of Samburu life emphasize is that between elders and *moran*. *Moran* are defined as outside normal life. At *ilmugit* rituals they build a separate enclosure outside the main settlement where they must eat; they may also sleep there. They are the herders, travelling far and wide to find new pastures, or just for the pleasure of travelling. Spencer records that the Samburu had no difficulty in classifying him as a *moran*; he was unmarried, prone to making pointless trips all over Samburu country and, they said, it was highly likely that his family did not even know where he was! The meat ban excludes the *moran* from eating in the village; their place is out in the bush, away from the encampments. This is vividly demonstrated by the taboo on a *moran* dying in the settlement; *moran* should die in the bush or disaster will befall.

The contrast between *moran* and elders appears in other contexts. The *moran* dress in a flamboyant, arresting manner, as do Gisu candidates for initiation into manhood, but for a whole period of their lives. They are vain about their appearance, while elders shave their heads and recognize that they look comparatively drab. The demeanour of elders is reserved and they are expected to act with restraint, in complete contrast to the emotional volatility of *moran*. *Moran*hood is a time of sexual freedom too: *moran* are free from the responsibilities of marriage and fatherhood. Indeed, most girls who are available to them then are forbidden as wives;[14] their future wives are still very young. Samburu say that even were a man able to marry his mistress, it would not be a good marriage, for the relationship between husband and wife is one of dominance and submission while that between lovers is more equal. The *moran* show off to the girls whom they court, and respond to their challenges by showing their daring in cattle-raids and fights among themselves. The girls tease the *moran* with lack of courage and encourage them to more extreme acts by singing taunting songs at the dances which occur at *ilmugit* gatherings, but also on other, less formal occasions. The *moran* are the epitome of masculine strength and beauty and it seems that many of them are loath to settle down into elderhood. One elder remarked to Spencer: 'Do not photograph me. I am dead! Go and photograph that young *moran*.'

Yet if the *moran* are seen as glamorous, the quintessence of virility, they are also said to be childish and irresponsible. They are expected to resort easily to violence and to steal beasts for their feasts; their outstanding characteristic is their lack of the quality of *nkanyit* which characterizes the elders. This concept means respect not only for seniors but for a whole body of rules which underlie Samburu society. Samburu say that the *moran* obey the rules because they have to, but a man with respect obeys them for what they are, the only honourable way to behave. It is the elders who judge when this has happened in each individual case, so that while Samburu say that a *moran* who develops respect has become an elder *de facto*, we can see that it is the elders' judgement of him which is vital. The *moran* are associated with strength, violence and physical power. The values of elderhood are quite different: marriage, fatherhood, reasoned discussion (Spencer, 1976: 166). The contrast can be summed up in the different ways thought proper to resolve disputes: *moran* may use physical violence; an elder must never do this but should settle disputes by discussion. The most potent weapon of the elders is the curse which they may invoke against an enemy, but to do so frequently or without just cause loses an elder his standing. They also have the power to bless; withholding a blessing is another sanction which elders may use, for it leaves the unblessed vulnerable to mystical dangers.

It is the elders who control Samburu society. They own and dispose of most of the cattle; a man may not dispose of beasts outside the clan without his father's permission. The elders control the marriages of their daughters, and may use their curse to prevent a marriage of which they disapprove, or to punish a young man who has offended them by making it impossible for him to find a wife. All these powers in the hands of elders depend on the recognition of the authority vested in them by virtue of the respect they have earned. Samburu elders do not claim authority from the ancestors, as senior Gisu do, but it nevertheless has religious connotations. Samburu believe that all events, both good and bad, and particularly unusual events, are caused by Nkai. Nkai is both a single remote spirit and a multiplicity of spirits. All human beings and some animals, like cattle, have protective spirits who may be strengthened by blessings or driven away by curses. The Samburu moral code and the ritual which accompanies it are designed to maintain the protectiveness of spirits and prevent the inauspiciousness which results in misfortune. Thus a Samburu elder told Spencer: 'Nkai likes respect.' Those with respect may invoke Nkai; his name itself is ritually powerful.

The lmugit rituals dramatize the difference between *moran* and elders in a striking fashion; the participants are divided into two groups, the colourful *moran* with their spears, and the quiet elders, who hold staffs, for their power lies in ritual not force. They harangue the *moran* and then give them a blessing, conditional on good behaviour in the future. This is a more developed and long-drawn-out version of the address given to initiates in other societies, such as that which invokes the ancestors' blessing on a Gisu initiand and commands him to follow the precepts of manhood. The Samburu case makes clear what is happening: it is a demonstration of the elders' power which is followed by a manifestation of its effect.

Spencer's description of the blessing from an *ilmugit* (the *ilmugit* of the bull, i.e. inaugurating the phase when *moran* will begin to get married) that he witnessed makes this vividly clear. The scene took place at the end of about ten days, during which each group had held separate discussions, and the elders had harangued the *moran* four or five times. It preceded the killing of the first ox for the *ilmugit*. About nine o'clock at night the *moran* were called over to the elders' enclosure. To the sound of a kudu horn, blown by a *moran*, a huge fire was built up. The elders, standing on one side of it, protected themselves from the intense heat by wrapping their blankets round them; the *moran* on the other side were wearing only short loincloths and so were fully exposed to it.

> Two firestick elders ... lead the blessing invoking the protection of God on the *moran*. 'May Nkai look after you ... May Nkai give you peace ... May Nkai give you good fortune ...' etc. ... At each pause the other elders waved their upraised staffs and chanted, 'Nkai ... Nkai ... Nkai ...' rhythmically and continued to do so even when the invocations were drowned by the general tumult. A *moran* was also blowing the horn in time with the rhythmical chanting.
>
> As they began their invocations, the two leading firestick elders splattered the bodies of the *moran* with a mixture of milk and water. The touch of the cool liquid on their bodies exposed to the heat of the fire caused many of them to squeal and jump. And immediately three started to shake and perhaps a dozen started to shiver [the preliminary to shaking]. Relentlessly the blessing continued and the gasps of the shaking *moran* and the chant of the elders and the sound of the horn practically drowned the words of the invocation.
>
> Some shaking *moran* partially recovered and others started to shake and had to be held. Eventually the *moran* blowing the horn fell shaking and had to be held by about five other *moran*. Another *moran* picked up the horn and started to blow, but he began to shake immediately and the horn was taken over by a third *moran* who had some difficulty in keeping the time and just blew it continuously. After about six minutes there were five shaking *moran* who were being forcibly held by both *moran* and elders and a dozen other *moran* who were either shivering

or shaking or holding a shaking *moran*. At this point the blessing
stopped.   [Spencer, 1965: 267–8]

This makes it quite clear that the elders are controlling the ritual; they
generate a contrast between their own controlled behaviour and the
uncontrolled response of the *moran*. The blessing is seen to have a powerful
effect, and when that effect is reached, the elders stop. The Samburu
themselves regard shaking as a sign of manliness and anger; the restraints
put on *moran* when they are shaking are said to prevent injury. *Moran*
themselves say they are angry and want to assert themselves. It would
seem as accurate to talk of uncontrolled feeling or frustrated aggression
as anxiety, which is the emotion Spencer attributed to the *moran*. There
is a parallel with the Gisu example, where the initiand is said to be filled
with *litima*, feelings of great violence which make him uncontrollable.
When this occurs, he too must be watched and guided lest he hurt himself
or others. This phase was explained as a further indication of how the Gisu
initiation candidate emphasizes more and more his non-social nature; in
that society it is a brief phase in a single ritual. Among the Samburu the
moran seem to embody all these attributes but for a longer period. The
words of the elders indeed seem to provoke a manifestation of just that lack
of control or respect, of which the elders accuse them. The scene described
above was part of the *ilmugit* of the bull, the ritual which ushers in a period
during which *moran* will, following their ritual leader, marry and settle
down to elderhood; it demonstrates most dramatically that they are still
moran. Significantly, the *ilmugit* of the milk and leaves, which is the rite
of accession to elderhood, does not contain a harangue. It is the only
ilmugit which does not.

The explicit purpose of this ritual, as expressed by the elders who
officiate at it, is to teach respect to the *moran*; they will call them together
for harangues more frequently when the *moran* have been particularly
unruly. They may also impose a collective fine on a group of *moran*. Six
ilmugit are necessary to mark the formal stages of transition, but the elders
may impose additional ones and seem to do so from time to time. Each
moran has to provide a beast for the feast at *ilmugit* so that fines and
additional rituals deplete the livestock of the fathers of the whole group,
without reference to the guilt or innocence of individuals. Collective
responsibility is thus instilled into the *moran* as an indirect consequence
of the elders' perception of them as lacking in respect. Indeed, collective
action is a guiding principle of the way of the elders, as opposed to the
egotistic violence of the *moran*. For the very exploits which the elders
deplore and which cause them to call the *moran* together for a harangue
and blessing, are those egotistical exploits which gain individual *moran*

prestige among their fellows: cattle-theft, fighting, adultery with the wives of elders. They are made individually responsible for their behaviour as *moran*. This, however, is achieved by collective fines and leaves unanswered the question of why Samburu elders see the ritual as a means of teaching respect.

Spencer sees the harangue, and the blessing which follows it, as the most effective part of the rituals which mark the transitional period of *moran*hood. He is concerned to show how the rituals inculcate in the young men a sense of respect, how they fulfil the purpose of the elders. In order to do this he postulates a psychological pattern of stress and suggestibility which seems very plausible. He uses the work of the psychiatrist William Sargant, who studied techniques of brain-washing used on prisoners of war, for he considers that the *moran* are undergoing a similar process. Sargant suggests that anxiety caused by stress induces increased suggestibility, which allows for attitudes to be changed or values reinforced. Spencer argues that anxiety in the *moran* is increased by their desire to acquit themselves well as *moran*, and also by the reiterated accusation of the elders that they are not developing the respect that they should be showing in their progress to elderhood. The anxiety is manifest in the fits of trembling or violent shaking which are described in the passage quoted above. These fits are characteristic of *moran*; during them they seem to lose control of themselves and have to be held to prevent their doing violence to themselves or others. This occurs more easily during harangues and blessings, before circumcision, at dances and (formerly) before battle. It appears rarely, if ever, among elders, in whom it is not thought appropriate.[15] In the ritual described above, the heat, noise and shouting which induced the *moran* to fall into fits of shaking appear to have had no effect on any of the elders, who are controlling it, although some of them will have anxieties which might emerge in physical reactions. Spencer records the growing tension of the elders about the success of the initial circumcision ritual, where they get more and more anxious about whether the candidates will flinch at the operation. There, by contrast, it is the elders who manifest anxiety and the initiates who show self-control. In this respect the circumcision ritual is the opposite of the *ilmugit* rituals; it resembles Gisu initiation, in which the ritual is directed towards ensuring that the ordeal is honourably surmounted. Any interpretation must encompass both types of rite.

Spencer notes that the *ilmugit* rituals instil in the *moran* 'an awe regarding their [the elders'] power to bless or to curse them' (1970: 138). The harangues assert this power and by implication attribute the lack of it in the *moran* to their misdemeanours, which indicate lack of respect. The *moran* also lack knowledge about the mystical aspects of the rituals. An aspect of what is entailed in the learning process of *moran*hood is that *moran* should accept that mystical forces are at work and that 'the older men alone know most of the ritual prescriptions'. It is the structure of the rituals which does this, both in the case of the *ilmugit* rituals and that of the circumcision rites of Samburu and Gisu.

The elders' blessing provokes a storm of shivering and shaking among the *moran* as the direct effect of their invocation. It can be seen as a demonstration of their power. Less obviously, circumcision has a similar place in its set of rites, and here the Gisu material gives the clearer evidence. Gisu boys are circumcised as the climax of ritual and secular preparations, which have gone on for months. The youths have been strengthened by hours of dancing as well as the blessing of the ancestors. This blessing is bestowed as the last act of the elders before the operation of circumcision itself. The ordeal is thus a double test: of the initiate's manhood and also of the effectiveness of the ritual. To the Samburu, flinching is not merely a matter of shame; it envelops the coward's father and brothers, and members of their lineage and clan, as well as their herds, in an aura of inauspiciousness, which may have dire effects in the future. For the Gisu it also involves the lineage in disgrace. Success, on the other hand, confirms the power of the ritual. Gisu initiates to whom I spoke during their convalescence showed two main preoccupations. First, they commented on their previous lack of knowledge of what the ritual would be like. 'You cannot know what the knife is like until you feel it,' one of them said, addressing me and some of the boys who were waiting on them. The second topic of conversation was their own courage; it was clear that the source of it was somehow mysterious to them. In so far as they felt transformed by their experience, and there was no doubt that they did, the transformation was the result of the whole ritual. The effect both of circumcision rites and the *ilmugit* is thus a direct confirmation of the elders' ability to conduct them, of their knowledge and hence of the power that the knowledge bestows. The effectiveness of ritual lies in the fact that it is self-validating.

NOTES TO CHAPTER VII

1. Baktaman do not make this final connection and do not seem to think that they will ultimately become ancestors themselves (F. Barth, personal communication).
2. All oral tradition reflects present perceptions of the past and can be used by historians only with great care.
3. See La Fontaine, 1968.

4. There was also ecological pressure against expansion. The Gisu inhabit the foothills of Mount Elgon, and in 1954 cultivated as high up as the boundary of the Forest Reserve at about 8,000 feet above sea-level. Above that, they told me, their staple crops would not flourish; the alternative was the plains to the west, which were much drier, and where more land was needed to support a family than in the hills. Moreover, down on the plains they were much more vulnerable to attack by their more warlike neighbours. They preferred to stay in the foothills, and until their pacification, in the first decade of the twentieth century, they were expanding northwards into the area occupied by the Sebei. They have also spread down into the plains and migrated elsewhere in Uganda in search of land; their density of population was remarked as early as 1902 (La Fontaine, 1959).

5. *Wanyala*, meaning literally 'You can [do it]', is used where English-speakers would say 'Thank you', and *Wanyala gimirimo*, 'You can do your work'. 'Thank you [for] the work', is one of the phrases used in greeting.

6. Land was also relatively plentiful in this area but boys were markedly younger at initiation than in other areas with similar population densities and no tradition of age-class organization.

7. Sexual maturity is achieved in two stages among the Samburu: when a youth becomes a *moran* he is free to sleep with uncircumcised girls, but a circumcised woman who becomes pregnant by him risks mystical dangers to herself and her baby. After the *moran* have been promoted at the *ilmugit* of the name, it is no longer dangerous for a senior *moran* to impregnate a woman, provided she is circumcised and their relationship is not incestuous. However, he still may not marry, a right only accorded him later.

8. Among the Masai, a youth may compensate for flinching at circumcision if he shows outstanding courage as a *moran*; however, this does not seem possible among the Samburu (P. Spencer, personal communication).

9. Blood is mixed with milk to eke out supplies of milk in the dry season but it is also considered a particularly strengthening food. Its use here is to promote convalescence, and has no ritual connotations.

10. The Turkana are an exception, for they, unlike other neighbours of the Samburu, do not recognize the immunity of newly circumcised youths.

11. They wear cloths tied in the manner of women (W. Thesiger, personal communication), indicating that they are still not fully male. They resemble recently circumcised girls and menstruating women in that they are in some ways considered sexless (P. Spencer, personal communication). See the discussion in Chapter VI of the parallels drawn between the bleeding boys and menstruating women.

12. Harangues and a blessing occur whenever the *moran* are assembled by the firestick elders; a special blessing is reserved for the *ilmugit* rites which promote the *moran* to senior status, permit their ritual leader to marry, or promote the whole class to elderhood.

13. This rule excludes the *moran* from meals in their own homes and within a village in general. They are forced to spend much of their time quite separately from the rest of the community.

14. They are often distant clan sisters. See also Spencer (1973: 95).
15. Some elders do shake and thereby lose the respect of their fellow-elders and find it hard to gain any influence thereafter (W. Thesiger, personal communication).

CHAPTER VIII

MARRIAGE,
MATERNITY
AND THE
INITIATION
OF GIRLS

Although there has been so much discussion of, and scholarly interest in, initiation, information on the rites of girls is lamentably sparse. Audrey Richards' monograph on the initiation of Bemba girls (1956) was characterized, seven years later, as 'the most complete and detailed description of a girl's initiation ceremony' (Brown, 1963: 837). Twenty years later still, it continues to deserve the compliment, although there have been a few more studies, most of them as yet unpublished.

One possible reason for this dearth of material is that such rites are relatively uncommon. While many societies perform rituals for girls, which are connected in some way with their maturation, few of these are initiation rites[1] and those that do exist may be less elaborate than the rituals for boys. The commonest life-crisis rite marking the maturity of girls is the wedding,[2] which also marks a change in status for the groom, although marriage is rarely discussed as a transition rite of significance for men. In certain societies, weddings may be the only life-crisis rites, but usually they are preceded by others, especially for girls. All the peoples discussed in the two previous chapters have puberty or nubility rites for girls; only those of Wogeo Island involve more than one girl at a time. Even in those cases where girls and boys are circumcised to mark their maturity, the character of the rituals in the two cases may be quite different. Among the Samburu, female circumcision involves a single individual, and the simple rite is timed to precede her marriage, rather than preparing her for admission to an age-class. The small-scale, individual nature of many rites for girls and their association with the physical events of menstruation, loss of virginity and childbirth[3] seem to have been taken to indicate a qualitative difference in the ritual treatment of girls and boys. This has also focused attention on the reproductive life-cycle as the dominant element in female rites.

The assumption that female life-crisis rites are concerned with physical changes has led to their explanation in terms of the society's concern with reproduction. Puberty rites follow the onset of menstruation and, since girls reach this stage of their physical development at different times, it is not surprising that puberty rites are celebrated individually. The lack of such clear indications of maturity in boys is held to explain why boys are usually initiated and puberty ritual is not performed for them. Further, the emphasis on menstruation as the universal sign of female maturation underlies the explanation of circumcision and other blood-letting operations on boys as an imitation of menstruation. It has also led to the mistaken conclusion that women mature 'naturally' while boys are more often inducted 'culturally' into manhood.

Consideration of the comparative evidence throws doubt on the accuracy of these judgements. Girls may undergo ritual which marks a new stage in their development at any age between eight and twenty, according to Brown (1963: 838), and even her broad definition of initiation excludes any ritual which is performed on girls younger than eight years old; it also excludes all marriage rites, as well as betrothals. A particular society's timing of the ritual appears to depend more on what it regards as significant than on the independent physical events of the female life cycle. By contrast, even these individual changes can be the occasion for initiation ritual. On Wogeo Island the onset of first menstruation in a girl necessitates an initiation rite for all girls in the area who are approaching the menarche. There is a sense in which the ritual most concerns the girl whose menstruation was the reason for performing it, since the others are not expected to keep the taboos as stringently as she is; but her companions are dressed the same, go through the same rites and are paraded round the village together at the end. There is also a clear parallel with boys' initiation. Many of the same features appear in both: the location on the beach, the ritual fights, washing in the pool, and the rite to keep the skin smooth. The islanders explain them as having the same purpose in each case: to cleanse the novices from the weakening effects of association with the opposite sex.

The Wogeo case is rather unusual. It is far commoner to find girls undergoing small-scale, domestic rituals individually as they reach menarche. Even where girls are initiated, they may undergo puberty ritual as well. However, the Wogeo case serves to demonstrate that the relative lack of female initiation rites cannot be explained by the character of female physiological development, or its difference from that of the male.

A more feasible explanation lies in the general fact that organized groups of women are rarely found as the building blocks of social structure. Male initiation rites have been shown to have an association with cohesive male groups (Allen, 1967; Y. Cohen, 1964; Herdt *et al.*, 1982; Young, 1962). As the last two chapters have shown, the rituals of male initiation are concerned with the authority of senior generations of men, and the newly initiated are incorporated into a male group by the experience which excludes women and children. The rites are often lineage-based, the male congregation being the descent group assembled in common action. The groups are recruited through male links, and women, though members of them, are in many senses peripheral. Gisu speak of descent groups as though they were composed of men; their female members marry outside them and are scattered, as individuals, among a range of nearby groups. They will become mothers of members of other lineages. Their role in the initiation rites reflects their marginality: they represent the association of women and children from which the novice is to be separated, and the major role for a woman in the rites is that of the outsider, the mother.[4] The fact that Gisu ritual for girls prepares each individual separately for marriage seems entirely appropriate. 'Daughters are enemies,' say the Gusii of western Kenya, whose social organization is very similar. Yet the Gusii hold true initiation rites for girls which are markedly more elaborate than those they perform for boys, so that the association between organized groups and initiation does not explain the incidence of such rites for women.

The existence of girls' initiation rites in parallel with those of boys has been dismissed as mere imitation (Huntingford, 1953) which draws attention to the similarities between the two types of rite performed in a single society and the lesser elaboration of the female ritual which is common. While there are ritual episodes which are identical in male and female initiations on Wogeo, there is no evidence that the people themselves think that one is 'real' and the other an 'imitation', so that this explanation seems unsatisfactory. It has been argued (Koloski, 1967; Hays & Hays, 1982; Comaroff, forthcoming) that both are part of a single ritual complex which must be analysed as a whole for either to be fully understood. Jean Comaroff has written of the Tswana that 'the rites of female initiation were considerably less elaborate than the male, and in the contrast between the two lay the full ideological significance of the whole ritual complex' (op. cit., p. 69). The adult sexual identity which is conferred at initiation is defined in opposition, not only to childhood, which is the point of departure for both sexes, but also, by contrast, to another distinct and different adult identity. Thus, where both sexes are initiated, there is the clear implication that childhood is a common state from which both men and women are moulded, in different forms, but by a similar ritual process.

This approach enables us to understand a particular feature of female initiation and women's rites in general which has drawn much attention from scholars but for which no satisfactory explanation has yet been given. Girls' rituals often differ from those of the boys in exhibiting sexual licence, privileged obscenity or mockery of men and male occupations; while nothing similar takes place during the transformation of boys. In the Gusii rites already mentioned, there is an episode in which married women, including the mothers of the novices, who are accompanying them, taunt men with obscenities and insults, mimic their behaviour and make fun of them generally. Women on Wogeo Island seem to enjoy their period of licence during the initiation of girls, where their licentious behaviour is interpreted by the men as showing lack of respect. Hogbin writes: 'Had I not been aware that everything was taking place according to the accepted pattern I might have assumed that an unexpected feminist upsurge was in progress and the males were resisting the loss of traditional privileges' (1970: 133). Such behaviour is not a spontaneous reaction to the occasion but a necessary part of the proceedings.

Similar episodes of licence have been noted as characterizing rites in which women play the dominant roles, even when they are not initiations but agricultural rituals designed to ensure a plentiful harvest. Gluckman describes how Zulu and Tsonga women dressed as men, imitated men's herding and other activities, and at certain stages in the rites 'went naked and sang lewd songs' (1962: 5). He emphasized that the men hid, not because they were embarrassed or at a loss, but because this was their role in a ceremony which was performed for the good of all. He interprets the rite as a ritual rebellion, allowing for the dissipation of strains engendered in the social system, by enacting the conflicts which result. A similar explanation is offered by Brown (1963)[5] and both she and Gluckman considered that the result is a strengthening of the structure of male authority.

Such explanations rely on selecting this one element to characterize the whole ritual, which includes much else besides. They also depend heavily on the attribution to the participants of feelings which seem to be represented in their actions. No evidence is offered that they do feel hostile or rebellious; some may do so, but there are others who perform the actions because they are enjoined to, or in order to amuse, to pay off grudges, or for many other reasons which will vary according to the particular and differing personalities of the women involved. A ritual is performed to accomplish a socially defined purpose; the licentious behaviour of women is part of a sequence of actions which are believed to achieve it.

These actions are not only a manifestation of lack of respect for men in general, and husbands, fathers or brothers in particular, but the reversal of normal feminine behaviour. Rigby has pointed out (1968) that such reversals are commonly a part of rites of passage, marking the marginal period between two states of being. The particular form of this reversal, however, can only be understood if it is seen as an opposition of symbols, a creative reordering of categories, rather than the manifestation of feminine resentment against men as human beings who exercise power and authority. Among the Tswana, female initiation rites assert a principle which is in tension with the social order symbolized by maleness, but also complementary to it. It is no less necessary for the continuity of society than women themselves, who link men in marriage and whose generative power is associated, not only with 'the wild' beyond the civilized village, but with the distant Modimo, the supreme spirit and creator of life (Comaroff, forthcoming). In considering the initiation of girls, it is therefore necessary to elucidate the components of a symbolic field that includes as one element the idea of 'woman'. Implicit in those meanings is a contrast with the polar idea, the cluster of meanings containing 'man'. The actual men and women who are the performers in any ritual represent the whole range of associations, not merely the categories 'male' and 'female'.

The initiation ritual of girls among the Pokot resembles that of boys in many respects. The Pokot themselves draw the parallel when they say: 'Women initiate girls as men initiate boys.'[6] The responsibility for transforming immature individuals into men and women is shared by the senior members of the community and their interdependence in everyday life is very clear (Meyerhoff, 1982). While the initiation rites for each sex exclude the other from much of the proceedings, there are important roles for both in each set of rites. Taken together the initiations emphasize the authority of age and experience in a manner which seems to override distinctions of gender, at least to a considerable extent.

The Pokot live in western Kenya, not far from the Gisu, in an area bordering on that of the Samburu, with whom they have both linguistic and cultural similarities. While those living in the more arid areas are pastoralists, the Pokot living in the highlands, which are better watered, grow maize and millet. The two sections differ from one another in other respects, including the details of their initiation rituals; those discussed here are the rites of the agricultural Pokot.

Pokot girls are circumcised at the outset of a series of rites which last three to four months and are seen as a preparation for marriage. Ideally a Pokot girl should marry while she is still wearing the decorations from the 'coming-out' ritual of her initiation, but the ideal may not be always followed. At the rituals observed by Meyerhoff a number of the girls were pregnant, which is also a departure from the proper course of affairs, in which pregnancy follows marriage. However, the greatest concern is reserved for a girl who gives birth before her initiation; this is both dishonourable and a grave sin, with mystical consequences. Sexual experience before initiation is unimportant but the rites must be performed before a child is born.

Girls' initiation rites are performed every year, in one or other of the neighbourhoods of the region formed by a cluster of co-operating neighbourhoods. Boys' initiation rites are also based on the region but take place only every three or four years as part of the constitution of the age-class system which forms the framework of their traditional political organization. During the whole period of the rites the boys live in a special hut, set apart from the homesteads, and are forbidden to see women, while girls, although circumcised as a group, convalesce at their parental homes.[7] Unless there is more than one hut in the homestead, the father of a novice must stay elsewhere during the whole period until the final rites, for he must not share a hut with his daughter. One girl's home is chosen as the centre for much of the ritual and as a meeting-place for the novices, but the segregation of the girls from the rest of the community is much less strict than it is for boys.

The operation is a severe ordeal, during the public part of which a girl must hold herself rigid and silent in front of the crowd assembled to watch. If she cries out or moves before the sign is given her by the operator, she will be excluded from the final ceremonies and her mother will not be allowed to wear the headband denoting the mother of a successful initiate; the shame is never lived down. This part of the operation consists of the excision of the labia with a few quick strokes; later, after the crowd has dispersed, the expert will complete the operation, whose aim is to remove sufficient tissue so that the edges of the labia will heal together, producing a neat scar which covers the clitoris. This part of the operation may take longer than the public ordeal, but the girl is held and no shame attends her if she shows pain during it. Pokot see this as merely corrective surgery to ensure the desired result. Meyerhoff notes that the effect of the operation is to recreate virginity;[8] a bride should bleed when she first has sexual intercourse with her husband. Until her 'coming-out', she should not sleep with any man and there are constant inspections of all the girls to check that they have not broken the rule. In addition it underlines a distinction between sexual intercourse between immature lovers, and procreation, which is the privilege of adult men and women. In the case of girls, the initiation rites define motherhood as a social role, which a girl's performance at the ordeal has demonstrated her fitness to assume. It is significant that the posture assumed by the novice during her ordeal is said to be similar to that adopted by Pokot women during childbirth: sitting, with head up, legs spread apart, back arched and arms outstretched, gazing at the sky.

Throughout the rites there is an emphasis on the need for self-reliance.

The songs sung during the night before the operation, during which neither the initiands nor the accompanying women sleep, refer to the initiands' social identity, their parentage and character, and reiterate that girls can only rely on the strength of their own hearts. They will be alone in their ordeal, like those who have endured it before them. Moreover, the decision to be circumcised is left to the girls themselves and a number may present themselves at the moment of circumcision despite their parents' unwillingness to agree. If they seat themselves on the stones which have been set out for the novices to sit on, they must be operated on. Meyerhoff reported that at every initiation she witnessed, some girls did this. At other points in the ritual, too, songs and exhortations refer to the fact that a girl will be married into a strange community where she must rely on herself to know how to behave.

The initiation opens with these themes of loneliness and endurance. When all the candidates have been circumcised, each is accompanied back to her home. She is known as *chemerion*, initiate, and the name designates her special status, which lasts until she 'comes out' as a young woman. Until the wounds heal she will be subject to various restrictions, severe to start with;[9] she will be ritually 'cleansed' and released from some of them, but others continue, as a mark of marginality, until the final rites. The lasting rules forbid washing and enjoin a *chemerion* to carry a branch, whitened like herself with chalk, to mark her approach and touch anything that might be polluted to purify it. This behaviour indicates a state known as *orus*. Boys in the marginal state during their initiation are also *orus*, which can be glossed as 'unclean' or 'undefined'.[10] She wears an enveloping garment, concealing her, particularly from senior male kin, whom she must not see till the final rite.

The second phase of the marginal state begins when the girls have healed and the scars have been inspected. They are occupied with light tasks to help their mothers but chiefly in making the ornaments they will wear at their 'coming-out'. They are also gathered together more than once to attend festivities known as *lapan*. These are feasts, regarded as payments to the older women of the community; they eat an animal provided by the parents of one of the girls and drink the beer which is also provided. It is an expected part of the proceedings that they will get progressively drunker and more indiscreet as time wears on, but the *lapan* has a serious overt purpose and significant, though implicit, social effects.

Pokot mothers are authority figures to their children, a fact that is demonstrated in the initiation of boys and girls. Women advise the officiants concerned with their sons what points in the boys' characters need correction by their mentors during their instruction; at the *lapan* they open proceedings by addressing their daughters, pointing out their faults. This sets off long harangues, during which the girls must kneel in submissive attitudes. They are struck with branches, to humiliate them and make them respond to the questioning, to show that they are absorbing the 'teaching'. They are castigated individually for their faults of character and behaviour, and constant reference is made to their futures as brides in other communities. They will be ignorant of local ways and alone, subject to the authority of their mothers-in-law and other senior women to whose ways they must adapt. The flood of words conveys both the ideals of marriage and the relationships it creates, but also the actuality of women's lives.

The purpose of these harangues is to 'teach' the girls so that they will be prepared for marriage. What emerges is a vivid demonstration of a community of married women whose mutual loyalty and authority derive from long-term residence and participating in many such occasions over the years. Pokot marriages are fragile and girls not uncommonly leave their first and even second husbands. Meyerhoff records that it is only after time, in a stable marriage, that a woman becomes integrated into a new community. The group of senior women at the *lapan* show in their own persons the rewards of marital stability and the adaptability of women which results in the authority they wield as senior and long-term residents. They are largely women who have married into the community and the senior ones are mothers-in-law to their juniors. The harangues enact the authority to which their words refer: that which older women exercise over younger, and the connections made by marriage which weld the community together. While concerned with the initiates' future as brides, the occasion adds another dimension to the significance of marriage and the social relations it establishes.

Another theme which emerges is the idea that Pokot women have of their own power. They connect their own childbearing capacities with a source outside themselves, which is somewhat mysterious but relates to the source of rain, so vital to the success of their agriculture. One of the most secret rites of female initiation involves a sacred pool, which links women's powers with water and a local spirit which inhabits the pool. The rites must never be revealed to men or other uninitiated persons; although Elizabeth Meyerhoff, who lived with the Pokot[11] for some six years, witnessed most of the ritual, she was not allowed to watch this. Only the old women know the details and meaning of what is done; they pass this knowledge to other senior women so that again only long-term resident women acquire knowledge of the local ritual. Each locality has its own version, and each set of initiates will acquire at their own initiation only a very general impression of what is done, leaving control of the rite firmly in the hands of the old, experienced women of the locality.

An explicit reference to women's powers which is made, both in the harangues and in obscene songs sung then and during the marginal stage of the boys' initiation, concerns the fact that men depend on women for descendants. A song sung by women during male initiation puts it succinctly:

> He poured my sons on the skin of the bed. If I could
> not hold them, there would not be any children.

> [Meyerhoff, 1982: 173]

Moreover, during the feasts women relate their own experience in manipulating men and using feminine power for their own ends. What is communicated to the girls is not only the power and authority of senior women but the general sense of power which Pokot women appear to feel.

The secret rite at the river (or sacred pool) precedes the 'coming-out' of the initiates as young women. Once again the themes of childbearing and of relations between generations of women are emphasized. The *chemeri* follow a leader, a woman whose first-born was a girl and none of whose children have died. There is an echo here of the initial stage, of circumcision itself, when an ingredient of the healing liquid put on the girls' wounds was the milk of a woman who was suckling a baby girl and none of whose children had died. The girls are ordered, both at circumcision and during this rite, by reference to the seniority of their fathers' age-class rank. The essence of this ritual is that each girl must beat the water of the pool and a rainbow should signify the spirit's approval of her; she must then drop an iron bead and some ghee into the water. The way the bead drops through the water is taken as an augury for her reproductive future. Songs are sung, indicating that the 'mother' has received them and 'mixed' them with the past. After the 'coming-out', the girls bury two beads in a secret place; a woman whose daughter's daughter has successfully been initiated digs up two beads which were buried there previously. There are further rites and instruction, but accounts were vague. What is clear is the representation of continuity through generations of women associated with the sacred places, and the symbolic link between water, the spirit and maternity.

The final 'coming-out' ritual is remarkably similar for boys and girls. They are both dressed as young women and are promised gifts of stock, the boys first by women and later by their senior female kin, the girls first by boys and later by their senior male kin. These gifts, recalling the inducements to a bride to undertake various actions in the new home, establish relations between the new adult and members of the opposite sex, emphasizing the Pokot theme of male/female interdependence.

The ritual of girls' initiation develops a counterpoint to the theme in that of the boys: where that of the boys emphasizes ranking by age-class, ancestors and hence descent, that of the girls represents a cluster of ideas which make the bearing of children more than just a matter of female physiology, but the focus of the conjugal relationship, relations established by marriage, the building of a community and its continuity in space and across the generations. It brings together in common action human beings whose organized activity demonstrates the power of the community and of experience acquired through living in it.

The significance of marriage is the major overt theme manifest in the initiation rites of girls among the Bemba of Zambia, who are a matri-lineally organized society. The Bemba form part of what has been called 'the matrilineal belt of Africa': the peoples stretching from Mozambique to what is now Zaire, northwards into Tanzania and Malawi and south into Angola. Many of these peoples use the same term as the Bemba use for the rites, *chisungu*. In an appendix to her monograph, Richards dis-cusses the distribution of the rites throughout this area. They are charac-terized by an absence of any physical mutilation but an emphasis on mimes, singing and dancing and the showing of various sacred objects. Perhaps the most intriguing remark is that the initiation rites of the Bemba seem to be the most elaborate, just as they 'are the only people in this group with ritual kingship and a centralized government'. While, as Richards herself remarks, there is not enough evidence to pursue this comparatively, the association in the Bemba case is clear enough to shed light on the issues this book is concerned with.

The societies discussed so far, with the exception of the Hopi, have all been characterized by patriliny, which gives an extra social dimension to the relationship of father and son and the solidarity of men. Not only does inheritance of property pass from father to son, but the relationship between successive generations of men is the means by which a major social grouping perpetuates itself. One might expect, then, that in societies where descent groups are founded on links through and between women, initiation rituals would be different in kind.

While matrilineal descent assigns individuals to groups according to the affiliation of their mother, this does not mean that women are the dominant sex. Men are still the authorities; their heirs are not their sons, but their sister's sons. Domestic authority over his children may be exer-cised by their father, but legal jurisdiction over them, particularly when they are adults, remains with their mother's brother, who may live elsewhere. The effect of this is to distinguish sharply between a household group, in which men have domestic authority over their children, and the descent group, in which their subordinates are their sister's children. In such a situation the father–son relationship is distinct from, and may contrast with, relationships between the generations in the descent group. Often, as with the Bemba, the core of a village community consists of women, related as mothers, sisters and daughters, who also form the core of a descent group. They may be influential but they do not wield much economic or political power. Authority in such systems is still male authority, but the model of the relation between successive generations within the descent group is female: the tie between mother and daughter. If rituals of initiation are manifestations of the legitimacy of authority, one would expect them to reflect differences in the distribution of authority in matrilineal systems.

In pre-colonial times, the Bemba, most of whom live in what is now Zambia, though there are also Bemba in south-eastern Zaire, formed a centralized state, based on the pre-eminence of the royal Crocodile clan who provided the Bemba king, the Citimukulu. Succession to this high office was determined by position in the genealogy which related members of the royal clan to the ruling line, but only in conjunction with the holding of a series of subordinate chiefships, which were ranked in order of precedence and for which there was competition. The kings were thus outstanding figures in the Crocodile clan, as well as qualified by matrilineal descent from a long line of predecessors, with whom they were closely identified. The Citimukulu in the 1930s claimed to be the thirty-first Citimukulu.

All powerful political positions were held by the Crocodile clan, although some headmen of villages, whose position depended on royal assent, were commoners. The Bemba state depended on military success and the exaction of tribute and slaves from dominated peoples. 'We Bemba cultivate with the spear and not the hoe' is the phrase Richards quotes. Another characteristic of Bemba society, which she emphasizes, is that there was little storable material wealth or transmissible property; power lay in the ability to command the services of other people. It is the organizing ability which enables a man to build up and maintain a village or command a following that Bemba admire, even though British colonial rule put an end to slaving and the tribute they exacted from a wide area.

As might be expected, the Bemba recognize not only the right to command exercised by the royal clan, who are expected to be arrogant, ruthless and generous to their commoner subjects, but also the rights of age. Richards describes it thus: 'Extreme deference is paid to age. Every child knows his exact position of seniority in a group of village children and is given precedence in games. Each group of men sitting in the village shelter does the same' (Richards, 1956: 48). Many of the ritual acts in *chisungu* consist of a repetition of acts by people in their exact order of precedence and there is more emphasis on precedence than on anything else. Bemba women were admired for industry in agriculture and as the mothers of children. Among neighbouring peoples they were famous for their independence, a measure of which is their right to plead their own cases in the courts. Bemba royal women also have a role in political and religious life. Two districts are ruled by senior princesses of the royal clan, and junior princesses may be village heads; royal women may also have charge of ancestral shrines. Even commoner women, as the mothers of their brothers' heirs, have a position which commands respect, and an assurance and influence which increase with age. A man's following is partly dependent on the ability of his sisters and daughters to attract husbands to live with and support him.

The Citimukulu and all political officials under him were responsible for the ritual welfare of their people. The Citimukulu's ritual powers derived from his ability to approach the royal ancestors, whose jurisdiction included all Bemba. No man might approach his ancestors unless he were married. The wives of headmen, lineage heads and the great chiefs, up to and including the Citimukulu himself, had the responsibility of ensuring the purity of their husbands so that the ancestral ritual might be effective. Royal ritual and the initiation of girls, the *chisungu*, formed the two major ritual complexes of the Bemba. In many ways they were direct contrasts: royal ritual was secret, reverent and involved only those qualified by descent; the *chisungu* was a public festival involving crowds of people, much singing and dancing, as well as secret rites. The office of *nacimbusa*, mother of secrets, is not inherited but achieved by apprenticeship and learning. Ancestral ritual consists largely of prayers and offerings to the ancestors, although there are ritual actions of great significance such as those to 'warm the country'; by contrast, the *chisungu* includes the showing of sacred objects, mimes, songs and tests of the novices.

The two ritual cycles are linked by their dependence on notions of purity, the maintenance of which is the responsibility of women, passed on in the *chisungu*. The symbol of this is the marriage pot, given to a girl at her marriage and represented in the *chisungu*; it will hold water with which a woman ceremonially cleanses herself and her husband after intercourse, so that they are pure and do not endanger others, including their own children.[12] It also represents a set of ideas about blood, fire and adult sexuality which underlies all Bemba ritual and much of their everyday life.

The details of this central complex of beliefs have been carefully analysed by Richards and will not be repeated here, apart from some significant meanings that are important in the argument. They play on similarities and differences, which shift slightly in context. In ritual action they emerge as the necessity to create 'new' – that is, pure – fire, and in ceremonial acts of sexual intercourse, performed by people in authority to 'warm the country' or remove a person from a dangerous state. Ritual fire is kindled by rubbing sticks, which is itself symbolic of the sexual act. People of sexual maturity, and particularly those who have had intercourse, are 'hot'; in this condition they pollute fires, and hence the food that is cooked on the fires. The giving and sharing of food is an important index of social relations in Bemba society so that food must be pure. Babies[13] are particularly endangered by such pollution and by persons in a 'hot' state. The chief's sacred fire and he himself are also specially vulnerable; both must be carefully protected. The shedding of blood, in menstruation or in the killing of animals or human beings in hunting or warfare, is also dangerously polluting. A chief's fire is usually tended by a senior wife who is past the menopause, and his food is cooked by a man, so that he is protected from the dangers of menstrual blood. Hunters and killers may not approach fires until they are ritually cleansed of blood; Richards records a case when two Bemba murderers were caught because it was remarked that they were eating their food cold, i.e. they could not approach a fire. Fire is equated with the principle of generation; old women give new (pure) fire, and the power to bear children safely, to the novices during an important episode in the *chisungu*.

The expressed purpose of the *chisungu* is to change the girls into women, not merely by teaching them the songs and dances, and showing them the sacred emblems, but by transforming them in the course of the experience. All the overt emphasis of the rites is placed on marriage, a woman's responsibilities, her subservience to her husband, to senior women and all others in authority. The rituals are opened by the headman of the village but men play little part in them, except that the girl's betrothed or a relative who stands in for him[14] must perform certain of the rites. No men of the descent group take part. Ideally, the *chisungu* is followed by marriage and a girl's future husband is expected to contribute to the expenses of his bride's *chisungu*.

The full ritual is long and complex. It took four weeks to complete in 1931 when Richards observed it, and it was said that formerly it would last several months, the rites intermingling with visits from kin, feasts and secular dancing. The mysteries, referred to by Richards as emblems, and called 'things handed down' by the Bemba, consisted of forty-three different pottery objects, as well as a number of unfired clay models, carefully made for a particular rite and then destroyed, nine different designs painted on the wall and more than a hundred different songs. The mistress of ceremonies has learnt over a long apprenticeship what is required of such a ritual, and her knowledge earns her prestige and respect. In the past these women were entitled to wear the plumed head-dress of chiefs and hereditary counsellors, as a sign of the respect due to their rank. The knowledge to which girls are introduced at their *chisungu* is esoteric and its significance is not explained. The initiates must serve as helpers at subsequent rites for another one or two occasions; even then it takes interest and perseverance on the part of a young woman if she is to become a *nacimbusa*. The corpus of 'things handed down' forms an area where women can become pre-eminent, just as men do by their social and organizational skills, as headmen and chiefs.

The emphasis on marriage in the *chisungu* included a role for the bridegroom, whose virility is symbolically tested when he shoots an arrow into a round mark on the wall above his bride's head. The wedding ritual includes tests and signs of virility. Richards considers these characteristics of the *chisungu* complex, for they are widely distributed among the matrilineal peoples of central Africa. The symbolic representation of male and female links the *chisungu* ritual both with the sex/fire/blood complex and with the structure of authority in the Bemba state. Bemba women and the *chisungu* ritual represent rank and social continuity, while chiefs and men are symbols of the power to shape events but also to destroy, a power which is beneficial only when contained by the constraints of descent and tradition. The *chisungu* is at one level a drama of the interdependence of kingship and the descent groups of commoners.

Chiefs, men and hunters are identified and symbolized in ritual as lions (and also the crocodile, the name of the royal clan). A man's bow and arrows are identified with him and inherited by his heir; hunting was an esteemed male activity. Bemba are proud of their fierce reputation and their former ability to dominate the neighbouring peoples by force. The spoils of war – ivory and slaves – were traded to the coast and brought in the wealth on which the autonomous Bemba state depended. Chiefs are expected to be generous to their dependants and more than one rite compares a husband with a chief in this respect. A particular rite, called 'begging for parenthood', displays these associations. I quote Richards' description and interpretation of the accompanying songs (1956: 77–8; see also 194):

An important stage in the ceremony had now been reached – the lighting of the new fire. This might be described as the first of the rites of aggregation. The senior 'father's sister' of one of the girls, wrinkled and bent with rheumatism, danced to the company and then lay down on her back. Nangoshye [the *nacimbusa*] picked up a firestick and started twirling it round in the groove on the old woman's thigh, telling the two girl novices to copy her afterwards. Then the two old women set out to make fire in earnest. Women do not commonly make fire among the Bemba. The work needs skill and practice as well as considerable strength. The two old women rubbed the firestick in turns, sweating and groaning with the effort. The company swayed to and fro, moaning the *chisungu* fire songs:

> *We have come to get fire*
> *Lion we beg it of you*

and

> *Scratch scratch* (the grating of the firesticks)
> *How many children have you borne?*

When at last the tinder caught fire it was greeted with relieved clapping. The father's sister plays the leading part in the ceremony and it is she who by tradition influences the fertility of the girl.

The interpretation of the songs was given as follows: the sticks are rubbed on the back of the girl's father's sister who can give or withhold parenthood (she represents the father's clan); the girl is told that she owes fire to the older woman whose hands ache from the rubbing; she must take over now. She must take her turn at the bearing of the children now; the lion is the bridegroom, the chief or the male principal throughout the ceremony; the bridegroom is begged for fire. The whole rite is called 'begging for parenthood'.

While several incidents emphasize that a husband 'gives' children, it is important to recognize that Bemba believe that the substance of a child is entirely that of its mother. The role of the father is to activate his wife's fertility, which makes the comparison with a chief in his role as organizer and leader even more apposite. The agricultural ritual performed by the chiefs, starting with the ritual performed by the Citimukulu, initiated the various seasons of the year. This cluster of associated ideas includes the continued and fruitful alliance between clans. Bemba must marry outside their own clan, so that the wives who protect their husbands' potency and receive 'parenthood' from them are representative of other clans. Chiefs are installed by ritual elders of commoner clans, whose knowledge of the correct ritual both protects and controls them. Any alliance is, ideally, perpetuated in the next generation, since the preferred form of marriage is one that repeats the link between two clans, a man's heir (his sister's son) marrying his daughter. The father's sister who 'gives fire' as representative of her clan recalls both her brother, father to the novice, and her son, the girl's future husband. So the conjunction of husband and wife, which is the ostensible end of the *chisungu* ritual, is also a continuing alliance between clans, between royals and commoners, chiefs and people, men and women, warfare and agriculture.

The emphasis on rank and precedence, on the necessary co-operation between clans, emphasizes the traditional rights which pertain to people as occupiers of social ranks and members of matrilineal clans. The 'things handed down from the ancestors', who founded the clans and established the ideal pattern of Bemba society, are the material embodiment of tradition. Their power is directed, as Bemba society was led, by an individual: a *nacimbusa*, the female equivalent of a chief, who held a position whose authority depended in large measure on ability and experience. The interdependence between hereditary rank and the ability of individuals were the twin ideas which supported the Bemba state. The destruction of that state by the colonial power probably contributed more to the decline of the practice of female initiation than either missionary endeavour or western education.

The apparent concern of girls' initiation rites with marriage and maternity is thus not only a concern with reproduction, but a dramatic enactment of the moral order which is a society's constitution. Nowhere is this more clear than in the case of the initiation of Nayar girls on the Malabar Coast of India. Their traditional system has been radically altered (Fuller, 1976; Gough, 1955) but the historical evidence is sufficient to establish the broad outlines of the system as it existed in the eighteenth and early nineteenth centuries.

The Nayar traditionally represented what one might call matriliny taken to its logical conclusion. Men and women lived in a joint household with its own land, called a *taravad*, the term also meaning segment of a descent group. Residents, men and women, were descended through women from a single ancestress; they were brothers and sisters, or mother's brothers and sister's children, mothers and children, to one another. The household contained no married couples and only the children of women of the *taravad* belonged to it. The joint household was under the authority of senior male kinsmen; the women and their children were strictly controlled. Women were, however, free to take lovers, as long as they were of the appropriate caste. The relationships might be short or long-standing affairs, but gave the man no legal rights to any children the woman might have, even if he was her only lover, which he might not be.

All Nayar girls went through the rituals at an early age; it was considered dangerously polluting for a girl to menstruate before initiation. Were this to become known, her kin would suffer public shame and worse. In order to ensure that this would not happen, the girls were initiated between the ages of five and eight, with some cases of girls as young as three being initiated. Since the ritual had to precede any physiological evidence of maturity, the rituals were not related to natural events; they could be organized when convenient, and could include girls of different ages. It seems to have been usual for the girls of a *taravad* who were of a suitable age to be initiated together. The ritual required the services of a male member of another *taravad*, linked to that of the girl by a series of ritual services in a continuing alliance known by a special name, *enangar*. This man went through the ritual with the girls, or girl, for it is not clear if each girl had a separate sponsor. The ritual included the man's tying a gold ornament (*tali*) round the girl's neck. The couple were then secluded for a varying period; some accounts indicate that the man was expected to deflower the girl. The final rite consisted of tearing a cloth in half, signifying the separation of the couple. The girl and her sponsor retained no special relationship after the rite was over, except that she and her children would observe mourning taboos when the sponsor died. He might or might not become her lover later on but she and her children had no claims on him nor he on them.

This Nayar ritual has been the centre of a controversy over whether the Nayar could be said to be the sole example of a society without the institution of marriage. Elsewhere in South India the tying of the *tali* round a girl's neck is part of wedding ritual and the ritual tearing of cloth a symbol of divorce. Further, the ritual services performed for each other by *enangar* lineages and sometimes, for the higher Nayar lineages, by high-caste Brahmins, resemble the duties of affines, people linked by marriage. Yet the rite established no conjugal relationship and no paternal rights to a girl's future children, which weddings commonly do, so that it has also been argued that this is an initiation rite, concerned with control over Nayar women and their sexual purity.

It is not necessary to come down on one or other side of the argument. The Nayar formed part of a society, a caste among other castes, whose fundamental tenet was that sexual contact between a woman of higher caste and a man of lower caste polluted her and all her kin (Dumont, 1966). The Nayar rite demonstrated the continuing purity of a lineage, guaranteed by the ritual exchange of services with other lineages of equal or greater purity. Descent and exchange of services were the two principles on which the hierarchy of society was founded. The little Nayar girls represented one means by which the legitimacy of the traditional order was periodically reaffirmed.

The rituals considered in this chapter, like all rituals, display symbols whose multiple meanings draw on many different layers of social life, from assumptions about the nature of the world and of human beings, to abstract ideas, often vague and ill-defined, which must be deduced from the context, not merely of one ritual, but of others performed in the same society, and from secular life. This many-textured quality makes rites difficult to analyse and even harder to write about. The problem is well put by Stephen Hugh-Jones, writing of initiation and cosmology in north-west Amazonia:

> Firstly, these rites, which are not simply rites of initiation but total religious phenomena, have no simple explanation. Rather they must be explained at a number of different levels and along a number of different axes. Secondly and related to this point, these explanations should ideally be given simultaneously, for *they are all there simultaneously* in the multidimensional nature of the rites themselves [1979: 10; my italics].

The divisions which must be introduced in order to make exposition possible can become destructive of the subtleties and richness of ritual. This chapter has taken some themes from the initiation of girls to show that they are not qualitatively different from those of boys; they demonstrate that the human beings who appear to be independent actors are also symbols with many meanings. From this point of view, initiation is a patterned performance whose purpose is action to achieve transformed individuals but whose effect is to demonstrate the power of traditional knowledge and legitimize a continuing social order.

NOTES TO CHAPTER VIII

1. In the sense of rites concerned with a set of novices, the sense used here.
2. Where an individual can marry more than once, either in polygamy or after divorce, it is obviously only the first wedding that has this significance.
3. Where a girl is not expected to be a virgin at marriage, loss of virginity is not a physical event with social significance.
4. There is also a role for the father's sister, but as one of many extra-descent group kin. The mother's role is part of the central acts, at the time of circumcision.
5. Brown is considering a category of rite defined by the infliction of 'severe pain' which she associates with similar male rites.
6. The information in this section is taken from Elizabeth Meyerhoff's thesis on the 'Socio-Economic and Ritual Roles of Pokot Women'. I am very grateful to her for allowing me to use her material on their initiation rites and for taking the time to comment on a draft of this chapter and correct inaccuracies of fact. I have tried to make clear when we disagree on an interpretation and the responsibility for the argument is mine, not hers.
7. If the girl's father is a polygynist, then she sleeps in her mother's hut and

her father moves in with his other wife or wives. The point is that the initiate retains a close association with her mother, rather than other novices. Among the pastoral Pokot, girls convalesce together. (E. Meyerhoff, personal communication.)

8. Dr Meyerhoff points out that the scarring makes it necessary for midwives to assist the passage of the first, and sometimes, the second child by cutting, but this is also often performed on western women who have not had this operation. As far as sexual enjoyment is concerned, some Pokot women have asserted that there was more pleasure to be had after circumcision, because of the possibility of conception. They stated they could feel the womb reaching for the children (a euphemism for sperm).

9. She may not drink water for about two weeks after the operation; this taboo also affects a woman who has just given birth. Both are bleeding but this does not seem to be the important similarity to Pokot. Dr Meyerhoff tells me, 'What the Pokot always stressed was their fear of polluting water, and other things, with menstrual blood; e.g. menstruating women should not wash in the irrigation channels, *chemeri* (initiates) must hit the channels (and the river) with their ritual sticks before crossing them, etc.' Given the association of water with fertility, I would interpret this taboo as marking the incompatibility of bleeding and conception.

10. Dr Meyerhoff translates the term as 'hazy'; given the characteristics of the marginal period I thought it permissible to change this gloss slightly.

11. Her personal friends told her what they knew but the accounts were confused.

12. Only a married couple may use such a pot, so adulterous sex is polluting, dangerous to a wife and her children. A similar belief is held by Pokot (E. Meyerhoff, personal communication).

13. The high mortality rate of children made this a very real anxiety at the time Richards undertook her study in the early 1930s.

14. The preferred husband for a girl is the son of her father's sister but if her betrothed is not a cousin of this sort, then the stand-in should be.

CONCLUSIONS

Initiation rituals have much in common with plays. They are artificial experiences, created by the people concerned and performed in a manner, time and place which the participants choose. Indeed, the timing, location and details of the performance may be a matter of intense debate between those who are concerned with directing it. Like theatrical performances, rituals make use of deceptions and 'special effects' to create impressions. The Masonic candidate undertakes a journey created for him by the Lodge members; the experience confuses him and demonstrates his helplessness, both to him and the directors of his movements. There are even more dramatic moments in other rituals: the mock killing of the initiate in the Nyoro spirit rituals was realistic enough to provoke terror in Beattie's informant. Meyerhoff describes listening to nervous discussions among Pokot women about whether the spirit had really killed the boys being initiated. Perhaps the most dramatic moment in Samburu rituals is the shower of milk falling on the naked, fire-scorched bodies of the *moran*, provoking a storm of physical reactions. In all initiation rituals there are highly dramatic moments, of excitement and tension, of solemnity and grandeur, and also of comedy. Observers vary in their concern to record or convey these moments but there is no doubt that they are there.

Nor must one ignore the element of entertainment provided by these rituals, particularly in societies where daily life may be drab, monotonous or full of anxieties. The singing, dancing and feasting that usually accompany them are enjoyed by the participants. Gisu attending circumcision rites clearly took pleasure in dressing up, adding bizarre touches to their costumes for the amusement of others. There was much laughter and mockery. The gathering together of people to hold ceremonies allows friends and kinsmen to meet, to entertain and be entertained, to flirt and gossip. Audrey Richards considered that much of the traditional Bemba *chisungu* ceremony was concerned with these pleasurable consequences of the rite; she added, 'A successful and well-run ceremony attracts large crowds and contributes to the prestige of the *nacimbusa* and to the village in which it is held.' No doubt Bemba headmen and chiefs sponsor the rites partly for this reason as well as to demonstrate in another context the generosity which is expected of them. Initiation rituals are often also festivals, a matter of pride for the participants. Even the rites of secret societies, who by their nature are not public, and may be quite small-scale, have an element of festival.

Plays are evaluated both as fixed forms and as performances which may vary from occasion to occasion. Rituals resemble them in this too. An observer can get an account of what will happen in any type of ritual; the salient features and their order can be discovered although informants will differ in their ability to recall and order details.[1] Nevertheless the performances vary and may be judged to be more or less successful, more or less close to what the ideal form is believed to be. Variations may be accepted, as Pokot songs vary from neighbourhood to neighbourhood, as an indication of the differences between localities. Among the Gisu, too, different lineages may define themselves by particular features of the initiation rituals which are peculiar to themselves. Variation is a feature of the rites of Hopi ritual societies and of the clan-based *ilmugit* of the Samburu. Other variations may be less legitimate and the fact that they happen at all may be denied or forgotten: this is particularly easy where no written record of the 'right' form exists.[2] Changes in the ritual may be imposed by outside authorities; those that are spontaneous developments are quickly assimilated to the ideal fixed form and given the sanction of long tradition. Not many people today know that the idea that the bride should wear a white dress is a relatively recent development in wedding ritual, fewer still that in medieval France marriage was not a church rite. Some imposed changes are remembered and even resented, as I know from my own experience. A few years ago in Britain, I was involved in filming Hogmanay in a Scots village. The regulations of the appropriate local authorities were ignored by the villagers, determined that the film should show the 'traditional' ceremony as it 'ought' to be. Earlier, during my field-work among the Gisu, I was caught in a dispute between the lineage elders, supported by the local people, and the chiefs, representing the colonial authorities. The elders had not ordered the construction of a fenced enclosure in which the candidates would be circumcised, although they had done so for nearly twenty years since the Uganda Government had made the regulation; they argued that I had wished to see traditional Gisu initiation and that was a ritual without fences. These two examples show that the idea of a fixed form which is the only right one can be a matter of pride, not merely a slavish following of customary procedure.

The full meaning of a ritual, like that of a play, relies on a set of shared conventions and assumptions that may be quite difficult for an outsider, first to elicit from people, and then to understand. Some of these refer to the symbols, which condense many layers of meaning, drawn both from tradition and from daily life. These may differ quite sharply in different societies: colour symbolism provides an example. In western societies black is the colour of funerals and mourning; in other countries, like China, white is used for the same purpose. The colours green[3] and orange take on a political and religious significance in Belfast that they do not have in London. The outsider has to learn the code in order to interpret the meaning of such elements as the significance of numbers or the reference to daily life in certain actions or objects that occur both in rituals and plays.

A whole range of assumptions about human beings and their social relations is embedded both in ritual and drama. Laura Bohannan published in 1956 an amusing account of her telling of the story of *Hamlet* to a group of Tiv, among whom she was doing field-work in Nigeria. They refused to believe that she had told the story 'right', excusing her on the grounds that she was young and a woman. The reasons for their disbelief are interesting: Tiv do not believe in ghosts, in the sense of the English word. The dead are not visible spirits who can communicate with the living; the only such spiritual beings are zombies, the spirits of living people stolen by witches to act as their servants. If Hamlet had truck with them, then he was dabbling in witchcraft. More important perhaps, it is the duty of a Tiv man to marry his brother's widow in order to care for her. The actions of the King in marrying Hamlet's mother led Tiv to conclude that he was a moral, upright man. Their judgement of the moral qualities of the characters knocked away the supports of the plot, leaving them understandably confused about what the point of the story was. No doubt many westerners would sympathize with them, being themselves too distant from Shakespeare's world to grasp the full meaning either. In the course of describing the initiation rituals of other societies I have often had to include information about their daily activities and the structure of their social relations in order to indicate the social context from which assumptions, like those implicit in *Hamlet*, derive. Or rather, to be more exact, the assumptions which are reaffirmed in the ritual, for ritual is not a passive reflection of the form of society. The relationship between sacred and secular is much more complex than describing it as a reflection or even a false picture[4] would imply. Understanding the relation between them is no simple matter.

The comparison of initiation with a theatrical performance is not a new idea. It dates back beyond Jane Harrison, the classical scholar, who made use of it to argue that classical Greek theatre had evolved from the earlier religious rituals of the Greeks. Lindgren saw particular significance in the gathering of people together and the entertaining aspect of similar rituals among the Tungus of Siberia. I have used it here to make the point that to understand these rituals one must consider them as wholes, not merely breaking them down into separate symbols, or sets of symbols, for symbols take meaning from their setting in the whole sequence of the rites. I follow Van Gennep in arguing that the fact that initiation rites form an ordered sequence is an important key to understanding them. His analysis showed that obscenity, such as that of the initiating shaman in Nyoro spirit ritual, and reversal of normal behaviour, like the fighting in Wogeo boys' rites, can most easily be interpreted in terms of their place in a sequence of events; the contrast with the normal social order emphasizes and manifests a boundary which the rites serve to create.

For the great distinction between ritual and drama lies in the fact that ritual, unlike a play, is purposeful activity; that is, it aims to affect the world. Whatever the purpose of the participants – and there are many of these aims reinforcing each other (for a full discussion, see Richards, 1956: 112–35), so that we should rather speak of purposes in the plural – ritual is not simply the expression of ideas and social meaning, although it is also that. It is seen as effective action. Whether it is the material world that is to be affected, as in the rituals for rain, at harvest or when bringing new ground under cultivation, or human beings who are to be redistributed among the groups and positions that make up social life, ritual is expected to produce results. The performance is not an end in itself,[5] but a means to achieve other ends. The analogy with the theatre brings out certain qualities of initiation rites but it does not get us very far.

There are other significant differences between plays and initiation rituals, of which one of the most important is that there is not usually an audience for the rituals. Indeed, many of these rites are secret so that a potential audience is excluded by definition. Those who are not eligible to participate serve to indicate by their very exclusion the separateness of the group concerned. Secrecy may be a political necessity, as it was for members of the Triad society or of Mau Mau, when those who did not join were at best neutral and at worst actively hostile, but even where it is not, some people may be excluded. The effect of the exclusion can be seen in initiation rites for the youth of one sex. On Wogeo Island when the flutes are played for the boys' initiation rites, women and children must hide in the huts, providing an antithesis to the men and boys engaged in ritual activity. Most rituals require general participation: Pokot women may insult or even assault one of their number who was missing from a neighbourhood initiation ritual. I doubt if any Gisu, bar the sick, old and infirm, and tiny children, would be absent from all of the events concerned with initiation, for fear of social ostracism. Public rituals often depend for their effect on large gatherings to make the singing loud and the dancing impressive. Often there are believed to be general benefits to all concerned. Moreover, participation is a means of demonstrating membership of the community and concern for public, rather than private, goals. In such circumstances, participation in ritual is not a matter of the choice open to a theatre-goer; it is an affirmation of loyalty.

Let us now abandon the comparison we have been considering, for it cannot take us any further in understanding initiation ritual and has, in some cases, even hindered it. In considering the effects of ritual it is important to distinguish between the participant's view and that of the observer. Since the expressed aim of initiation rites is simple, to change the status of individuals, we can take that first. The rites are self-fulfilling in one sense. If men are defined as those who have been circumcised in an initiation ritual, as Gisu do define them, then boys who undergo this initiation become men. There is no universal 'natural' definition of adulthood; such definitions are always social. Even menstruation is not a universally recognized sign of adult womanhood; Bemba girls are not women because they have reached the menarche but because 'their *chisungu* has been danced', they have been initiated. Membership of a secret society is conferred by initiation rituals; a man who has been initiated into a Masonic Lodge is a Mason, though he may not participate much in its activities from then on. In so far as initiation rituals mark the dividing line which distinguishes between social statuses, like adult and child, and between membership of groups and outsiders, crossing it changes one's state. Hence the very common insistence on large-scale participation; those who are not being initiated are affected by the change in those who are, and must, therefore, witness it. New members will be the subordinates of the others who participate in their initiation; and where the change is one involving the assumption of adult status, existing relationships will be altered. In most of these rituals the final act is one in which the new status of the initiate is recognized by gifts, greetings or eating together, acts which publicly recognize that the purpose of the rite has been achieved.

However, the question is more complex than this simple, observer's point of view, particularly when, as in maturation rituals, it is claimed that some existential change in the human beings has taken place. I well remember the eager questions of two Herero men[6] who, on hearing that I was writing a book on initiation, demanded that I explain what they had always wondered about. It seems that they had a playmate, a girl of their own age, who was a good friend and joined in all their games, 'like a boy'. Then she was taken off to the girls' initiation rite, and afterwards 'she was not the same'. She did not wish to associate with them, nor join in their games; she even spoke and behaved differently. They wanted to know what could explain this. The ritual experience had changed her; she had become a woman and they were still little boys.

All initiation rituals involve secrets, even those like Gisu initiation where what is mysterious, because it is not communicable, is the nature of the experience itself. The nature of the secrets may be trivial, merely, as in the case of Mende, Wogeo and Hopi rituals, the knowledge that other people do not know. That is sufficient to create a barrier between people, to impede communication between those who know and those who do not. Of course, the areas of life in which such a barrier is significant may not be very extensive: nevertheless where the need to conceal secrets is as strongly emphasized as it is in most of the rites I have been considering, the new initiates may have to be guarded in their conversations with those they formerly could talk freely to. The Baktaman of New Guinea discourage discussion of the initiation rites, even among initiates, and the Zuni fear that the power of their knowledge may be diminished if it is shared. Outsiders are kept at a distance by the fact that there are things they cannot be told.

By contrast, shared secrets create a bond. This bond is the basis of the solidarity of members of a secret society, underlying their expressed loyalty to one another. It is also fundamental to groups based on age, whether or not they are formalized into age-sets. The ritual itself and the experience of initiation are a most important part of what is shared. The dramatic form of the rites heightens the significance of the experience, to create a lasting impression. But the impression is also regularly reinforced by participation in subsequent rituals. All the rituals give some place to initiates other than the directing elders: senior *moran* sponsor new entrants into an age-set, newly initiated Nyoro shamans assist in the initiations conducted by their seniors, and a Bemba girl has an explicit obligation to assist her *nacimbusa* for further performances of *chisungu*. Among the Lovedu, an initiate is only considered fully mature when she has witnessed the rites six times (Krige cited in Richards, 1956: 128). The experience must then be considered part of the shared and organized activity which sustains the common identity of those concerned, whether secret societies like the Triad, the men of a clan or village among Samburu or Wogeo, or the women of a Pokot community.

Initiation rituals include, as part of the ordered series of events, elements which may be called tests. The word includes what may at first sight seem rather different elements: the formal taking of an oath of allegiance, as among the Masons, ordeals involving privation or severe pain, the harangues from the elders to which Samburu boys and Pokot girls are subjected, or the teasing of Bemba initiands to make them cry. They have in common that successfully passing them demonstrates the candidate's fitness for his or her new status, and are also indications of the efficacy of the rites themselves. What seems to be significant is that they all entail proper responses to the initiators, demonstrating submission to the authority which the initiates now accept. An oath is administered by a senior Mau Mau member, Gisu boys are judged by their performance during circumcision, and Pokot women insist that the girls must respond, by answers or tears, to the women who harangue them. It is a necessary part of the ritual, not merely spontaneous bullying; Richards indicates that the Bemba women saw the teasing of the girls as a rather tiresome necessity, quite different from the pleasure they took in other parts of the *chisungu*. The tests make an important contribution to the ritual, by demonstrating that it is working, having an effect.

The experience of initiation is usually identified by the participants as conferring on the initiate knowledge or rights which underline and justify an increase in his or her status, whether this is publicly acknowledged by a community or recognized only in the closed circle of the group. The rights acquired in initiation also entail duties, of which one of the most important is that of obedience to seniors. It is characteristic of secret societies that initiation reveals, in whole or in part, a hierarchy of positions, like a ladder seen from the bottom rung. However, it *is* a ladder, leading to further increments in knowledge and status. Wogeo boys are shown the flutes and told that they will be taught to play them. Contrary perhaps to their naïve expectations, all is not revealed to initiates; in some respects one can say they learn enough to know what they do not know. Just as their own improved status is directly linked to the experience they undergo and what it reveals to them, so the hierarchy above them associates further knowledge with greater powers and higher positions.

Much of what is imparted as ritual knowledge consists of rules of what is to be done and the materials to be used. Regular participation in rituals may transfer much of this information so that experienced participants can direct rituals on their own responsibility. Some of the meanings may be the subject of direct exegesis by ritual experts, who impart specialized knowledge to those of their juniors who are interested, or qualified, to learn. But much of the understanding conveyed in ritual depends on impression and association, on experience of the lived-in world and its social relationships. It is difficult to convey the way in which the meanings of ritual are implicit in the process of life, rather than systemized into an intellectual schema. Ritual may express concepts and ideas which order experience and give moral authority to the ideal form of social relationships, but experience also informs one's understanding of ritual as it is performed. To take a brief and personal example: the Gisu who accompanied me to the first funeral I attended found it virtually incredible that I had not seen a dead body in my life before. The Gisu do not shut their dead away in coffins and the mortality rate is such that even quite small children have experience of death. My reactions to the funeral clearly differed from those of the Gisu attending it, not merely because of my unfamiliarity with their language and funerary practices, but as a result of widely different experiences.

If repeated participation in ritual is the means whereby the next generation learns what is to be done, and experience of life informs understanding, then ritual knowledge clearly supports the authority of older men and women. This is a generalized authority; in all societies individuals differ in their capacity to absorb and remember information and in their sensitivity to associations and meanings. Nangoshye, the Bemba *nacimbusa*, was quite clear that some of the girls she initiated would be eager and able to learn more, others would not. An emphasis on the acquisition of knowledge and on individual achievement was characteristic of the secret societies, whether or not promotion through the ranks depended on ritual knowledge, or some other quality, such as wealth or political skill. The ritual itself associates the authority and status of officiants with knowledge and this appears as the basis of their authority. The efficacy of the ritual serves to confirm the power of what is known, equating knowledge with power and supporting legitimate authority.

Maturity rituals also serve to distinguish the powers mobilized in ritual from other kinds of power. The means by which this is done is symbolic: the association of the states before and after initiation with distinct sets of qualities, which are thus displayed as opposites. In Gisu and Samburu initiation rites, the candidates are associated with physical strength and uncontrolled violence, whether of feelings or behaviour; the elders represent respect for rules of behaviour, self-control and the wisdom of experience. The ritual then demonstrates the elders' control of their juniors, through their access to mystical powers. The message of the *ilmugit* is particularly clear: the mystical power of experienced elders is greater than physical force. Among the other peoples discussed, the dominant themes may vary. In particular, the girls' initiation rites contrast sexual maturity in the physical sense with the social roles of responsible mother and wife. The right to bear children which is conferred by initiation is inextricably involved with submission to authority, both of husbands and of experienced, older women. Another theme relates physical growth to ritual powers as effect to cause: the islanders of Wogeo stress that the rites ensure that the boys will grow, and the Bemba believe that *chisungu* induces maturation.

In the initiation rites of both boys and girls, parenthood is always associated with enhanced authority; this is not final authority, since the domestic group that is founded on the roles of spouses/parents is defined by, and is subordinated to, the wider society.

A common theme can be found in the symbolism of all these rituals: a reference to sexuality and birth. It appears in the rites of secret societies as it does in those of other transitions, such as funerals, as well as in initiations where it might seem most appropriate, since they are overtly concerned with parenthood. Where a direct reference to sexuality seems out of keeping with the occasion, it is common to find interpretations which assert Van Gennepian ideas of rebirth, (Eliade, 1958) or social continuity (Bloch & Parry, 1982). Yet this hardly explains why sexual symbols are so ubiquitous; are they just 'natural symbols', material available? In many of the rites discussed here, there are other symbols – fire, water or beer – which are linked with sexuality. They are usually interpreted as metaphors for it, in a way that assumes that the primary meaning is sexuality. If we approach rituals as actions designed to achieve a purpose, and consider the objects and acts which appear in rituals not only as designating meaning but containing qualities which are used, then a different explanation is possible. These are substances and processes which are generative; they create change. Fire, yeast, water, all change the substances they come in contact with; they are potent. The processes are not metaphors for procreation but parallel to it, used as much for their own powers as for the representation of the power of reproduction. The self-validating quality of ritual confirms the power of the ingredients of ritual as much as it supports the elders' knowledge of how they should be used. What we see as symbols may be the means of affecting the world.

Ritual knowledge, unlike science, is antithetical to change. It is conceived of as the property of the ancestors, the founders of all social life. It must be handed on, not tested, altered, improved or even discarded. Since it supports experience and validates the seniority of elders, it is not surprising if they throw the weight of their secular powers behind it. But traditional societies are not unchanging, even if they see themselves as attempting to maintain the moral order as it was freshly created in the beginning. On the other hand, there are elements of traditional authority and traditional wisdom even in those societies which define themselves as accumulating knowledge and see change as progressive evolution. It should not be thought that rituals discussed in this book constitute the whole of social life, even where they are still very important. In seeking to understand them as a form of ritual, we isolate them artificially from the processes in which they are embedded. Ritual is one element in the very intricate and complex pattern that is created as people live out their lives within a particular moral order.

NOTES TO CONCLUSIONS

1. Richards has an interesting discussion of the difference between various accounts of the *chisungu* given her which were crude outlines of the complex series of events that she actually witnessed (1956: 135–8).
2. I do not intend to give the impression that I think writing excludes the possibility of variation, by providing a fixed 'script'. That would be a naïve conclusion, as the large literature on Shakespearian drama and the very varied performances of his plays show. It is also true that where people must commit things to memory in order to preserve and perpetuate, not only rituals, but myths, history and family genealogies, they display feats of memory that members of literate societies can admire but rarely emulate.
3. Green, the Catholic colour, is, in Irish tradition, the colour worn by the leprechauns, 'the little people', so that it has a triple significance at least: national identity, traditional folk system and politico-religious identity.
4. By this I mean the labelling of religion, and hence ritual, as 'mystification' or false consciousness, used by some Marxist writers. This begs the question of what is the reality that is being concealed and leads all too easily to simple-minded conspiracy theories which see people as the dupes of priests and kings. The arrogance of intellectuals who claim to be the only ones who can see through this fraud to what is 'real', owes much to the anti-clerical tradition in European society but possibly more to the kind of authority without power that knowledge confers in western society.
5. Malinowski distinguished magic and religion in terms of their ends: he argued that magic was concerned with individual aims and desires, while religious ceremonies were performed for the general good of the community and for more general purposes such as pleasing the gods, or not angering the ancestors, or as a duty imposed on the faithful. I do not make this distinction here because the purposes and intentions of the performers may be mixed. What is more important is to distinguish clearly between expressed purposes and those which may be deduced by the observer.
6. The Herero live mostly in Namibia though a section of them are to be found in Botswana, where they fled as refugees from German rule.

BIBLIOGRAPHY

Allen, M. 1967. *Male Cults and Secret Initiations in Melanesia*, Melbourne University Press, Melbourne.

Almagor, U. 1978. 'Gerontocracy, Polygyny and Scarce Resources' in *Sex and Age as Principles of Social Differentiation*, ed. J. S. La Fontaine, Academic Press, London.

Ampthill, Lord. 1934. Preface to H. S. Banner, *These Men Were Masons*; see below.

Banner, H. S. 1934. *These Men Were Masons: A Series of Biographies of Masonic Significance*, Chapman & Hall, London.

Barnett, D. L. & Njama, K. 1966. *Mau-Mau from Within: Autobiography and Analysis of Kenya's Peasant Revolt*, MacGibbon & Kee, Letchworth.

Barth, F. 1975. *Ritual and Knowledge among the Baktaman of New Guinea*, Yale University Press, New Haven.

Bateson, G. 1936. *Naven: A Survey of the Problems suggested by a Composite Picture of the Culture of a New Guinea Tribe Drawn from Three Points of View*, Cambridge University Press, Cambridge.

Baxter, P. T. & Almagor, U. 1978. 'Observations about Generations' in *Sex and Age as Principles of Social Differentiation*, ed. J. S. La Fontaine, Academic Press, London.

Beattie, J. H. M. 1957. 'Initiation into the Cwezi Spirit Possession Cult in Bunyoro', *African Studies*, Vol. 16, No. 3.

Beattie, J. H. M. 1961. 'Group Aspects of the Nyoro Spirit Mediumship Cult', *Rhodes Livingstone Journal*, No. 30.

Beattie, J. H. M. 1969. 'Spirit Mediumship in Bunyoro' in *Spirit Mediumship and Society in Africa*, ed. J. H. M. Beattie & J. Middleton, Routledge & Kegan Paul, London.

Beattie, J. H. M. 1971. *The Nyoro State*, Oxford University Press, London.

Beidelman, T. 1966. 'Swazi Royal Ritual', *Africa*, Vol. 36, No. 4.

Bettelheim, B. 1954. *Symbolic Wounds*, Free Press, Glencoe, Illinois.

Bloch, M. E. F. n.d. Paper presented at seminar, London School of Economics, 1972.

Bloch, M. E. F. 1974. 'Symbols, Song, Dance and Features of Articulation', *European Journal of Sociology*, Vol. 15 (1).

Bloch, M. E. F. 1975. 'Property and the End of Affinity' in *Marxist Analyses and Social Anthropology*, ed. M. Bloch, ASA Studies, Dent, London.

Bloch, M. & Parry, J. 1982. Introduction to *Death and the Regeneration of Life*, ed. M. Bloch & J. Parry, Cambridge University Press, Cambridge.

Bohannan, L. 1956. 'Miching Mallecho That Means Witchcraft' in *From the Third Programme*, ed. J. Morris, Nonesuch Press, London. Republished in *Magic, Witchcraft and Curing*, ed. J. Middleton, American Museum Source Books in Anthropology, The Natural History Press, New York.

Brown, J. K. 1963. 'A Cross-Cultural Study of Female Initiation Rites among Pre-Literate Peoples', *American Anthropologist*, Vol. 65, No. 4.

Buck, P. S. (translator). 1948. Shui Hu Chuan, *All Men are Brothers*, with an Introduction by Lin Yutang, Heritage Press, New York.

Buijtenhuijs, R. 1982. *Essays on Mau-Mau: Contributions to Mau-Mau Historiography*, Research Reports, No. 17, African Studies Centre, Leiden.

Caplan, A. P. 1976. 'Boys' Circumcision and Girls' Puberty Rites among the Swahili of Mafia Island, Tanzania', *Africa*, Vol. 46, No. 1.

Chesneaux, J. 1965. *Sociétés Secrètes en Chine*, René Juilliard, Paris.

Chesneaux, J. *et al.* 1970. *Mouvements Populaires et Sociétés Secrètes en Chine aux XIXe et XXe siècles*, Maspero, Paris.

Cohen, A. 1971. 'The Politics of Ritual Secrecy', *Man* n.s., Vol. 6, No. 3.

Cohen, A. 1981. *The Politics of Elite Culture*, University of California Press, Berkeley and Los Angeles.

Cohen, Y. 1964a. *The Transition from Childhood to Adolescence: Cross-Cultural Studies of Initiation Ceremonies, Legal Systems and Incest Taboos*, Aldine, Chicago.

Cohen, Y. 1964b. 'The Establishment of Identity: The Special Case of Initiation Ceremonies and the Relation to Value and Legal Systems', *American Anthropologist*, Vol. 66, No. 3.

Comaroff, J. forthcoming. *Body of Power: Spirit of Protest*, University of Chicago Press, Chicago.

Corfield, F. D. 1960. *Historical Survey of the Origins and Growth of Mau-Mau*, HMSO, London.

Davis, Fei-ling. 1977. *Primitive Revolutionaries of China: a study of secret societies in the late nineteenth century*, Routledge & Kegan Paul, London.

Douglas, M. 1970. *Natural Symbols*, Barrie & Rockliff, London.

Dozier, E. P. 1970. *The Pueblo Indians of North America: Case Studies in Cultural Anthropology*, Holt Rinehart & Winston for Stanford University, Stanford, California.

Dumont, L. 1966. *Homo Hierarchicus: The Caste System and its Implications*, Weidenfeld & Nicolson, London.

Durkheim, E. 1912. *Les Formes Elémentaires de la Vie Religieuse*. English translation, 1915, *The Elementary Forms of the Religious Life*, Allen & Unwin, London.

Eggan, F. 1950. *Social Organization of the Western Pueblos: an integrated analysis of the Hopi, Hano, Zuni, Acoma and Laguna Indians*, University of Chicago Press, Chicago.

Eliade, M. 1958. *Rites and Symbols of Initiation: The Mysteries of Birth and Rebirth* (English translation, paperback edition), Harper, New York.

Firth, Sir R. 1973. *Symbols, Public and Private*, Allen & Unwin, London.

Fortes, M. 1945. *The Dynamics of Clanship among the Tallensi*, Oxford University Press, London.

Fortes, M. 1949. *The Web of Kinship among the Tallensi*, Oxford University Press, London.

Fortes, M. 1962. 'Ritual and Office in Tribal Society' in *Essays on the Ritual of Social Relations*, ed. M. Gluckman, Manchester University Press, Manchester.

Frazer, Sir J. G. 1907-15. *The Golden Bough* (12 vols), London. Abridged edition, 1922, Macmillan, London.

Frazer, Sir J. G. 1913. *The Belief in Immortality and the Worship of the Dead*, Macmillan, London.

Freedman, M. 1960. 'Immigrants and Associations: Chinese in Nineteenth-Century Singapore', *Comparative Studies in Society and History*, Vol. 3.

Freedman, M. 1970. 'Ritual Aspects of Chinese Kinship and Marriage' in *Family and Kinship in Chinese Society*, ed. M. Freedman, Stanford University Press, Stanford, California.

Fuller, C. J. 1976. *The Nayar Today*, Cambridge University Press, Cambridge.

Furedi, F. 1974. 'The Social Composition of the Mau-Mau Movement in the White Highlands', *Journal of Peasant Studies*, Vol. 1, No. 4.

Gell, A. 1975. *Metamorphosis of the Cassowaries: Umeda Society, Language and Rituals*, LSE Monographs on Social Anthropology, No. 51, Athlone Press, London.

Gell, A. 1979. 'Reflections on a Cut Finger: Taboo in the Umeda Conception of the Self' in *Fantasy and Symbol: Studies in Anthropological Interpretation*, Academic Press, London, New York, San Francisco.

Glick, C. & Hong Sheng-hwa. 1947. *Swords of Silence: Chinese Secret Societies – Past and Present*, New York.

Gluckman, M. 1949. 'The Roles of the Sexes in Wiko Circumcision Ceremonies' in *Social Structure: Studies presented to A. R. Radcliffe-Brown*, ed. M. Fortes, Oxford University Press, Oxford.

Gluckman, M. 1954. 'Ritual of Rebellion in South-East Africa', the Frazer Lecture, Manchester University Press, Manchester.

Gluckman, M. 1962. Introduction to *Essays on the Ritual of Social Relations*, ed. M. Gluckman, Manchester University Press, Manchester.

Goody, J. R. 1961. 'Religion and Ritual – the definitional problem', *British Journal of Sociology*, Vol. 12.

Gough, E. K. 1955. 'Female Initiation Rites on the Malabar Coast', *Journal of the Royal Anthropological Institute*, Vol. 85.

Grant, J. A. 1864. *A Walk Across Africa*, Blackwood, London.

Harley, G. W. 1941. 'Notes on the Poro in Liberia', *Peabody Museum of Natural History and Ethnology Papers*, Vol. XIX, Harvard University, Cambridge, Massachusetts.

Hays, T. E. & Hays, P. H. 1982. 'Opposition and Complementarity of the Sexes in Ndumba Initiation' in *Rituals of Manhood*, ed. G. H. Herdt; see below.

Heald, S. 1982. 'The Making of Men; the Relevance of Vernacular Psychology to the Interpretation of a Gisu Ritual', *Africa*, Vol. 52, No. 1.

Heckethorn, C. W. 1875. *The Secret Societies of All Ages and Countries*. Reprinted 1965, University Books, New York.

Herdt, G. H. (ed.). 1982. *Rituals of Manhood: Male Initiation in Papua New Guinea*, University of California Press, Berkeley, Los Angeles, London.

Hogbin, I. 1944–5. 'Marriage in Wogeo', *Oceania*, Vol. 15.

Hogbin, I. 1945–6. 'Puberty to Marriage: A Study of the Sexual Life of the Natives of Wogeo', *Oceania*, Vol. 16.

Hogbin, I. 1963–4. 'Wogeo Kinship Terminology', *Oceania*, Vol. 34.

Hogbin, I. 1970. 'The Island of Menstruating Men: Religion in Wogeo, New Guinea', *Chandler Publications in Anthropology and Sociology*, Chandler Scranton, London, Toronto.

Holman, D. 1964. *Bwana Drum*, W. H. Allen, London.

Hopkins, E. 1970. 'The Nyabingi Cult of Southwestern Uganda' in *Protest and Power in Black Africa*, ed. R. L. Rotberg & A. A. Mazrui, Oxford University Press, Oxford. Paperback edition 1971.

Hopkins, E. 1971. 'The Kyanyangire, 1907: Passive Revolt against British Overrule' in *Protest and Power in Black Africa* (paperback edition), ed. R. L. Rotberg & A. A. Mazrui, Oxford University Press, Oxford.

Horton, R. 1968. 'Neo-Tylorianism: sound sense or sinister prejudice?', *Man* n.s., Vol. 3, No. 4.

Hugh-Jones, S. 1979. *The Palm and the Pleiades: Initiation and Cosmology in Northwest Amazonia*, Cambridge University Press, Cambridge.

Huntingford, G. W. B. 1953. 'The Southern Nilo-Hamites', *Ethnographic Survey of Africa*, Part VIII, International African Institute, London.

Itote, Waruhiu. 1967. *Mau-Mau General*, East African Publishing House, Nairobi, Kenya.

Jones, M. 1967. 'Freemasonry' in *Secret Societies*, ed. N. MacKenzie, Aldus Books, London.

Junod, H. A. 1927. *The Life of a South African Tribe* (2nd edition), Macmillan, London.

Kariuki, J. M. 1963. *Mau-Mau Detainee*, Oxford University Press, Oxford.

Koloski, E. 1967. *Initiation Ritual in Selected African Societies*, M.A. thesis, University of London.

Kuper, H. 1944. 'A Ritual of Kingship among the Swazi', *Africa*, Vol. 14.

Kuper, H. 1947. *An African Aristocracy*, Oxford University Press, London.

Kuper, H. 1973. 'Costume and Cosmology: The animal symbolism of the Ncwala', *Man* n.s., Vol. 8, No. 4.

La Fontaine, J. S. 1955. 'Symposium on ritual circumcision of the Bagishu', *The East African Medical Journal*, British Medical Association (Uganda Branch), Vol. 32, No. 1.

La Fontaine, J. S. 1957. *The Social Organisation of the Gisu of Uganda with Special Reference to their Initiation Rites*, Ph.D. thesis, University of Cambridge.

La Fontaine, J. S. 1959. 'The Gisu of Uganda', *Ethnographic Survey of Africa*, Part X, International African Institute, London.

La Fontaine, J. S. 1968. 'Parricide in Bugisu: a study in inter-generational conflict', *Man* n.s., Vol. 2, No. 2.

La Fontaine, J. S. 1969. 'Tribalism among the Gisu' in *Tradition and Transition in East Africa*, ed. P. H. Gulliver, Routledge & Kegan Paul, London.

La Fontaine, J. S. 1972. 'Ritualisation of Women's Life-Crises in Bugisu' in *The Interpretation of Ritual*, ed. J. S. La Fontaine, Tavistock, London.

La Fontaine, J. S. 1977. 'The Power of Rights', the Henry Myers Lecture, *Man* n.s., Vol. 12, No. 3/4.

La Fontaine, J. S. 1979. 'Land and the Political Community in Bugisu' in *Politics in Leadership: A comparative perspective*, ed. William A. Shack & Percy S. Cohen, Clarendon Press, Oxford.

La Fontaine, J. S. 1981. 'The Domestication of the Savage Male', *Man* n.s., Vol. 16, No. 2.

La Fontaine, J. S. 1982. Introduction to A. I. Richards, *Chisungu: A Girls' Initiation Ceremony among the Bemba of Zambia* (2nd edition), Tavistock, London.

Leach, E. R. 1976. *Culture and Communication: The Logic by which Symbols Are Connected*, Cambridge University Press, Cambridge.

Leakey, L. S. B. 1952. *Mau-Mau and the Kikuyu*, Methuen, London.

Lévi-Strauss, C. 1958. Translated by C. Jacobson & B. Grundfest Schoeps, 1963, *Structural Anthropology*, Chapters IX & X, Basic Books, New York, London.

Lévi-Strauss, C. 1971. *L'Homme Nu: Mythologiques IV*, Plon, Paris.

Lewis, G. 1980. *Day of Shining Red: An Essay on Understanding Ritual*, Cambridge University Press, Cambridge.

Lewis, I. M. 1971. *Ecstatic Religion*, Penguin, Harmondsworth.

Lieberthal, K. 1973. 'The Suppression of Secret Societies in post-Liberation Tientsin', *China Quarterly*, No. 54.

Little, K. L. 1951. *The Mende of Sierra Leone: A West African People in Transition*, Routledge & Kegan Paul, London.

MacCormack, C. P. 1979. 'Sande: The Public Face of a Secret Society' in *The New Religions of Africa* ed. B. Jules-Rosette.

MacCormack, C. P. 1980. 'Nature, Culture and Gender: A Critique' in *Nature, Culture and Gender*, ed. C. MacCormack & M. Strathern, Cambridge University Press, Cambridge.

Maclean, S. (ed.). 1980. *Female Circumcision, Excision and Infibulation: the facts and proposals for change*, Report No. 47, Minority Rights Group, London.

Mair, L. 1962. *Primitive Government*, Penguin, London.

Mauss, M. 1950. Translated by R. Brain, 1972, *A General Theory of Magic*, Routledge & Kegan Paul, London.

Meyerhoff, E. 1982. *The Socio-Economic and Ritual Roles of Pokot Women*, Ph.D. thesis, University of Cambridge.

Middleton, J. & Kershaw, G. 1965. 'The Kikuyu and Kamba of Kenya', *Ethnographic Survey of Africa*, East Central Africa, Part V, International African Institute, London.

Morgan, L. H. 1877. *Ancient Society*, Henry Holt, New York.

Ortner, S. 1974. 'Is Female to Male as Nature is to Culture?' in *Woman, Culture and Society*, ed. M. A. Rosaldo & L. Lamphere, Stanford University Press, Stanford, California.

Parsons, E. C. 1939. *Pueblo Indian Religion* (2 vols.), University of Chicago Publications in Anthropology, Chicago.

Porter Poole, F. 1982. 'The Ritual Forging of Identity: Aspects of Person and Self in Bimin-Kuskusmin Male Initiation' in *Rituals of Manhood: Male Initiation in Papua New Guinea*, ed. G. H. Herdt; see above.

Radcliffe-Brown, A. R. 1929. 'The Sociological Theory of Totemism', *Proceedings of the Fourth Pacific Science Congress, Java*. Republished 1952 in *Structure and Function in Primitive Society*, ed. E. E. Evans-Pritchard & F. Eggan, Cohen & West, London.

Radcliffe-Brown, A. R. 1945. 'Religion and Society', the Henry Myers Lecture, *Journal of the Royal Anthropological Institute*. Republished 1952 in *Structure and Function in Primitive Society*, ed. E. E. Evans-Pritchard & F. Eggan, Cohen & West, London.

Richards, A. I. 1956. *Chisungu: A Girls' Initiation Ceremony in Northern Rhodesia*, Faber, London. Reissued 1982 with an Introduction by J. S. La Fontaine, as *Chisungu: A Girls' Initiation Ceremony in Zambia*, Tavistock, London.

Richards, A. I. 1960. 'Social Mechanisms for the Transfer of Political Rights in Some African Tribes', *Journal of the Royal Anthropological Institute*, Vol. 9, pp. 175–90.

Richards, A. I. 1969. 'Keeping the King Divine', *Proceedings of the Royal Anthropological Institute*.

Rigby, P. 1968. 'Some Gogo Rituals of "Purification": An Essay on Social and Moral Categories' in *Dialectic in Practical Religion*, ed. E. R. Leach, Cambridge Papers in Social Anthropology, No. 5, Cambridge University Press, Cambridge.

Rosaldo, M. A. & Lamphere, L. 1974. *Woman, Culture and Society*, Stanford University Press, Stanford, California.

Rosberg, C. G., Jnr, & Nottingham, J. 1966. *The Myth of Mau-Mau Nationalism in Kenya*, Hoover Institution on War, Revolution and Peace, Stanford University, E. A. Publishing House, Nairobi.

Schwab, G. 1947. 'Tribes of the Liberian Hinterland', *Peabody Museum of Natural History and Ethnology Papers*, Vol. XXXI, Harvard University, Cambridge, Massachusetts.

Simmel, G. 1905–6. 'The Sociology of Secrecy and Secret Societies', *American Journal of Sociology*, Vol. 11.

Skorupski, J. 1976. *Symbol and Theory: A Philosophical Study of Theories of Religion*, Cambridge University Press, Cambridge.

Spencer, P. 1965. *The Samburu: A Study of Gerontocracy in a Nomadic Tribe*, Routledge & Kegan Paul, London.

Spencer, P. 1970. 'The Function of Ritual in the Socialization of the Samburu Moran' in *Socialization: The Approach from Social Anthropology*, ed. P. Mayer, ASA Monograph 8, Tavistock, London.

Spencer, P. 1973. *Nomads in Alliance: Symbiosis and Growth among the Rendille and Samburu of Kenya*, Oxford University Press, London.

Spencer, P. 1976. 'Opposing Streams and the Gerontocratic Ladder: Two Models of Age Organisation in East Africa', *Man* n.s., Vol. 11, No. 2.

Stanton, W. 1900. *The Triad Society or Heaven and Earth Association*, Kelley & Walsh, Hong Kong.

Stephen, A. M. 1936. *Hopi Journal* (3 vols), ed. E. C. Parsons, *Columbia Contributions to Anthropology*, Vols 22 & 23, Columbia University Press, New York.

Strathern, M. 1972. *Woman in Between: Female Roles in a Male World*, Seminar (Academic) Press, London.

Strathern, M. 1981. 'Self-Interest and the Social Good: Some Implications of Hagen Gender Imagery' in *Sexual Meanings*, ed. S. Ortner & H. Whitehead, Cambridge University Press, New York.

Tamarkin, M. 1973. *Social and Political Change in a Twentieth-Century African Urban Community in Kenya*, Ph.D. thesis, University of London.

Taylor, B. K. 1962. 'The Western Lacustrine Bantu', *Ethnographic Survey of Africa*, Part XIII, International African Institute, London.

Titiev, M. 1944. 'Old Oraibi: A Study of the Indians of Third Mesa', *Peabody Museum of Natural History and Ethnology Papers*, Vol. XXII, Part I., Harvard University, Cambridge, Massachusetts.

Turner, T. S. 1977. 'Transformation, Hierarchy and Transcendence: A Reformulation of Van Gennep's Model of the Structure of Rites de Passage' in *Secular Ritual*, ed. B. Meyerhoff & S. Moore, Van Gornum, Assen.

Turner, V. W. 1962. 'Three Symbols of Passage in Ndembu Circumcision Ritual: an interpretation, in *Essays on the Ritual of Social Relations*, ed. M. Gluckman, Manchester University Press, Manchester.

Turner, V. W. 1964. 'Symbols in Ndembu Ritual' in *Closed Systems and Open Minds*, ed. M. Gluckman, Manchester University Press, Manchester.

Turner, V. W. 1969. 'Mukanda: the Politics of a Non-Political Ritual' in *Local Level Politics*, ed. M. Swartz, University of London Press, London.

Van Gennep, A. 1909. *Les Rites de Passage*, Emile Nourry, Paris. Translated by M. B. Vizedom & G. L. Caffee, 1960, *The Rites of Passage*, with an Introduction by S. T. Kimball, Routledge & Kegan Paul, London.

Ward, B. E. 1967. 'Chinese Secret Societies' in *Secret Societies*, ed. N. MacKenzie, Aldus Books, London.

Ward, J. S. M. & Stirling, W. G. 1925. *The Hung Society*, Hong Kong.

Watson, J. 1977. 'The Chinese: Hong Kong Villagers in the British Catering Trade' in *Between Two Cultures: Migrants and Minorities in Britain*, ed. J. Watson, Basil Blackwell, Oxford.

Whalen, W. J. 1966. *A Handbook of Secret Organizations*, Bruce Publishing Co., Milwaukee.

Whiting, J. W. M., Kluckholn, R. & Anthony, A. 1958. 'The Function of Male Initiation Ceremonies at Puberty' in *Readings in Social Psychology*, ed. E. E. MacCoby *et al.*, Holt, New York.

Wilson, M. 1957. *Rituals of Kinship among the Nyakyusa*, International African Institute, Oxford University Press, London.

Wilson, M. 1959. *Communal Rituals among the Nyakyusa*, International African Institute, Oxford University Press, London.

Young, F. W. 1962. 'The Function of Male Initiation Ceremonies', *American Journal of Sociology*, Vol. 67, No. 4.

INDEX